The Little Inspirational™ Bathroom Bible™ Book

W. B. Freeman

STARBURST PUBLISHERS®

P. O. Box 4123, Lancaster, Pennsylvania 17604

Visit **www.starburstpublishers.com**

CREDITS:
    Cover design by Richmond & Williams
    Text design and composition by John Reinhardt Book Design

Bible references are from the King James Version of the Bible unless otherwise designated.

Other Bible versions used are indicated by the following abbreviations:
    The Living Bible (TLB)
    New American Standard Bible (NAS)
    New International Version (NIV)
    New King James Version (NKJV)
    New Revised Standard (NRS)

THE LITTLE INSPIRATIONAL™ BATHROOM BIBLE™ BOOK

    First printing, May 2002
    ISBN: 1-892016-68-0
    Library of Congress Catalog Number: 2002102277
    Printed in USA

Manuscript prepared by W. B. Freeman Concepts, Inc., Tulsa, Oklahoma.

CONTENTS

Note: Shorter items are between one and two pages long. Longer items are over two pages.

Church Chatter

Church Humor

Know Your Bible Better

Movies, Books, and the Arts

Stop to Think

Today's Christians

SHORTER

LONGER

Top Ten

SHORTER

The Word's Words

SHORTER

LONGER

Under His Wings

Several years ago *National Geographic* magazine described an incident that occurred in the aftermath of a forest fire that razed much of Yellowstone National Park.

As forest rangers began their trek up a mountain to assess the damage, a ranger found a bird literally petrified in the ashes. It was perched statuesquely on the ground at the base of a tree.

Somewhat sickened at the eerie sight, a ranger knocked over the bird with a stick. As he did so, three tiny chicks scurried from under their dead mother's wings.

This loving mother bird, keenly aware of impending disaster, had carried her offspring to the base of the tree and had gathered them under her wings, instinctively knowing that the toxic smoke would rise. She could have flown to safety, but she had refused to abandon her babies. When the blaze arrived and the heat scorched her small body, she remained steadfast. Because she was willing to die, those under the cover of her wings lived.

> **A BIT OF CHURCH HUMOR**
>
> During a children's sermon, a pastor asked the children what "amen" means.
>
> A little boy raised his hand and said: "It means tha-tha-tha-that's all, folks!"

The psalmist wrote this about God: "He shall cover you with his feathers, and under His wings you shall find refuge" (Psalm 91:4 NKJV).

God has loved you so much that he gave his only begotten son to die in your place, that you might live (John 3:16).

At the Center of It All

Consider these questions and answers:

What is the shortest chapter of the Bible?   Psalm 117
What is the longest chapter of the Bible?   Psalm 119
Which chapter is in the center of the Bible?   Psalm 118

Fact: There are 594 chapters before Psalm 118
Fact: There are 594 chapters after Psalm 118
   Add these numbers together and you get 1188.

What is the center verse in the Bible?   Psalm 118:8

The next time a person tells you that they want to be in the center of God's perfect will for their lives, direct them to the very center of God's Word—which is his will for our lives. Psalm 118:8 NAS says: "It is better to take refuge in the LORD than to trust man."

> What is most valuable is not *what* we have in our lives, but *who* we have in our lives.

Trusting God is at the heart of knowing God, and doing what God says to do. It is at the heart of believing and obeying. When there is nothing left but trusting God, you discover that trusting God is all that is required.

Born Again Spin-Offs

It seems like everything and everyone is born again. A restaurant changes its menu, and it's labeled born again. A man changes jobs, and his career is born again.

The first time "born again" appears in the Bible is in John 3:3 when Jesus talks to Nicodemus. Jesus says, "I tell you the truth, no one can see the kingdom of God unless he is born again."

Like a movie that generates a bunch of sequels, "born again" is constantly being born again. Here are some other uses:

- Born Again™—a trademarked line of skin creams
- Born-Again Boards—makers of surfboards and other hand-crafted wood products
- Born Again Used Books—a store in Colorado Springs.
- Born Again Records—the third biggest independent gospel record label in the United States
- Born Again—a CD title with explicit lyrics by the Notorious B.I.G.
- Born Again Card™ Recycling Program, which turns Christmas cards into ornaments
- Born Again Motorcycles, Inc.—a store that sells used parts for vintage cycles
- Born Again Creations—a company that produces one-of-a-kind dolls and other collectibles
- Born Again Bears—a company that recycles furs into teddy bears

Source: Lin Johnson, *John—God's Word for the Biblically-Inept*™ (Lancaster, PA: Starburst Publishers, 2000), 33.

Bible Oddities

Over the years our fascination with the Bible has taken some odd turns in printing and use:

The World's Smallest Bible

Less than one-fourth inch thick and containing 838,380 letters on its 520 pages, this tiny Bible is about one-third the size of a postage stamp. It required four years to complete, and is parchment-bound and sewed with silk thread. The Bible was printed in 1895 by David Bryce & Son, Glasgow.

The Vinegar Bible

In 1716 an edition of the Bible was printed in England with the headline: "The Parable of the Vinegar." It should have read "The Parable of the Vineyard" (Luke 20:9–19). Rare book collectors have paid amazing sums for copies of the "The Vinegar Bible."

Thou Shalt?

One printing of the Bible omitted the word "not" from one of the Ten Commandments. Most of the copies of this Bible were destroyed, but a few remain. In those still existing Exodus 20:14 reads, "Thou shalt commit adultery."

Light-Bulb-Changing Techniques

How many Christians does it take to change a light bulb?

Charismatics: Only one. Hands are already in the air.

Presbyterians: None. Lights will go on and off at predestined times.

Roman Catholic: None. Candles only, please.

Baptists: At least 16. One to change the light bulb and three committees to approve the change and decide who brings the potato salad.

Episcopalians: Three. One to call the electrician, one to mix the drinks, and one to talk about how much better the old one was.

Mormons: Five. One man to change the bulb and four of his wives to tell him how to do it.

Unitarians: We choose not to make a statement either in favor of or against the need for a light bulb. However, if in your own journey you have found that light bulbs work for you, that is fine. You are invited to write a poem or compose a modern dance about your light bulb for the next service, in which we will explore a number of light bulb traditions, all of which are equally valid paths to luminescence.

Methodists: Undetermined. Whether your light is bright, dull, or completely out, you are loved. You can be a light bulb, turnip bulb, or tulip bulb. A lighting service is planned for Sunday. Bring the bulb of your choice.

Nazarenes: Six. One woman to replace the bulb while five men review church lighting policy.

Lutherans: None. We don't believe in change.

Amish: What's a light bulb?

Extra! Extra! Read All about It! Part 1

Construction Project Stalls, Foreman Stymied

Today's events in Babylonia left many scratching their heads, not least of all the foreman of a massive building project at the heart of the city.

"It was the craziest thing," said "Jobe," who declined to give his real name. "A bunch of us moved here a little while back and decided it looked like a great place to settle down. We all know about that flood, and we figured it'd be safer to hang together.

"Well, we started baking bricks to build ourselves a nice city, and someone, I don't remember who, said, 'Why don't we build a tower that reaches all the way to heaven? Then we can knock on God's door and say hi!' We all laughed at first, but then we said, 'Oh, why not? Let's see how high we can make this thing!'

"The work was going great," Jobe said before lapsing into silence, a confused look on his face. "I asked one of the crew to hand me a brick, and he just stared at me. Then he started talking, but I have no idea what he said. It sounded like jibberish. That's when I realized that I couldn't understand what hardly *anyone* was saying anymore."

Jobe looked down at the ground and kicked the dirt with the toe of his sandal.

"We're moving on," he said with a sigh. "We're going back to my wife's family's place. Of course, my mother-in-law is going to say, 'I told you so!'"

From the number of people on the road today, it looks like Jobe's family is just one of many leaving Babylonia because of this unexplained breakdown in communication. Attempts to interview other city dwellers failed, due to language difficulties.

Construction of the tower, now referred to as "Babel," has been halted. Officials would not say—or more accurately, could not be under-

stood to say—when construction might resume (For more on this story, read Genesis 11:1-9.)

Loaf of Bread Dooms Troops

Those rascally Midianites, who have been treating the Israelites like dirt for the past seven years, finally got their comeuppance last week.

Reports from the field tell us that a man named Gideon used a ridiculously small army of 300 men to deliver a knockout punch to the enemy, without even breaking a sweat.

Inside sources revealed that Gideon and his servant, Purah, sneaked into the Midianite camp one night and overheard a soldier describing a dream he'd had in which a loaf of barley bread figured prominently. No other details were given. "It's a sign that we're going to get squashed like bugs!" the soldier cried, which greatly heartened the eavesdropping duo.

Of course, it took more than bread to win this battle. Gideon continued his unorthodox ways, equipping his men with trumpets, empty jars, and torches. With shouts of "For the Lord and for Gideon!" this ragtag "army" struck fear in the hearts of the Midianites who, in great confusion, started stabbing each other with their swords. Those who survived the frenetic slashing ran away, only to be pursued by men from several of Israel's twelve tribes.

Gideon's father, Joash, was not known for his musical ability, so the source of Gideon's trumpet technique remains a mystery. (For more on this story, read Judges 7:7-25.)

Lions Sleep Tonight, Man Lives

In what is being billed as a narrow escape from certain death, a young Judahite named Daniel emerged today from a den of hungry lions with "nary a scratch on him," as one witness described the young administrator for King Darius.

How Daniel came to be consigned to this punishment in the first place is a matter of debate.

Friends of Daniel say he was set up by jealous satraps—officials in the Persian Empire who are required to report to the king's three administrators. Rumor has it that the king planned to put the exceptionally talented Daniel over the whole kingdom, which infuriated both the satraps and the other two administrators and led them to try to dig up some dirt on the king's obvious favorite.

The satraps and administrators, in the hours before dawn, claimed they were only trying to pay homage to the king when they asked him to make a law that said all the people had to pray only to the king for a period of 30 days, and not to any other god, under penalty of being tossed to the lions.

The king's media director said the palace had no comment on the law, except to confirm that Darius did indeed sign it.

Daniel freely admits that in spite of the law, he continued to kneel and pray to his God three times a day, and that he was caught in the act by the king's men.

An interior designer who wishes to remain anonymous speculated that new window treatments in Daniel's apartment may have prevented the whole mess. Sources say that Darius tried to find a way to exempt Daniel from the law, but was unsuccessful.

At the moment when Daniel was thrown into the den of bloodthirsty carnivores, the king was heard to shout, "May your God, whom you serve continually, rescue you!"

It was the king himself who returned to the den at dawn today to determine Daniel's fate. He and others on the scene were shocked when Daniel called out that an angel of his God "shut the mouths of the lions" and kept him from harm.

The lions did not go hungry. Daniel's accusers, along with their wives and children, became the beasts' next meal.

Darius has made no secret of the fact that he now believes in the God of Daniel.

Separation of church and state is at an all-time low. (Read more about this story in Daniel 6:3–27.)

Grace for Ice Cream

A woman took her children to a restaurant, and her six-year-old son asked if he could say grace. He prayed, "God is good. God is great. Thank you for the food, and I would even thank you more if Mom gets us ice cream for dessert! And liberty and justice for all! Amen!"

Along with laughter from other customers, a woman nearby remarked, "That's what's wrong with this country. Kids today don't even know how to pray.

"Asking God for ice cream! Why, I never!"

Hearing this, the boy burst into tears. "Did I do it wrong? Is God mad at me?"

As the mother assured her son that he had done a terrific job, an elderly gentleman approached the table. He winked at the six-year-old and said, "I happen to know God thought that was a great prayer."

"Really?" the boy asked.

"Cross my heart," the man replied. He nodded toward the critical woman and whispered, "Too bad she never asks God for ice cream. A little ice cream is good for the soul sometimes."

When the mother bought her children ice cream for dessert, her son did not eat his sundae right away. He stared at it for a moment, and then without a word he picked it up, walked over, and placed it in front of the woman. With a big smile he said, "Here, this is for you. Ice cream is good for the soul sometimes, and my soul is good already."

Touching Lives

The story line of the original **Touched by an Angel** television pilot was about an angel watching over children whose destinies were in danger. Roma Downey played the angel of mercy, who was a deceased human who had returned to earth. Della Reese and Michael Pollard were cast in the original script, which had all the angels at odds with one another.

As an employee of CBS in 1994, Martha Williamson was asked to critique that pilot show of *Touched by an Angel*. Williamson was critical of the first show. She left CBS shortly after but the "Angel" script stayed in her mind. She made it a matter of prayer—and asked friends to join her in this prayer effort—to determine if she was to have anything to do with the program. She got an opportunity to interview with CBS to be the executive producer of the "Angel" show and landed the job on the spot.

Asking Difficult Questions

She changed the entire premise of the show, but Williamson wanted to work with the original cast including Della Reese and Roma Downey. In Williamson's version, angels weren't going to be "fairies flapping their wings" but messengers of God, a "God who had to be reckoned with." She said, "We have to ask the hard questions every week. 'If God is good, then why did my baby die? Why did my marriage end? Where was God when I needed Him?' We had to meet head-on the inevitable criticism that faith is a cop-out to avoid dealing with reality, that belief in God is the opiate of the masses. Instead, faith is the most powerful weapon we have."

Angel Works

Just as she thought, that premise worked and appealed to an enthusiastic audience. "Angel" became the first overtly religious drama to break into the Nielsen's Top 10 rating during the 46-year history of the ratings service. The popular show is now in its eighth season.

Della Reese, who plays the part of the angel Tess, often reflects her own perspective in the character that she plays. "The humans we touch have to churn their own butter," she says. "Tess, Monica, and Andrew don't come to fix people in trouble. They come to teach them how to fix themselves. They provide assistance for people at a crossroads. If people see the hope, see that life is not all about oppression, depression and suppression, and have their eyes opened, they can become their own miracle."

A "God Thing"

Della Reese also believes the program is a "God thing." In her book *Touched by an Angel,* Williamson tells about the time she and Reese were getting their physical exams for insurance coverage before they began shooting the show.

Della Reese refused to sign the insurance papers. When asked why she wouldn't, she explained that in the blank where it asked for "anticipated length of employment," it said six episodes. Reese refused to sign the form until the anticipated length of employment was changed to read "ten years." Reese believed God had brought them together to do this show and that it would last at least that long.

A Fresh Look at Psalm 23

Have you ever thought or looked at this favorite Psalm in this way?

"The Lord is my Shepherd." .... *That's Relationship!*
"I shall not want." .... *That's Supply!*
"He maketh me to lie down in
    green pastures." .... *That's Rest!*
"He leadeth me beside the still waters." .... *That's Refreshment!*
"He restoreth my soul." .... *That's Healing!*
"He leadeth me in the paths
    of righteousness." .... *That's Guidance!*
"For His name sake." .... *That's Purpose!*
"Yea, though I walk through the valley
    of the shadow of death." .... *That's Testing!*
"I will fear no evil." .... *That's Protection!*
"For Thou art with me." .... *That's Faithfulness!*
"Thy rod and Thy staff they comfort me." ... *That's Discipline!*
"Thou preparest a table before me
    in the presence of mine enemies." .... *That's Hope!*
"Thou anointest my head with oil." .... *That's Consecra-
tion!*
"My cup runneth over." .... *That's Abundance!*
"Surely goodness and mercy shall
    follow me all the days of my life." ... *That's Blessing!*
"And I will dwell in the house
    of the Lord." .... *That's Security!*
"Forever." .... *That's Eternity!*

Wrunken

In the sixteenth century, Philip II ordered the execution of all Protestants found reading the Bible in their own language.

While inspecting the house of the Mayor of Brugge (a city in Belgium), the Inquisitors found a Bible. The mayor's family members claimed to know nothing about the Bible.

Finally the officials asked a young maid-servant, Wrunken. She boldly said, "I am reading it!" The mayor, knowing the penalty, defended her: "Oh, no, she only owns it. She doesn't read from it."

Wrunken, however, declared, "This book is mine. I am reading from it, and it is more precious to me than anything."

Sentenced

She was sentenced to die by suffocation—tied to a hollow carved into the city wall, with the opening then bricked over.

As she was placed in the wall and the bricks were laid, officials pleaded, "Recant. You will suffocate and die!" She answered, "I will be with Jesus." Just before the wall was completed, the official repeated, "Recant, and you will go free." She refused, saying, "O Lord, forgive my murderers."

The final brick was laid. Her bones were removed from the wall years later and buried in the cemetery of Brugge.

Information from dcTalk and The Voice of the Martyrs, *Jesus Freaks* (Tulsa, OK: Albury Publishing, 1999, 41–42.

PAX

When PAX Network founder, Lowell "Bud" Paxson, "retired" from his Home Shopping Network in 1991, his friends told him to enjoy retirement, go to the beach, and relax. He said, "I took their advice. It was a great day!"

Then Paxson, a committed Christian, began his most ambitious enterprise yet: PAX TV, now the nation's seventh largest broadcast television network. Paxson had his sights set on establishing a network with quality programming with family values, free of excessive violence, explicit sex, or foul language.

Ratings Run

In June 2001, PAX TV tied its highest rated week ever with a 1.1 household rating, or 1.5 million viewers—a 22 percent increase over the same time a year ago. The network features off-network runs of popular shows including the CBS hit series *Touched By An Angel*, *Dr. Quinn*, *Medicine Woman*, and *Diagnosis Murder*, in addition to a number of original programs and theatrical and made-for-television movies.

In his book, *Threading the Needle,* Paxson said, "Frankly, when I look at the deluge of trashy programming that's flooding the market today, I don't believe for a second we can fail."

That isn't the only reason he expects PAX TV to succeed. He said, "Each of us has three threads, or elements, of life we need to get through the needle's eye: the business or career thread, the spiritual thread, and the family thread."

According to Paxson, PAX TV combines all three.

Time Out

Even machines need time out for maintenance in order to operate efficiently. Time out is even more necessary for people because that is the way God made us. In fact, people need daily rest and weekly down time, a vital dose of R and R.

Rest and relaxation should be taken seriously. Americans particularly have a hard time "getting away from it all" with their propensity to multitask and overload. One out of two Americans say fatigue affects their on-the-job performance. According to the National Sleep Foundation, about 100,000 automobile crashes annually are attributed to drowsy drivers.

God-Ordained Rest

Regular rest is ordained in the 10 Commandments: "Remember the sabbath day to keep it holy. Six days shalt thou labour, and do all thy work: but the seventh day is the sabbath of the Lord thy God: in it thou shalt not do any work" (Exodus 20:8–10). Since New Testament times most Christians have observed the Sabbath on Sunday.

British author G. K. Chesterton said leisure is a matter of freedom:

- freedom to do something (for instance taking time to pursue a hobby),
- freedom to do anything (to climb a mountain simply because it is there),
- freedom to do nothing.

The Sabbath is not just a time to stop doing the work we

normally do throughout the week; it is a time to do something else—rest! Rest is essential for physical, mental, emotional, and spiritual well-being. It restores perspective and rejuvenates creativity.

Restful Reasons

One of the main reasons for people to rest is simply to enjoy creation and our Creator. One can be surprised, delighted, or calmed by seeing cloud formations, an exquisite sunrise or sunset, a beautiful garden, or enjoying a walk along a sandy beach.

Play is another important part of rest. Play is an activity that is pursued for its own sake. Some activities, such as golf, can lose their play value if taken too seriously. Play brings a freedom of mind and spirit simply to enjoy.

Helpful Hobbies

Hobbies, likewise, can be a good way to engage a person in activities for the sheer fun of it. Pursuing a hobby, such as coin collecting or quilting, helps take the drudgery out of the day-to-day world of work. By taking our thoughts off urgent or pressing problems, our minds relax and we often find new and creative solutions to longstanding dilemmas. For example, during World War II, Winston Churchill took time to paint. No doubt it helped him do some fresh thinking about the overwhelming challenges he faced as prime minister of England.

Put in proper perspective, leisure is needed to energize us, enhance our enjoyment of life and loved ones, and increase our love for our Creator.

Dig This One!

Archaeology is a relatively new science (only about 200 years old) about a very old subject. It is the chief means for learning about ancient cultures and civilizations that existed before the invention of writing over 5,000 years ago.

Biblical archaeology is the study of excavated materials of the cultures and civilizations from the time of the Bible. It is said to have begun in 1799 with the discovery of the Rosetta Stone, which provides the key to be able to translate ancient Egyptian language. The findings of biblical archaeologists shed light on what life was like in biblical times and help us understand the Bible better by understanding the culture and the context in which the Bible was written.

Until the 1800s, little was known of biblical times and customs except what was recorded in the Old Testament; knowledge of New Testament times came from Greek historians who recorded and preserved significant materials from that era.

Papyri

The discovery of large quantities of papyri (manuscripts written on paper made from papyrus reeds) in Egypt at the beginning of the twentieth century has helped establish a grammar of ancient languages and consequently to positively date the writing of the New Testament books to the first century. It has also confirmed that New Testament Greek was the common language used during the first century of the Christian era, and not a language invented for the writing of the New Testament.

City of Ur in Ancient Babylon

Abraham lived in the city of Ur around 2000 B.C. Archaeological findings reveal that the city was destroyed suddenly and reduced to ruins about 1960 B.C. From that time it has been covered up until modern archaeologists excavated the site on the Euphrates River in present-day Iraq. Evidence from the site confirms that idolatry was widespread in that area. Abraham lived there until God called him to leave those surroundings and to begin a people of God separated from idols to follow the one true God.

COOPERATION PLUS

Walking up stairs requires the cooperation of 300 different muscles. The sense receptors in your foot let your brain know exactly what kind of surface you're walking on—rocks, ice, soft sand—and your foot immediately adapts.

In the course of your life, you will walk about 100,000 miles. If you walk or jog for exercise, of course, that number will be higher. Speaking of running—when you run, you are putting three to four times the weight of your body on each foot.

Dead Sea Scrolls

The discovery of ancient manuscripts in the caves near the Dead Sea in 1947 is unquestionably the greatest manuscript discovery of modern times. The scrolls have been dated from as early as 250 B.C. to about A.D. 68. These documents are the oldest existing manuscripts of the Bible in any language.

Code of Hammurabi

Hammurabi was a Babylonian king who lived at the same time as Abraham. The code of law that governed his kingdom was engraved in ancient cuneiform on a stone found in 1902. Hammurabi claimed he received the laws from the sun-god Shamash. The laws dealt with worship, justice, taxes, wages, interest, money lending, property, disputes, marriage, public works, and commerce. Written 300 years before the laws of Moses, the Hammurabi code is so significantly different that it could not have been the basis for the Mosaic law, which Moses received directly from God.

Death of Pharaoh's Firstborn

Experts are not certain who the pharaoh was when Moses came to deliver the children of Israel from his control, but mummies of four pharaohs have been found from that time—one of which was the ruling pharaoh of Egypt when the plague of the death hit the firstborn Egyptians. Two of those four rulers were not succeeded by their firstborn sons indicating something happened to the firstborn.

These are but a few of the enormous finds of modern biblical archaeologists. It is obvious that archaeology is far from being a "dead" science. It brings Bible history and people to life and helps us understand the Good Book.

If God Could . . . Then God Can

- If God could stop the world from spinning so Joshua could have daylight in which to win his battle, then he can stop your world from spinning out of control so *you* can win your battle!
- If God could make a donkey talk, then God can speak to you!
- If God could part the sea to make way for the Israelites, then he can part the seas of circumstances to make a way for you.
- If God could make a woman from a rib, then he can make a new outlook out of your tired, worn out one.
- If God could hang a rainbow of promise in the sky, he can shelter you through your rainiest days.
- If God could make a mighty warrior and king out of a small boy with five smooth stones and a slingshot, then he can use your talents to change the world.
- If God could give a son to the elderly Abraham and Sarah, then God can fulfill your desires for a family.
- If God could heal the 10 lepers, then he can heal you!
- If God could use a murdering, stuttering, runaway to lead a mighty people out of captivity, then he can make a great leader out of you.
- If God could feed an entire nation with heavenly manna during a desert sojourn, then he can feed your body and soul during the dry spells you go through.
- If God could bring water from the rock in Kadesh, then he can supply all your physical needs.

- If God could send ravens and angels to feed Elijah, then he can send the right job to you!
- If God could cause the widow's jar of oil never to run out, then he can provide an unending supply of what you require to serve him.
- If God could cause an axe to float, then he can make a way for you to get out of debt.
- If God could bring down the walls of Jericho, then he can bring down the walls that separate you from his perfect will.
- If God could speak to Moses through a burning bush, then he can speak to you in unexpected ways.
- If God could close the lions' mouths, then he can close the mouths of your enemies.
- If God could keep the three Hebrew children from burning in the fiery furnace, then he can protect you and your family from Satan's harm.
- If God could send a battalion of angelic warriors to surround Gideon's enemies, then he can send his angels to do battle for you.

> **WHAT'S OLD?**
>
> Gray hair was a mark of honor in Bible times. Noah lived to be 950 years old; Moses, 120; Aaron, 123; Joshua, 110; Eli, 98; Anna, 84. Today the average life expectancy in America is 77.26 years.

At a Theater Near You

"Cast of thousands" is an understatement when it comes to the team of actors, producers, and technical crews it took to produce **Lord of the Rings**, the three films based on J.R.R. Tolkien's fantasy fiction published in 1954–55. The more than 100 million readers of Tolkien's works are a built-in audience for the movie.

Director-writer-producer Peter Jackson of New Zealand is himself a long-time Tolkien fan. About the *Lord of the Rings* series Jackson said, "I am interested in themes about friendship and self-sacrifice. This is a story of survival and courage, about a touching last stand that paved the way for the ascent of humankind."

Beginning with Caution

Jackson was born in New Zealand and began making movies with his parents' Super 8 camera as a young boy. By age 17 he purchased a 16mm camera and began making his own no- to low-budget movies and even appearing in the films himself. It wasn't long before he moved into the ranks of professional film producer and he received an Oscar nomination for Best Screenplay for *Heavenly Creatures*.

Jackson believed that visual effects technology had reached the state where it could do justice to the film series, but he waited for someone else to step forward to take on the project. When no one else did, Jackson took on the challenge and signed a contract to produce the trilogy in 1998. He and his wife, Fran Walsh, and writer Philippa Boyens wrote the screenplay. Filming began in 1999 and continued for more than a year.

Filming a Trilogy

Jackson is the first person to direct three major feature films simultaneously, which he did for the *Lord of the Rings* series in order to save production costs. The budget for the trilogy was nearly $300 million. The first film, *The Fellowship of the Ring,* was released at Christmas 2001 to record box-office crowds, with the remaining two films to be released Christmas 2002 and 2003.

The production team alone numbered some 2,500 people who worked at everything from attaching latex hobbit feet to coaching actors in Middle-earth dialect. The crew included digital experts, medieval weapons designers, basket makers, stone sculptors, glassblowers, boat builders and boot makers, linguists, tanners and coopers, thatched-roofers, milliners, costume designers, make-up artists, blacksmiths, and model builders.

Besides the leading cast members, 26,000 extras were used.

International Celebrity

What is all the excitement about? Tolkien himself was baffled by the international celebrity status that followed him after the publication of his *Lord of the Ring* book series in the 1950s. He wrote the fantasy series out of his lifelong interest in languages, myths, and legends.

Tolkien was born in South Africa to English parents. After the premature death of his father, Tolkien moved back to England at the age of four. He converted to Catholicism and studied at Oxford. His Christian worldview is evident in his work. Although there are no explicit references to God in the hobbit stories, Tolkien draws a clear contrast between good and evil.

Interest in Language

Why did Tolkien write the series? He had invented languages and wanted to put them to use. He didn't expect others to be interested in his work because to him it was "primarily linguistic" in inspiration. As a storyteller, however, he also wanted to try a "really long story" that would "hold the attention of readers, amuse them, delight them, and at times maybe excite them or deeply move them."

Wearing of the Green

What was originally a holy day honoring a Christian saint has become a day to celebrate all things Irish. Saint Patrick, known as the apostle to Ireland, is attributed with the conversion of the Irish from paganism to Christianity in the 400s.

He was the second bishop of Ireland and died on March 17, 461, the day honored and celebrated as St. Patrick's Day. When economic hardship forced the Irish to leave Ireland, they took their national holiday with them, and it spread throughout the world.

Kidnapped

Patrick was born in Britain in 389 to a nobleman's family and was given the name Maewyn Succat. He had a privileged life until, at age 16, he was kidnapped by Irish raiders and taken to Ireland as a slave. There he was sold to a local king who put him to work herding sheep and livestock.

As a slave he recalled his Christian heritage and became closer to God than he had been as a boy. He spent his days alone tending the flocks and reciting the prayers he had learned as a child. Later, in his writings, he described those days: "Many times a day I prayed. The love of God and His fear came to me more and more, and my faith was strengthened. In a single day I would say as many as a hundred prayers, and almost as many in the night. I used to get up for prayer before daylight whatever the weather—snow, frost, rain—without suffering any ill effects. The spirit within me was fervent."

A rabbi and his two friends, a priest and a minister, played poker for small stakes once a week. The only problem was that they lived in a very conservative town. The sheriff raided their game and took all three before the local judge.

After listening to the sheriff's story, the judge sternly inquired of the priest, "Were you gambling, Father?"

The priest looked toward heaven, whispered, "Oh, Lord, forgive me!" and then said aloud, "No, your honor, I was not gambling."

"Were you gambling, Reverend?" the judge asked the minister. The minister repeated the priest's actions and said, "No, your honor, I was not."

Turning to the third clergyman, the judge asked, "Were you gambling, Rabbi?" The rabbi eyed him coolly and replied, "With whom?"

Escape and Return

Patrick dreamed of escape and after six years as a slave he seized a perilous opportunity to run away and return to his home. He caught a ride on a boat and then journeyed some 200 miles to be reunited with his family. He returned with a profoundly deepened faith, convinced that the terrible suffering he endured and his miraculous escape were ordained for a divine purpose.

He traveled to Gaul and began the studies that eventually led him into the priesthood. In the monastery he had a series of dreams in which the voices of the Irish called him back to Ireland. In 432, Patrick returned to Ireland. He spent 30 years there as a wandering bishop and established monasteries, schools, and churches throughout the island. He baptized tens of thousands of converts and ordained hundreds of priests.

Patrick looked back on his life, amazed at the conversion of the formerly pagan people: "Those who never had a knowledge of God but worshiped idols and things impure, have now become a people of the Lord, sons of God." The Christian faith grew to be so strong in Ireland, the Irish sent missionaries to Scotland, England, France, Germany, and Belgium.

Abundant Folklore

Much folklore surrounds this popular saint. One such belief is that Patrick drove the snakes out of Ireland by commanding them to rush into the sea and drown. This could not have been true as there were no snakes native to Ireland, but the legend is taken as a metaphor for St. Patrick's driving paganism out of Ireland.

Trinity Image

Another tale, which is quite probable, is that of the shamrock. Legend has it that Patrick used the three-leaf shamrock to explain the Trinity—that it represented the Father, Son, and Holy Spirit, and how all the persons of the Godhead could exist as separate elements but of the same entity. His followers later began the custom of wearing a shamrock on his feast day.

The custom of wearing green on St. Patrick's Day comes from the green of the shamrock, and the beautiful green countryside of the "Emerald Isle." St. Patrick's Day was first celebrated in America in 1737 in the city of Boston.

Theories of Jesus' Missing Body

To explain away Jesus' missing body at his resurrection, people have made up several theories.

Theory .... Fraud Theory
Description .... Someone stole it.
Evidence against It .... Roman guards were posted, so no one could steal it.
Disciples didn't believe Jesus was going to rise.
If Jesus' enemies had taken it, they would have produced the body to show he didn't rise.
Disciples wouldn't have died for a fraud.

Theory .... Swoon Theory
Description .... Jesus didn't really die; he passed out.
Evidence against It .... Jesus' wounds (hands and feet pierced with nails, side pierced with sword) were so bad he couldn't have gotten up and walked away.
Soldiers didn't break his legs because he was dead.
After hanging on the cross, he wouldn't have had enough strength to roll away a rock that weighed two tons and fight the guards to escape.

Theory .... Ghost Theory
Description .... Disciples only thought they saw Jesus alive.
Evidence against It .... Disciples didn't expect to see Jesus alive.
Jesus had a real body after the Resurrection.

Source: Lin Johnson, *John—God's Word for the Biblically-Inept* (Lancaster, PA: Starburst Publishers, 2000), 280.

Staff of Life

Bread was the most essential basic food of Bible times. To "eat bread" in Hebrew meant to have a meal. The price of grain was an indicator of the economic conditions at any time. The wealthy people ate white bread; poor people ate barley bread. Shepherds who were nomads ate unleavened bread.

Several types of bread are particularly significant in the Bible: manna, unleavened bread, and shewbread.

Manna

Manna was the bread supernaturally provided by God during the years of the Hebrew exodus from Egypt to the Promised Land. It was crisp sweet bread that appeared on the desert floor six days a week. Manna has spiritual significance in that it represents the presence of God with his people and his concern and provision for their daily well-being. Jesus referred to himself as the "true bread from heaven" meaning he was a source of nurture unto eternal life to those who participate in him.

Unleavened Bread

Unleavened bread was the bread of the Passover and was made without yeast. It is a reminder of the Israelites' hasty departure from slavery in Egypt. They had to make bread quickly for their journey and did not have time to wait for bread to rise.

Showbread

Showbread or shewbread was bread set aside "before the face of God" as an offering. Each Sabbath, 12 loaves of unleavened

bread were set on the table in the tabernacle and later in the Temple. The loaves were replaced weekly, and only the priests could eat the old loaves.

Jesus and Bread

One of the most well-known miracles in the Bible involves the multiplication of a young boy's five barley loaves and two fishes to feed thousands. In Capernaum the day after the miracle, Jesus referred to himself as the "bread of life": Those who came to Jesus, the "true bread from heaven," would never hunger again.

At the Last Supper Jesus told his disciples that the bread he broke was his own body. As Christians celebrate Communion around the world they eat bread that has been consecrated as the body of Christ for the nourishment of their souls.

In addition to the significance of bread in religious life, the "breaking of bread" has come to mean the fellowship that Christians enjoy with one another.

TOP 10 QUESTIONS ASKED BY NOAH'S WIFE AND CHILDREN

10. What do you mean, you think you forgot the other unicorn?
9. How many rabbits did you say we now have?
8. Where did you last see the tarantulas, dear?
7. Who told you that April showers bring May flowers?
6. What did the cruise brochure list as our destination ports?
5. Why didn't you tell me this tar-covered box would float?
4. Did you remember to bring the seasickness tablets?
3. May I go outside and play?
2. Where are the bathrooms?
1. Are we there yet?

How Do You Know?

How can you tell if you are in a Texas church? Here's how!

The preacher says, "I'd like to ask Bubba to help take up the offering" and five people stand up, three of which are women.

The choir group is known as the "OK Chorale."

Baptism is called "branding."

When people hear the story of Jesus feeding 5,000 people, they immediately wonder if the two fish he used were catfish or bass.

People grumble about Noah letting coyotes and gophers on the ark.

Opening day of deer season is an official church holiday.

A member of the church requests to be buried in his pickup truck because "It ain't never been in a hole it couldn't get out of."

The pastor wears boots.

Four generations of the same family sit together in one pew.

There is no such thing as a "private" sin.

Every year there's a fund-raiser to help someone in the congregation buy a new septic tank.

Finding and returning lost sheep isn't just a parable.

High notes on the organ set the dogs to howling.

People think "rapture" is the result of lifting something too heavy.

The final words of the benediction are "Ya'll come back now, ya hear."

Fruit and Vegetable Basket Upset!

How well do you know your Bible fruits and vegetables? Familiarity with the King James Version will help with this quiz. Check your answers on page 41.

1. Which food did the Israelites *not* mention when they complained about no longer being in Egypt?
   a. cucumbers
   b. melons
   c. onions
   d. grapes

2. Which plant tasted bitter and symbolized tragedy and sorrow to the Israelites?
   a. mallow
   b. mandrake
   c. calamus
   d. wormwood

3. Which of these fruits were *not* among the products that the twelve spies of the Israelites brought out of Canaan?
   a. pomegranates
   b. apples
   c. figs
   d. grapes

4. Jacob did *not* use a rod from which of these fruit trees to breed his flocks?
   a. cherry
   b. poplar
   c. almond
   d. none of the above

5. The likeness of which of these fruits was stitched into the pattern of the high priest's vestments?
   a. grapes
   b. pomegranates
   c. cherries
   d. apples

6. The prophecy of Joel did *not* mention the withering of which of the following trees (symbolizing the doom of God's people)?
   a. palm
   b. apple
   c. peach
   d. pomegranate

7. Which of these herbs did Jesus cite as being tithed by the Pharisees?
   a. cumin
   b. anise
   c. mint
   d. all three

8. Which kind of fruit did the chief cupbearer of Pharaoh dream about and ask Joseph about?
   a. grapes
   b. figs
   c. pomegranates
   d. apples

Answers:

1. d (Numbers 11:5) **2.** d (Lamentations 3:19) **3.** b (Numbers 13:23) **4.** a (Genesis 30:37) **5.** b (Exodus 39:24) **6.** c (Joel 1:12) **7.** d (Matthew 23:23) **8.** a (Genesis 40:9–10)

Nuggets of Loveliness

"Whatsoever things are lovely, whatever things are of good report, if there is any virtue and if there is anything praiseworthy—meditate on these things" (Philippians 4:8 NKJV).

How "lovely" are these moments!

- Watching your child sing with gusto in the church choir
- An hour to browse at leisure through a bookstore
- Finding a lost pet
- The smell of breakfast cooking as you awaken
- Perfumed love letters
- Birds watching bird-watchers
- Old hats that bespeak good old memories
- Tickets to a matinee performance
- A day without deadlines
- A dash of unusual spice added to an otherwise bland dish
- Freshly baked bread with homemade strawberry preserves
- A friend with whom you can "talk over the day"
- A giant sigh of relief
- A clear-sky morning after a stormy night
- The first night of fall that requires an extra blanket
- Fog lifting before you head out on the open road
- A surprise visit from a loved one
- A good report
- Feeling snug and safe in your bed
- A party in your honor

True Reflection

Has there ever been a time in your life when things were so tough, you felt as if you were going "through the fire?" Perhaps this story will give you a new way of looking at trials and tribulations.

Solving the Mystery

A women's Bible study group was reading Malachi 3:3, which says, "And he shall sit as a refiner and purifier of silver."

"What does that mean?" one of the women asked. Another member of the group volunteered to find out.

The group's detective, Sylvia, found the name of a silversmith in town and called to make an appointment. "I want to see how you work with silver," she told him. At the artisan's shop, Sylvia watched as he took a piece of silver, held it over the fire, and let it get hot. "To refine silver," he explained, "you have to hold it right in the middle of the fire—the hottest part—so that all the impurities will burn away."

"Do you have to sit here through that whole process?" Sylvia asked.

"Oh, yes," the silversmith said. "If you keep the silver in the fire for too long, it will be destroyed."

"How do you know when the silver is refined?" Sylvia asked. The silversmith smiled.

"When I can see my image in it," he said.

No matter what you're going through, you can rest in the knowledge that God is refining you to reflect *his* image.

A Prayer for Protection

One of the greatest prayers in the Bible is Psalm 71. It is a prayer for God's protection in times of trouble and terror. The excerpt below is from *The Promise* version of the Bible (Thomas Nelson Publishers):

I run to you, LORD, for protection.
    Don't disappoint me.
You do what is right, so come to my rescue.
    Listen to my prayer and keep me safe.
Be my mighty rock,
    the place where I can always run for protection.
You brought me safely through birth,
    and I always praise you.
Come closer, God! Please hurry and help.
Embarrass and destroy all who want me dead;
    disgrace and confuse all who want to hurt me.
I will never give up hope or stop praising you.
All day long I will tell the wonderful things you do
    to save your people.
You made me suffer a lot,
But you will bring me back from this deep pit
    and give me new life.
You will make me truly great and take my sorrow away.
I will praise you, God, the Holy One of Israel.
You are faithful.

Wilderness Logistics

As the children of Israel left Egypt, they crossed the Red Sea on dry ground. Many illustrations depict them walking double file through a narrow gorge bordered by "walls of water." In that configuration, the line of Israelites would have been 800 miles long. Thirty-five days and nights would have been required for full passage of the 2 to 3 million people involved. To get over the Red Sea in a single night, the path needed to be at least three miles wide, with the people walking 5,000 abreast.

Once the children of Israel had left Egypt and were wandering in the wilderness, Moses faced a series of monumental logistics problems.

> **A BIT OF CHURCH HUMOR**
>
> I was at the beach with my children when my four-year-old son ran up to me, grabbed my hand, and led me to the shore, where a sea gull lay dead in the sand. "Mommy, what happened to him?" he asked.
>
> "He died and went to heaven," I replied.
>
> My son thought a moment and then asked, "Why did God throw him back?"

Food

The people needed to have 1,500 *tons* of food each day, according to the Quartermaster General of the United States Army. It would take two freight trains, each a mile long, to convey that much food.

Firewood

The amount of firewood necessary for cooking this amount of food would be 4,000 tons of wood—that would mean several more freight trains, each a mile long, every day.

BUG COUNTRY

The Stick Bug from the Borneo rain forests has a record length of 20 inches including its legs. The ugly Malaysian Stick Bug, 7 inches long and 5 inches wide, has 100 spikes covering its body. It has an alien face and two sets of wings—one pink and one green.

Water

Eleven *million* gallons of water would be required each day as a bare minimum for drinking and washing. It would take a freight train with tank cars 1,800 miles long to convey that amount!

Campground

Each time the Israelites camped, a campground two-thirds the size of Rhode Island was required—a total of 750 square miles.

Could Moses have calculated all this in advance? Could he have organized the people to provide for themselves these vital provisions and space? Hardly.

If God could take care of these logistics, surely he can take care of the details associated with the your life today!

A Woman's Tears

A little boy asked his mother, "Why are you crying?"

"Because I'm a woman," she told him.

"I don't understand," he said.

His mum just hugged him and said, "And you never will."

Later the little boy asked his father, "Why does Mother seem to cry for no reason?"

"All women cry for no reason," was all his dad could say.

The little boy grew up and became a man, still wondering why women cry.

Finally he put in a call to God; and when God got on the phone, he asked, "God, why do women cry so easily?"

God said:

"When I made the woman she had to be special. I made her shoulders strong enough to carry the weight of the world; yet, gentle enough to give comfort."

"I gave her an inner strength to endure childbirth and the rejection that many times comes from her children.

"I gave her a hardness that allows her to keep going when everyone else gives up, and take care of her family through sickness and fatigue without complaining.

"I gave her the sensitivity to love her children under any and all circumstances, even when her child has hurt her very badly.

"I gave her strength to carry her husband through his faults and fashioned her from his rib to protect his heart.

"I gave her wisdom to know that a good husband never hurts his wife, but sometimes tests strengths and her resolve to stand beside him unfalteringly.

"And finally, I gave her a tear to shed. This is hers exclusively to use whenever it is needed.

"You see: The beauty of a woman is not in the clothes she wears, the figure that she carries, or the way she combs her hair.

"The beauty of a woman must be seen in her eyes, because that is the doorway to her heart—the place where love resides."

AN UNBROKEN CHAIN

The remains of three monks are entombed at St. Catherine's Monastery near the traditional site of Mt. Sinai, Egypt. The remains are preserved in accordance with the last requests made by the monks more than 12 centuries ago. One monk was a doorkeeper and he asked to hold his job forever. His mummy has been sitting beside the door he guarded in life.

The other two monks were men who had made a vow when they were young to devote their lives to perpetual adoration—one praying while the other was asleep and vice versa.

From the time they made their vow, they never saw nor spoke to each other again although they occupied adjoining cells. Their only connection was a chain, which ran through the wall and was fastened to their wrists. Each monk would tug on the chain as a signal to begin or end a session of prayer. The two monks died the same day, and today, their skeletons lie side by side in caskets that are still united by the same chain.

Adapted from Paul Lee Tan, *Encyclopedia of 7,700 Illustrations* (Dallas, TX: Bible Communications, Inc., 1979), entries 4515.

Fearfully and Wonderfully Made

No two of your fingerprints are alike. Neither are they like those of any person who has ever lived, or will ever live.

Your handprint is completely unique . . . so, too, your footprint.

Your voiceprint is one of a kind. The pattern in the iris of your eye is also an "original" creation.

Unique Time

Not only is your physical body constructed in a way that is unique—based upon DNA that is unlike that of any other human being—but also your place and time in history is unique. No other person has lived in precisely "your" time, in the environment in which you live and move and work and play, or in the context of the same people you meet from day to day and the relationships you forge from year to year.

Unique Thoughts

In addition to your physical uniqueness, you have unique thoughts and feelings and prayers. Every sentence you speak flows from an "original" thought in time and space. Every word you say has never been said before in *precisely* the context you speak it.

God not only knows us in the uniqueness of our creation but also knows who we are uniquely at every moment of our existence. His renewal of us is ongoing; his provision for us is everlasting.

Hymns for All People

The Dentist's Hymn .... "Crown Him with Many Crowns"

The Weatherman's Hymn ...... "There Shall Be Showers of Blessing"

The Contractor's Hymn .... "The Church's One Foundation"

The Tailor's Hymn .... "Holy, Holy, Holy"

The Golfer's Hymn .... "There Is a Green Hill Far Away"

The Politician's Hymn .... "Standing on the Promises"

The Optometrist's Hymn .... "Open My Eyes that I Might See"

The IRS Agent's Hymn .... "I Surrender All"

The Gossip's Hymn .... "Pass It On"

The Electrician's Hymn .... "Send the Light"

The Shopper's Hymn .... "Sweet By and By"

The Realtor's Hymn .... "I've Got a Mansion Just over the Hilltop"

The Pilot's Hymn .... "I'll Fly Away"

The Paramedic's Hymn .... "Revive Us Again"

The Judge's Hymn .... "Almost Persuaded"

The Psychologist's Hymn ...... "Just a Little Talk with Jesus"

The Architect's Hymn .... "How Firm a Foundation"

The Credit Card User's .... "A Charge to Keep I Have"

The Zookeeper's Hymn .... "All Creatures of Our God and King"

The Postal Worker's Hymn .... "So Send I You"

The Waiter's Hymn .... "Fill My Cup, Lord"

The Gardener's Hymn .... "Lo, How a Rose E'er Blooming"

The Lifeguard's Hymn .... "Rescue the Perishing"

The Criminal's Hymn .... "Search Me, O God"

The Baker's Hymn .... "When the Roll Is Called Up Yonder"

The Shoe Repairer's Hymn .... "It Is Well with My Soul"

The Travel Agent's Hymn ...... "Anywhere with Jesus"

The Geologist's Hymn .... "Rock of Ages"

The Hematologist's Hymn ..... "Are You Washed in the Blood?"

The Men's-Wear Clerk's Hymn .. "Blest Be the Tie"

The Umpire's Hymn .... "I Need No Other Argument"

The Librarian's Hymn .... "Whispering Hope"

A Queen's Journey

Many people know about the Queen of Sheba's journey to test the wisdom of Solomon. Do you know this?

Where was Sheba? Sheba was located about 1,300 miles south of Jerusalem on the southwest tip of the Arabian peninsula. The nation of Yemen is located there today.

What was the strength of Sheba? Sheba was well-known for exotic treasure, including gold from Ophir (an area of Africa directly across the sea from Sheba). Sheba is mentioned several times in Scripture for its gold, frankincense, precious stones, spices, purple fabric, colorful embroidered garments, and sturdy woven cords. (See Psalm 72:10,15; Isaiah 60:6; Jeremiah 6:20; Ezekiel 27:22–23.)

How long did the queen's journey take? Her caravan trip is estimated to have taken more time than it presently would take to circle the world in a small boat.

What did she give to Solomon? She gave Solomon 120 talents of gold (about 4 million dollars worth of gold—likely small nuggets and hammered ingots), spices ("never again came such abundance of spices" [1 Kings 10:10 NKJV]), and precious stones. She also brought enough algum wood (extremely rare red sandalwood, found today only in remote areas of southeast Asia and Australia) for Solomon to make steps to the Temple, harps, and other stringed instruments.

Ten Wise Sayings

1. "Trust in the Lord with all your heart, and lean not on your own understanding; in all your ways acknowledge Him, and He shall direct your paths" (Proverbs 3:5 NKJV).

2. "Keep your heart with all diligence, for out of it spring the issues of life" (Proverbs 4:23 NKJV).

3. "The fear of the Lord is the beginning of wisdom, and the knowledge of the Holy One is understanding" (Proverbs 9:10 NKJV).

4. "The fruit of the righteous is a tree of life, and he who wins souls is wise" (Proverbs 11:30 NKJV).

5. "He who oppresses the poor reproaches his Maker, but he who honors Him has mercy on the needy" (Proverbs 14:31 NKJV).

6. "A gentle answer turns away wrath, but a harsh word stirs up anger" (Proverbs 15:1 NKJV).

7. "Pride goes before destruction, and a haughty spirit before a fall" (Proverbs 16:18 NKJV).

8. "A friend loves at all times, and a brother is born for adversity" (Proverbs 17:17 NKJV).

9. "A merry heart does good, like medicine, but a broken spirit dries the bones" (Proverbs 17:22 NKJV).

10. "Like a city whose walls are broken down is a man who lacks self-control" (Proverbs 25:28 NKJV).

The Amazing Brain

The human brain is a three-pound bundle of gray and white matter so incredibly made that only God knows exactly how it works. When God made the human being, he made the brain distinct and superior to that of all other creatures.

One way it is unique is that it has consciousness, the awareness of its existence. Although the brain is often compared to a computer, all the computers in the world put together could not match what your brain can do.

What We Know. . .

The brain has 100 billion nerve cells, called neurons, which connect with one another in complex networks. All physical and mental functioning depends on the establishment and maintenance of these networks. A person's habits, such as nail biting, and skills, such as playing the piano, become embedded within the brain when neural networks are frequently activated. When a person stops performing an activity, the networks for the activity eventually may disappear.

Each neuron (brain cell) receives information from thousands of other neurons. The region of the brain where information is transferred from one neuron to another is called a synapse, where there is a small gap between the neurons. Molecules, called neurotransmitters, are the messengers that travel across the gap to reach a receiving neuron. They are chemical signals that neurons use to talk to each other, which is what makes your brain work.

Interesting Tidbits

- **Your brain reached its full weight** of about three pounds by the time you were six years old.
- **The left side of your brain** controls movements on the right side of your body, and the right side of your brain controls movements on the left side of your body.
- **The brain does not feel pain directly** because it has no pain receptors. As a result, doctors can perform some types of brain surgery on patients who are conscious.
- **The brain requires about 20 percent** of the body's oxygen supply though it makes up only about 2 percent of a person's total body weight. Brain cells begin to die if they are deprived of oxygen for three to five minutes.
- **A study of German-born physicist Albert Einstein's brain** revealed that while the overall size was average, the portion of his brain related to mathematical ability was about 15 percent larger than average. Scientists think this key difference may explain the great physicist's genius.
- **Scientists think dreaming may help the brain** restore its ability to focus attention, to remember, and to learn. Elias Howe, the inventor of the sewing machine tried for months to think of a way to attach the thread to the needle. One night he dreamed he was being attacked by a group of natives who challenged him to invent the sewing machine or die. He noticed in his dream that the tips of their spears had holes. He woke up and decided that was how the thread was going to be attached to the needle.

Maximize Your Brain Power

Just as with other parts of your body, your brain responds to the way you treat it. You can increase your brain function with these tips:

- Focus on the things you are grateful for in your life.
- Spend time with people you want to be like.
- Build a library of wonderful experiences.
- Be nice to others.
- Exercise.
- Deal with situations that cause you conflict.
- Have meaning and purpose in your life.
- Sing and hum whenever you can.
- Wear a helmet in high-risk situations.
- Eat healthy.
- Read more.
- Memorize inspirational sayings and Scriptures that are worth remembering.
- Engage in active study.
- Never stop learning.
- Limit the amount of television you watch.
- Choose active modes of information processing, such as working puzzles, playing logic games, and solving mysteries.

Which Old Testament Book?

You probably know more about the Bible than you realize. Complete this multiple-choice quiz by circling the book in the Bible where you will find the event, subject, or verse. When you are finished, check your answers on page 59.

1. Noah and the ark
   a. Deuteronomy   c. Genesis
   b. Micah   d. Matthew

2. Joseph and the coat of many colors
   a. Genesis   c. 1 Kings
   b. Joshua   d. Nehemiah

3. David slays Goliath
   a. 1 Samuel   c. 2 Chronicles
   b. Acts   d. Philippians

4. "The Lord is my shepherd I shall not want."
   a. Proverbs   c. Daniel
   b. Psalms   d. Romans

5. The 10 Commandments
   a. Matthew   c. Revelation
   b. Exodus   d. Psalms

6. "Behold a virgin shall conceive, and bear a son, and shall call his name Immanuel."
   a. Isaiah   c. Malachi
   b. John   d. Genesis

7. Saul is anointed as Israel's first king
   a. 1 Samuel   c. Daniel
   b. 1 Kings   d. Amos

8. Children of Israel spend 40 years in the wilderness
   a. Leviticus   c. Exodus
   b. Nehemiah   d. Jeremiah

9. "Entreat me not to leave you."
   a. Ruth   c. 1 Timothy
   b. Song of Solomon   d. Proverbs

10. David tells Solomon to build a temple.
   a. 2 Kings   c. 2 Chronicles
   b. 1 Samuel   d. Daniel

11. King Nebuchadnezzar sees the handwriting on the wall.
   a. Lamentations   c. Daniel
   b. Ezekiel   d. Amos

12. "What does the Lord require of you but to do justly, to love mercy, and to walk humbly with your God?"
   a. Matthew   c. Micah
   b. Psalms   d. Ruth

13. "To everything there is a season, a time for every purpose under heaven."
   a. Joshua   c. Revelation
   b. 2 Chronicles   d. Ecclesiastes

Answers

1.c 2.a 3.a 4.b 5.b 6.a 7.a 8.c 9.a 10.b 11.c 12.c 13.d 14.a

Hollywood Insiders

Is it possible to work in Hollywood and not compromise your faith? The answer is "yes" for at least three Hollywood insiders who strive to integrate their faith with their art in the movie industry.

Touched by an Angel

Brian Bird writes for CBS's highest-rated drama series, *Touched by an Angel.* He said he was "called" to his work in Hollywood while watching an installment of *Fantasy Island* at a hotel in Ethiopia. This wasn't just any episode, but one from a script he wrote and sold four years earlier before he gave up on his screenwriting career. It was a "coincidence" that this show aired, and it renewed his desire to work in the entertainment industry.

Bird recounts that he fell on his knees and said, "God, put me back in the game." When he realized the far-reaching potential for the advancement of "life and faith-affirming messages" through the television and entertainment industry, Bird said he felt that Christians had to be "at the table." Bird's prayer was answered and now 14 years later he is the senior writer and co-executive producer for *Touched by an Angel,* which is seen in 200 nations every day.

Bird says that he and executive producer, Martha Williamson, are convinced that God must be the star of *Touched by an Angel.* For that reason, the show's writers guidelines are based on Scripture—"every episode features biblical truths, and the angels are God's angels, not reincarnated human beings."

Judging Amy

Karen Hall is a writer for the television show *Judging Amy*. While writing for shows like *M*A*S*H, Hill Street Blues,* and *Moonlighting,* Hall was an agnostic. Five years ago she committed her life to Christ. Hall has written for television for more than 20 years and has been nominated for seven Emmys. She says she can include a pro-Christian message in a script because she is a longtime veteran of Hollywood and had established her reputation as a Hollywood writer before she became a Christian.

TOP 10 THINGS MONEY CANNOT BUY

10. A bed but not sleep
9. Books but not brains
8. Food but not appetite
7. Finery but not beauty
6. A house but not a home
5. Medicine but not health
4. Luxuries but not culture
3. Amusements but not happiness
2. Companions but not friends
1. Flattery but not respect

X-Men

Ralph Winter is a producer whose credits include *X-Men* and the *Planet of the Apes* remake. Winter states that Christian screenwriters who are more focused on sharing an evangelistic message than on following the structural principles of good storytelling often end up with stories that are "more cliche than compelling."

An Alphabet of Bible Facts

Authors of the Bible: The Bible was written under the inspiration of the Holy Spirit by more than 40 authors from all walks of life: shepherds, farmers, tentmakers, physicians, fishermen, priests, philosophers, and kings.

"Bible" is the anglicized form of the Greek word for "book." The word *Bible* does not occur in the text of the Bible. There are 66 separate books in the Bible: 39 in the Old Testament and 27 in the New Testament.

"Canon" is derived from the Greek word *Kanon*, meaning a measuring rod. The books of the Bible were "canonized," which means they passed the test of divine inspiration and authority. The Bible became the collection of books or writings accepted by the apostles and leadership of the early church as a basis for Christian belief.

David is the man who is mentioned most in the Bible other than Jesus. He is mentioned 1,118 times.

Enoch and Elijah were the two men in the Bible who never died but were caught up to heaven. Enoch walked with God and was no more (Genesis 5:22–24) and Elijah was caught up by a whirlwind into heaven (2 Kings 2:11).

First five books of the Bible, referred to as the Pentateuch, were written by Moses. They are Genesis, Exodus, Leviticus, Numbers, and Deuteronomy.

Gutenberg was the first person to print the Bible. He invented the type mold for the printing press and printed the Bible in 1454. It was the first book ever printed.

Hebrew, Aramaic, and Greek were the original languages of the Bible.

Isaiah is the Old Testament book that is most referred to in the New Testament. It is quoted 419 times.

"Jesus" is in both the first and last verses of the New Testament.

King James Version of the Bible, also known as the Authorized Version of the Holy Scriptures, dates to 1611 and is considered one of the great works of English literature. It became the most printed book in the history of the world.

Longest name in the Bible is Maher-shalal-hash-baz (Isaiah 8:1). It means "quick to the plunder, swift to the spoil."

"*Mamusse Wunneetupanatamwe Up*—*Biblum God naneswe Nukkone testament kah wonk Wusku Testament Ne quoshkinnumuk neshape Wuttineumoh Christ noh osc ¥wesit John Eliot*" is the title of the first Bible printed in the United States. It was printed in the Algonquin Indian language in 1663. In English it is known as *Eliot's Indian Bible*.

Name of God is not mentioned in the Book of Esther, which is the only book in the Bible that does not mention the word *God*.

Oldest man recorded in the Bible was Methuselah who lived to be 969 years old (Genesis 5:27).

Paul wrote the most books in the New Testament: 14.

Q is the only letter of the alphabet not found in Daniel 4:37.

Revelation is the New Testament book containing material from the greatest number of Old Testament books. It contains material from 32 Old Testament books.

Shortest prayer in the Bible is Peter's: "Lord, save me!" (Matthew 14:30).

"Testament"—as in the Old and New Testaments—means "covenant" or "contract."

Ultimate sacrifice was paid by William Tyndale who translated the New Testament into English in 1525–26 giving us the first New Testament ever printed in the English language. Tyndale was hunted by inquisitors who opposed his work. After 11 years on the run, Tyndale was caught and incarcerated, and in 1536 he was burned at the stake. His last words were, "Lord, open the eyes of the King of England."

Verse that is the longest in the Bible: Esther 8:9—"So the king's scribes were called at that time, in the third month, which is the month of Sivan, on the twenty-third day; and it was written, according to all that Mordecai commanded, to the Jews, the satraps, the governors, and the princes of the provinces from India to Ethiopia, one hundred and twenty-seven provinces in all, to every province in its own script, to every people in their own language, and to the Jews in their own script and language."

The verse that is the shortest: John 11:35—"Jesus wept."

Wycliffe made the first translation of the Bible into English in 1382. It was handwritten.

Xerxes, also known as Ahasuerus in the Book of Esther, ruled Persia from 486 to 465 B.C. Esther became queen in the seventh years of his reign, about 478 B.C.

You can read the Bible through in a year by reading three chapters Monday through Saturday and five chapters on each Sunday.

Zimri was king of Israel for only one week before he committed suicide by setting the palace on fire around himself (1 Kings 16:15–20).

The Ultimate Sacrifice

The week before September 11, 2001, 32-year-old Todd Beamer and his wife, Lisa, had spent a five-day getaway in Italy. Both 1991 graduates of Wheaton College in Illinois, the couple returned home glad to be reunited with their sons, David, 3, and Andrew, 1.

The following morning Todd, a software executive, had to be at a sales meeting in northern California. He kissed Lisa good-bye, left for the Newark, New Jersey airport, and there boarded United Flight 93 for San Francisco.

Hijacked

About 90 minutes into the flight as the Boeing 757 approached Cleveland, three hijackers onboard the aircraft identified themselves as such to the 34 passengers and seven crew members. The hijackers proceeded to take control of the aircraft—both the cabin and the cockpit—and the plane took a sharp turn south.

The cabin passengers were herded to the back of the plane and guarded by a hijacker with a bomb strapped around his waist. Todd was able to get an Airfone in the back of one of the seats and connect to a GTE supervisor on the ground. He explained to her what was happening, telling her that he and the other passengers would not likely survive. He said he presumed the pilot and copilot were already dead or seriously injured.

Plane Plans

Having been told the news of terrorist attacks that had already happened at the World Trade Center and the Pentagon, Todd

apparently realized that the hijackers were intent on crashing the plane into another prominent building, probably in or near Washington D.C., which was the direction they were now heading.

The former Wheaton College baseball player told the GTE representative that he and a few others had determined to do whatever they could to disrupt the terrorists' plan.

Final Prayer

He then asked the person on the other end of the phone to call his wife and report their conversation to her and tell her how much he loved her. Then this committed Christian and devoted family man, who taught Sunday school each week, asked the GTE representative to pray the Lord's Prayer with him.

With the sound of passengers on board the aircraft screaming in the background, she complied. Following the prayer, Todd said calmly, "Help me, God. Help me, Jesus."

Now Famous Words

The GTE employee then heard Todd say, apparently to the other three businessmen he'd alluded to earlier: "Are you ready, guys? Let's roll!" With that the phone went dead.

Within minutes, Flight 93 began its fatal nosedive into a field 80 miles southeast of Pittsburgh. Because Todd Beamer was committed to Jesus Christ and his kingdom, he was willing to do whatever was necessary to put the needs of others above his own fear of danger and imminent death. Thanks to him and the other passengers on the flight who joined with him, the intended target in the nation's capital was not reached, and who

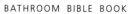

knows how many lives were saved because of that. No one on the ground was killed.

Legacy of Courage

According to Todd's wife, Lisa, "His example of courage has given me, my boys, and my unborn baby a reason to live." Lisa Beamer had suspected her husband played a role in thwarting the hijackers, and when she learned the news she said, "Obviously the future remains the same. But with this information he leaves a tremendous legacy to his sons."

> ### ONE BIG BOAT
>
> Noah's ark was 450 feet long by 450 feet high. By comparison, a football field is 360 feet long and the Statue of Liberty is 302 feet high.

Lisa continued, "Todd's death was not in vain and I see evidence of it all over. People have come up to me and said, 'What an inspiration.' I just hope that it leads to a revival of faith in this country and this world. It's clear that's what we need right now.

Heavenly Plans

"I know that Todd is in heaven and I'm going see him again and I know that his death was part of God's plan. The evil in this world will ultimately be conquered by God, and he used Todd to be a part of that."

That, Lisa concluded, is something she can hold onto in the challenging times that are ahead.

The Devil's Beatitudes

If the Devil were to write his beatitudes, they would probably go something like this:

- Blessed are those who are too tired, busy, or distracted to go to church weekly—they are my workers.
- Blessed are those who don't help people until asked and expect to be thanked—I can use them.
- Blessed are the touchy—with a bit of luck they may stop going to church and become my missionaries.
- Blessed are those who show off their good works and get on everyone's nerves—they are mine forever.
- Blessed are the troublemakers—they shall be called my children.
- Blessed are those who have no time to pray—they are easy prey for me.
- Blessed are the gossips—for they are my undercover agents, whether they know it or not.
- Blessed are the complainers—I'm all ears for them.
- Blessed are you if you read this and think it is only about *other* people—I want you!

The Authentic Beatitudes

In contrast, Jesus blessed the poor in spirit, those who mourn, the meek, those who hunger and thirst for righteousness, the merciful, the pure in heart, the peacemakers, and those who are persecuted for righteousness. They receive the kingdom of heaven, comfort, the earth, are filled, obtain mercy, see God, and are called sons of God. (See Matthew 5:3–10 NKJV.)

The Marriage Feast

When God created Eve from Adam's rib, he intended that "a man will leave his father and mother and be united to his wife, and they will become one flesh" (Genesis 2:24 NIV). In those words, God blessed the marriage relationship of men and women as his plan.

Jesus performed his first miracle at a wedding in Cana when he turned water into wine. The wedding was a joyous, festive occasion and to run out of wine was a social embarrassment (John 2:1–11). The marriage supper of the Lamb (Revelation 19:7) is regarded as the culmination of the relationship between God and his people. Throughout Scripture, marriage is honored and is to be protected by society.

Marriage and wedding customs of ancient Jewish culture centered in two events: the betrothal and the wedding.

Choice of the Bride

Usually the parents of a young man chose the wife and arranged for the marriage. Sometimes the young man did the choosing, and his parents did the negotiating with the bride's father. A man rarely married against the wishes of his parents. A woman was sometimes asked if she consented to the marriage, but her consent was not essential. Once the bride was chosen, a price was established for the bride.

Exchange of Gifts

The father of the bride was given payment for his daughter as compensation for the loss of a worker. The payment of the bride price formalized the oral or written contract between the families, and the couple was then considered betrothed. The gift could be either money or service as in the example of Jacob who agreed to work for seven years for Rachel (Genesis 29:18–20). The groom also gave gifts to his bride, and the father gave a dowry to his daughter.

The gift given to a bride by her father was considered her property and remained with her in the event of a divorce. For this reason, coins on the headgear, and rings and necklaces, become important wealth in the hour of the divorced woman's great need.

The gift given the bride by her father often took the form of coins, with holes drilled in them so they could be worn on a string. It was no doubt one of these coins that the woman in Jesus' parable had lost and was upset to find (Luke 15:8–9). In the event of a divorce, a woman was allowed to keep all her apparel, and the husband was not allowed to take anything that she had upon her person.

Betrothal

In the Near East, betrothal was a binding agreement, which could only be ended with divorce or death. A betrothed man and woman were sometimes called "husband" and "wife." A betrothal was considered binding when the father accepted the payment of the bride price.

There was usually a time elapsed between the betrothal and the marriage ceremony when the young man prepared a place in his father's house for his bride, and the bride prepared her trousseau for married life. This was an important time, particularly when the couple scarcely knew each another.

Vanished Bell Rings Again!

When residents of the Baltic sea town of Enmaste, Estonia, hear their church bell toll throughout their village it signals more than the usual call to worship. For the village's 289 residents, it reverberates the fulfillment of a long-awaited hope.

Soviet armies first invaded the Baltic nations of Estonia, Latvia, and Lithuania in 1940 during World War II.

Daring Decision

During their occupation, the Germans were desperate for anything brass to make into bullets. Car parts, doorknobs, and even church bells went into the artillery melting pot. The Enmaste villagers assumed the worst when they no longer heard the bell ring from atop the Lutheran church. What they didn't know was that six young men had carried out a daring mission to save the bell.

One of two survivors of the group, Theodor Pruul, then 21 and now 80, said, "We were thinking, 'We just can't let the Nazis take our church bell.'" Without saying a word to anyone else, the six men crept through a church window, climbed the church spire, and then pulled, pried, and sawed the bell from its wooden frame.

Long Wait

In silence, they lowered the 450-pound bell to the ground, hauled it 500 yards into the woods, and buried it. Their hope was to retrieve it within a few months. However, the occupying

Soviets severely restricted religious practice, and those months turned to years and the years to decades.

Only as Soviet repression eased in the 1980s did survivors reveal the secret and attempt to retrieve the bell. But a car wash and other new construction had changed the landscape and the bell couldn't be found. Searches continued on and off over five years but were fruitless. Some concluded that the secret had been betrayed and the bell recovered and sold.

The Search Continues

Villager Jeter Tull, however, refused to give up. Tull contacted Douglas Wells who was a Peace Corps volunteer in Estonia with access to a metal detector. Wells thought the story was too farfetched to be true, but for days he dragged his detector across the floor of the wet forest. His skepticism grew until one icy December day, the metal detector screeched.

Tull rushed over to Wells where the metal detector went off and thrust his shovel into the ground. When he did, he hit metal. "This is it!" Wells shouted. "We've found it!"

Tears of Joy

Tull and Wells ran to tell the church pastor, Guido Reinvalla. They led him back to the half-buried bell. As Reinvalla approached the bell he stared at it, and then fell to his knees. Tears streamed down his face as he bowed his head in prayer.

So, whenever the church bell rings through the village, it also sounds happiness and hope for the villagers of Enmaste.

Lessons from a Mule

Once there was a farmer who owned an old mule that accidentally fell into the farmer's well. The farmer heard the mule braying.

After carefully assessing the situation, the farmer sympathized with the mule, but decided that neither the mule nor the well was worth the trouble of saving.

Instead, he called his neighbors together and told them what had happened . . . and enlisted them to help haul dirt to bury the old mule in the well and put him out of his misery.

Initially, the old mule was hysterical! But as the farmer and his neighbors continued shoveling and the dirt hit his back . . . a thought struck the mule. It suddenly dawned on him that every time a shovel load of dirt landed on his back, he should shake it off and step up! This he did, blow after blow.

"Shake it off and step up! Shake it off and step up! Shake it off and step up!" he repeated to encourage himself.

No matter how painful the blows or distressing the situation seemed, the old mule fought panic and just kept right on shaking it off and stepping up! His determination to stay alive just kept getting stronger.

Then a strange thing happened. It wasn't long before the old mule, battered and exhausted, stepped triumphantly over the wall of that well!

What seemed like it would bury him, actually blessed him . . . all because of the manner in which he handled his adversity.

Prophecies Come True

God didn't waste any time before he began telling his children about Jesus. He started in Genesis and continued throughout the Old Testament. Following are some of the Old Testament prophecies about Jesus that were fulfilled:

- **He will be born of a woman** (Genesis 3:15). Jesus began his life on earth in Mary's womb and was born in the same manner as all other people (Matthew 1:18–25).
- **He will be from the house of David** (2 Samuel 7:12–16). Joseph, Mary's husband and Jesus' earthly father, was a distant relative of David (Matthew 1:1–16).
- **He will have a forerunner** (Isaiah 40:3–5). This was John the Baptist, who said, "Prepare the way of the Lord" (Matthew 3:1–3 NKJV).
- **He will be a healer** (Isaiah 53:4). This prophecy came true repeatedly in the gospels as Jesus healed the sick and raised people from the dead (Matthew 8:5–13, 16; 9:22; John 11:14–45).
- **He will make a triumphal entry into Jerusalem** (Zechariah 9:9). Shortly after healing two blind men, Jesus rode into Jerusalem on a donkey. As he entered the city, the people shouted, "Hosanna to the Son of David! Blessed is he who comes in the name of the Lord!" (Matthew 21:1–11 NKJV).
- **He will be buried with the rich** (Isaiah 53:9). After Jesus was crucified, Joseph, a rich man from Arimathea, buried Jesus' body in his own newly-hewn tomb (Matthew 27:57–60).

Makes Sense to Me

The following essay was written by Danny Dutton, age eight, from Chula Vista, California, for his third-grade homework assignment to "Explain God":

One of God's main jobs is making people. He makes them to replace the ones that die so there will be enough people to take care of things here on earth. He doesn't make grown-ups, just babies. I think because they are smaller and easier to make. That way, he doesn't have to take up his valuable time teaching them to talk and walk, he can just leave that to mothers and fathers.

God's second most important job is listening to prayers. An awful lot of this goes on, since some people, like preachers and things, pray at times besides bedtime. God doesn't have time to listen to the radio or TV on account of this. Since he hears everything, not only prayers, there must be a terrible lot of noise in his ears, unless he has thought of a way to turn it off.

God sees everything and hears everything and is everywhere, which keeps him pretty busy. So you shouldn't go wasting his time by going over your parents' head asking for something they said you couldn't have.

Atheists are people who don't believe in God. I don't think there are any in Chula Vista. At least there aren't any who come to our church.

Jesus is God's Son. He used to do all the hard work like walking on water and performing miracles and trying to teach the people who didn't want to learn about God. They finally got tired of him preaching to them and they crucified him. But he was good and kind like his Father and he told his Father that they didn't know what they were doing and to forgive them and God said OK.

His Dad [God] appreciated everything that he had done and all his hard work on earth so he told him he didn't have to go out on the road anymore, he could stay in heaven. So he did. And now he helps his Dad out by listening to prayers and seeing things which are important for God to take care of and which ones he can take care of himself without having to bother God. Like a secretary, only more important, of course. You can pray anytime you want and they are sure to hear you because they got it worked out so one of them is on duty all the time.

If you don't believe in God, besides being an atheist, you will be very lonely, because your parents can't go everywhere with you, like to camp, but God can. It is good to know he's around you when you're scared in the dark or when you can't swim very good and you get thrown into real deep water by big kids. But you shouldn't just always think of what God can do for you.

I figure God put me here and he can take me back anytime he pleases. And that's why I believe in God.

Twelve Ways to Be a Better Dad

1. **Love your children's mother.** One of the most important things a father can do for his children is to show love and respect to their mother. If you are married to her, show honor and demonstrate care and understanding to your children's mother. Think of new ways to keep your marriage strong and exciting to help them feel valued and secure and as an example to your children. If you are not married, show respect and support to the mother of your children.

2. **Spend time with your children.** How a father uses his time signals to his children what is most important to him. If you are always too busy for your children, they will feel neglected no matter what you tell them. Find ways to spend time with your children individually as well as together as a family.

3. **Earn the right to be heard.** A dad needs to have good communication with his children *before* problems occur in their lives. Good communication results from mutual respect, from taking time to listen to your child's point of view, and by giving encouragement as well as correction when needed.

4. **Discipline with love.** Discipline is a means of providing your child with guidance and direction, and setting age-appropriate boundaries for behavior. Be sure your child understands what those limits are and the consequences of violating those limits. Reward good behavior and discipline bad behavior by keeping your word.

5. **Be a role model.** Whether they realize it or not, fathers are role models for their children. A child will learn—both good and bad—from his or her father. A daughter who is loved and cherished by her father grows up knowing that she deserves to be treated with respect by boys. Fathers can teach their sons what is important in life by demonstrating honesty, humility, and responsibility.

6. **Be a teacher.** Take time to intentionally teach your children good values and morals and right from wrong. Time invested in teaching your children pays off when you see your children make good choices that will have positive effects on their lives.

7. **Eat together as a family.** Sharing meals together even though it requires deliberately adjusting your schedule to do so, gives a time when you can share one another's experiences for the day and help look forward to the day ahead.

8. **Have fun together as a family.** A family that can laugh together will grow stronger when they face challenges and difficulties. Enjoy one another's company and

> ### ALMOST-HOLY LAUGHTER
>
> A pastor stood up one Sunday and announced to his congregation: "I have good news and bad news. The good news is, we have enough money to pay for our new building program. The bad news is, it's still out there in your pockets."

choose to spend your discretionary time together in activities you all can enjoy.

9. **Read to your children.** A child who is read to, learns to value reading and develops good reading skills and habits that are crucial to his or her personal development and eventually career growth. Let the reading time become an opportunity to discuss differences of opinion and a time to create your own stories to share with one another.

10. **Show affection.** Regular physical affection sends a child the message that he or she is loved and valued. Children who are hugged by their fathers know they are accepted.

11. **Worship together.** The most important lessons you want your children to learn should be demonstrated and not just verbalized. Research has shown that regular church attendance as a family and times of prayer together strengthen family connections. Making a practice of living out the Word of God in your daily life is one of the greatest gifts a father can give to his children.

12. **Pray for your children daily.** Let your children hear you praying for them and praising God for them. Pray with them about their needs, concerns, and the challenges they face daily. Thank the Lord frequently for giving your child to you to love, nurture, and train.

The Status of Our Relationship

Each of us is continually moving toward God or away from God. Nobody remains static in his or her relationship with the heavenly Father.

How can we tell if we are moving away from God?

- When we begin to act as if genuine joy is dependent on the state of circumstances surrounding us . . . we are moving away.
- When we begin to feel or act as if our self-worth and acceptance are dependent on how well we perform . . . we are moving away.
- When we act as if victory or success depends on us and our ability, rather than on the adequacy of God and the power of the Holy Spirit . . . we are moving away.
- When the praises of men and women around us become more important than the approval of God . . . we are moving away.
- When relating to and caring for people is less important than programs, planning, meetings, and budgets . . . we are moving away.
- When our requests outweigh our praise . . . we are moving away.
- And finally, when our rights become more important than God's will and his commandments . . . we are moving away.

What You Probably Don't Know about *Ben-Hur*

Most people over 30 have seen the movie or video of *Ben-Hur*—the story of a young Jewish prince and his friend turned rival who became a Roman ruler. Those who have seen the movie likely recall the stirring performance given by Charlton Heston in the lead role, as well as the thrilling chariot race. But do you know the following facts related to this powerful tale?

Bookish Beginning

The movie was based upon a novel written in 1880 by General Lew Wallace. Wallace undertook the writing of the book after the famous atheist Robert Ingersoll challenged him to "prove" that Christ was the Son of God.

Wallace was not a Christian at the time he began writing his novel, but he came to believe the claims of Christ while completing the manuscript. Wallace took seven years to write the novel, which is divided into eight "books."

Military Background

Wallace fought under General Grant at Shiloh and saved the city of Cincinnati from being taken hostage. He also was a key figure in keeping Washington, D.C. from a surprise Confederate attack, a feat that may have changed the course of the Civil War.

Wallace's novel was originally titled *Judah: A Tale of the Christ*. The lead character's name is Judah Ben-Hur—literally Judah, the son of Hur. The publisher of the book, Harper and Brothers, felt that the name Judah was too similar to Judas, who betrayed Christ, so he changed the title of the book to *Ben-Hur: A Tale of the Christ.*

The book was considered one of the top five best-selling books in the world throughout the 20th century. It has been translated into more than 30 languages.

Ben-Hur the Broadway Show

For many years, Wallace resisted the offers of those who wanted to dramatize the book. He considered the theme too sacred, and he did not want his work to become the subject of "buffoonery" by troupes eager to please sensation-seeking crowds. He also confided to friends that he could not see how the full story could ever be recreated on a standard stage.

Ben-Hur was produced as a play on Broadway in 1899. It ran for 21 years. More than 20 million people saw it on Broadway and in touring companies. That number represented 25 percent of the U.S. population at the time! More than 6,000 performances were given, mostly in big cities.

The Light of the World

Wallace insisted from the outset that Christ not be impersonated on the stage. The Broadway producers proposed using a 25,000-candlepower shaft of light to represent the presence of Christ. After consulting a number of Christian leaders at the time, he agreed to this arrangement, with the strict admonition that neither the face nor figure of Christ be depicted. Wallace also insisted that the play use the exact *Ben-Hur* text phraseology whenever possible.

The chariot scene in the Broadway version of the show was recreated by using two actual chariots, each drawn by four real Arabian horses lunging forward as they ran on treadmills.

From opening night, *Ben-Hur* generated so much excitement that there was standing room only. The play was one of the longest in Broadway history—3 hours and 29 minutes.

Closed by Flu

In 1918, the play temporarily closed because of a worldwide influenza epidemic that killed more than 30 million people. In 1920, it was performed again and then closed that April.

Ben-Hur at the Movies

The first of several *Ben-Hur* movies was produced in 1907 on one reel. This brief silent film was produced by a pioneering production company called Kalem, and it was promoted as "positively the most superb moving picture spectacle ever made in America." Wallace sued Kalem for copyright infringement—it was the first time the newly launched movie industry was seriously challenged in a copyright action. The suit was fought all the way to the Supreme Court, where a final verdict in 1910 was found in favor of Wallace. The film's producers were required to pay $25,000 in damages. That made this version of *Ben-Hur* the costliest one-reel film in movie history.

Big Bucks

In 1921, Abraham Erlanger, a key figure in the Broadway production, joined with two others to pay Wallace a million dollars for the film rights to the novel. They sold the rights to

Metro-Goldwyn-Mayer, which spent $4 million and three years filming the story in locations from Hollywood to Rome.

The sea fight was enacted in the Mediterranean using 14 vessels and 2,800 actors. Two thousand actors and 198 horses were used for the chariot race. A specially constructed grandstand was built—3,000 feet in length. Forty-two cameras, one of them mounted in an airplane, were used to film the chariot race. In all, that one scene cost $250,000 to produce—it was the most expensive scene ever produced to that point.

Sound Effects

The film opened in 1925 and was circulated across America for a nonstop run of more than 22 months before traveling to the rest of the world. It was received positively in Germany and England, but it was banned in China as "pro-Christian propaganda." In 1931, sound effects were added to the film.

The First Epic

The film version of *Ben-Hur* that most people recall was released by MGM in 1959, and it set new standards for the entire movie industry. This film was 212 minutes long (3 hours and 32 minutes) and was shown with an intermission. It was the first movie to be widely described as an "epic"—and it became the standard of "epic" status for films thereafter.

More than 50,000 people were part of the 1959 film cast for *Ben-Hur.* The chariot race lasted 40 minutes in this film version—one actor died in one of the chariot crashes.

The 1959 film version won 11 Academy Awards, out of 12 nominations, a record that stood until the movie *Titanic* tied it in the late 1990s.

Endearing Acts of Friendship

The best way to have a friend is to be a friend. Here are simple ways to extend friendship or forge a deeper friendship—and none of them require an excessive amount of time or money:

1. Send a note of encouragement.
2. Be present in the crisis.
3. Give a certificate of appreciation.
4. Provide a helping hand.
5. Invite the person to accompany you in a service activity.
6. Pass on a meaningful inspirational message.
7. Give a sincere compliment.
8. Provide meaningful touch.
9. Provide a place of rest and nurture for a weekend or Saturday morning.
10. Offer a prayer.

CHILDREN AND CHURCH

One Sunday in a Midwest city, a young boy was "acting up" during the morning worship hour. The parents did their best to maintain some sense of order in the pew but were losing the battle. Finally, the father picked the little fellow up and walked sternly back the aisle on his way out. Just before reaching the safety of the foyer, the little one called loudly to the congregation, "Pray for me! Pray for me!"

A Prayer to Remember

When the Reverend Joe Wright was asked in 2000 to open the new session of the Kansas State Senate with a prayer, everyone expected the usual generalities. Instead, the following prayer is what they heard. The prayer subsequently was aired by commentator Paul Harvey on his radio program, *The Rest of the Story*. Harvey received a larger response to this program than any other program he had aired to that time.

Heavenly Father, we come before you today to ask your forgiveness and to seek your direction and guidance. We know your Word says, "Woe to those who call evil good," but that is exactly what we have done.

We have lost our spiritual equilibrium and reversed our values.

We confess that:

We have ridiculed the absolute truth of your Word and called it pluralism.

We have worshiped other gods and called it multiculturalism.

We have endorsed perversion and called it "alternative lifestyle."

We have exploited the poor and called it "the lottery."

We have rewarded laziness and called it "welfare."

We have killed our unborn and called it "choice."

We have shot abortionists and called it "justifiable."

We have neglected to discipline our children and called it "building self-esteem."

We have abused power and called it "politics."

We have coveted our neighbor's possessions and called it "ambition."

We have polluted the air with profanity and pornography and called it "freedom of expression."

We have ridiculed the time-honored values of our forefathers and called it "enlightenment."

Search us, O God, and know our hearts today; cleanse us from every sin and set us free. Guide and bless these men and women who have been sent to direct us to the center of your will, to open our hearts and ask it in the name of your Son, the living Savior, Jesus Christ. Amen.

ALMOST-HOLY LAUGHTER

A Sunday school teacher began her lesson with a question, "Boys and girls, what do we know about God?"
A hand shot up in the air.

"He is an artist!" said the kindergarten boy.

"Really? How do you know?" the teacher asked.

"You know—Our Father, who does art in Heaven"

The response to Wright's prayer was immediate. Several legislators walked out during the prayer in protest. In six weeks, Central Christian Church, where Wright was the pastor, logged more than 5,000 phone calls—only 47 of those calls were negative. The church received requests internationally for copies of the prayer, including requests from India, Korea, and several nations in Africa.

The Bible According to Kids

Elementary school children were asked questions about the Bible. Here are some of their answers—spelling and grammar have *not* been corrected!

In the first book of the bible, Guinesses, God got tired of creating the world, so he took the Sabbath off.

Adam and Eve were created from an apple tree. Noah's wife was called Joan of Ark. Noah built an ark, which the animals come on to in pears.

Lot's wife was a pillar of salt by day, but a ball of fire by night.

The Jews were a proud people and throughout history they had trouble with the unsympathetic Genitals.

Samson was a strongman who let himself be led astray by a Jezebel like Delilah.

Moses led the Hebrews to the Red Sea where they made unleavened bread, which is bread without any ingredients.

The Egyptians were all drowned in the dessert.

Afterwards, Moses went on Mount Cyanide to get the ten amendments.

Moses died before he ever reached Canada.

Then Joshua led the Hebrews in the battle of Geritol.

The greatest miracle in the Bible is when Joshua told his son to stand still and he obeyed him.

David was a Hebrew king skilled at playing the liar, he fought with the Finkelsteins, a race of people who lived in Biblical times.

Solomon, one of David's sons, had 300 wives and 700 porcupines.

When Mary heard she was the mother of Jesus, she sang the Magna Carta.

When the three wise guys from the east side arrived, they found Jesus in the manager.

Jesus was born because Mary had an immaculate contraption.

Jesus enunciated the Golden Rule, which says to do one to others before they do one to you. He also explained, "a man doth not live by sweat alone."

It was a miracle when Jesus rose from the dead and managed to get the tombstone off the entrance.

The people who followed the lord were called the 12 decibels. The epistles were the wives of the apostles.

One of the oppossums was St. Matthew who was also a taximan.

St. Paul cavorted to Christianity. He preached holy acrimony, which is another name for marriage.

Christians have only one spouse. This is called monotony.

Untiring Commitment

Although he did not enter full-time ministry until he was 35, John Wesley became one of the most prolific Christian preachers and authors of all time.

- He traveled an average of 250 miles a day for 40 years by horseback and carriage. In 44 years of traveling ministry, he traveled more than 200,000 miles.
- He preached 44,000 sermons.
- He produced 400 books.
- He knew 10 languages.

Wesley's Works

Wesley's published works include a four-volume commentary on the whole Bible, a dictionary of the English language, a five-volume work on natural philosophy, a four-volume work on church history, histories of England and Rome, grammars on the Hebrew, Latin, Greek, French, and English languages, three works on medicine, six volumes of church music, seven volumes of sermons and papers. He also edited a library of fifty volumes known as *The Christian Library*.

He arose at 4 A.M. daily and retired at 10 P.M., allowing himself only brief periods for meals and an occasional nap as he traveled by carriage.

At age 83 he was annoyed that he could not write more than 15 hours a day without hurting his eyes. At age 86 he was ashamed that he could not preach more than twice a day. He complained in his diary that he had an increasing tendency to lie in bed until 5:30 in the morning.

On his 85 birthday, Wesley wrote this (paraphrased) in his diary:

I find some decay in my memory with regard to names and things lately past, but not at all with what I had read 20, 40, or 60 years ago. Nor do I feel any weariness either in traveling or preaching. To what cause can I impute this? First, to the power of God, fitting me to the work to which I am called; and next, to the prayers of his children. Then, may not I also impute it to these inferior means:

1. my constant exercise and change of air,
2. my never having lost a night's sleep, sick or well, on land or at sea,
3. my having slept at command, whether day or night,
4. my having risen constantly at 4 A.M. for about 60 years,
5. my constant preaching at 5 A.M. for above 50 years, and
6. my having so little pain, sorrow, or anxious care in life.

When you think that perhaps you are spending too much time in your efforts to spread the gospel or encourage fellow believers, stop to think again.

Adapted from Paul Lee Tan, *Encyclopedia of 7,700 Illustrations* (Dallas, TX: Bible Communications, Inc., 1979), 932–934, 1668.

Little Mysteries

God's creation is filled with little mysteries—"quirks of nature" that intrigue us, puzzle us, and compel us to learn more about what God *may* have had in mind for us to learn and to know. Consider these little mysteries:

How Many Moons?

Mars has two. Neptune has eight. Mercury and Venus have none. Saturn has eighteen moons. Earth is the only planet in our solar system that has just one moon.

The Helicopter of Birds

A hummingbird flies rings around most other birds. It flies forward, backward, and even upside down. Its wings beat from 18 to 80 times a second, and its heart can beat from 550 to 1,200 beats a minute. A person whose body burned energy like a hummingbird's would have to eat 155,000 calories a day, about 70 times the normal calorie intake of an average human adult. The tiny rufous hummingbird weighs only one-tenth of an ounce, yet each year it migrates between Alaska and central Mexico. Measured in body lengths, this is the longest round-trip migration of any bird.

Forty Days of Fluttering

More than 12,000 different kinds of butterflies are fluttering around on earth today! The orange and black monarchs fly up to 5,000 miles round-trip each year to spend the winter in one secluded area—the high sierra mountains of Mexico, about 80 miles west of Mexico City. In the summer months, however, monarchs can be found as far north as Canada. As they migrate, monarchs may reach a top speed of 35 miles an hour—some have been discovered to fly 265 miles in a single day. The average migration trip takes about 40 days.

While in the Mexican mountains, more than 10,000 feet above sea level, the monarchs—about 300 million of them—rest on thick fir trees. The monarchs that leave Mexico lay eggs in places such as Texas and Louisiana and it is their offspring who, after transforming themselves from caterpillars to butterflies, fly on as far north as Canada and then begin the trip to Mexico the following August.

The Eyes Have It

Most adult insects have a pair of compound eyes made of facets—each facet is a lens. A housefly's eyes have 4,000 facets each. When a fly looks at a flower, each facet sees a tiny part of the flower. The fly's brain then combines the thousands of images into one whole flower image, like a jigsaw puzzle.

Some lizards have a third eye in the upper part of their skulls. This eye is specialized to sense light and darkness but not shapes.

The four-eyed fish of Mexico and Central America really has only two eyes, but each is "divided" horizontally by a band of tissue. The upper halves of the eyes are for seeing above water. The lower halves are good at seeing underwater objects.

Adapted from Kathy Wollard, *How Come? Planet Earth* (New York: Workman Publishing, 1999).

Some of the most famous preachers of all time are not only well-known for the words they have spoken or written but also for their great zeal in preaching and teaching the gospel.

Martin Luther preached almost daily. He lectured frequently as a professor, in addition to caring for the churches he helped establish. His correspondence filled volumes. Even though he was perpetually harassed with controversies, which required response in both word and deed, he was one of the most prolific writers of his day.

John Calvin preached or lectured every day while in Strasburg. He supplied preachers to 2,150 reformed congregations throughout Europe.

Oliver Heywood, in one year besides his work on Sundays, preached 150 times,

---

TIDBITS

Isaiah 1:18 speaks symbolically of sin as being scarlet and red as crimson. Crimson or scarlet dye was the most difficult to bleach out of any material.

• • •

There are 66 books in the Bible, and they are divided into 1,189 chapters of 31,173 verses. The chapter divisions were created in 1228 by Stephen Langton.

• • •

The first Bible printed with verse divisions was an a Latin Old Testament, by Pagninus, printed in 1528. The first complete English version of the Bible divided into verses was the Geneva Bible, printed in 1560.

kept 50 days of fasting and prayer, set aside nine days for thanksgiving, and traveled 1,400 miles in his ministry on foot or horseback.

John Wesley preached an average of three sermons a day for 54 years. His first sermon was usually at 5:30 A.M. at a service of Morning Prayer.

Dr. F. E. Clark, father of the Christian Endeavor movement, once preached nine services on one Sunday at Bethany Presbyterian Church in Philadelphia.

John Wanamaker, a Sunday school teacher, taught 11 times that same day, and after the last service, went to visit a sick student.

George Whitefield's last hours were spent preaching. Upon returning from a journey, he lighted a candle and went upstairs to retire for the night. People, however, had gathered in front of his house and filled the street to hear him preach. So there, on the stairway with a lighted candle in his hand, he preached a message to them. He then retired and died in his sleep.

John Knox, even in old age when he had to be supported by assistants to climb the steps to his pulpit, spoke with such passion that one of his friends noted, "So mighty was he in his yearning that I thought he would break the pulpit into bits."

A church in Kansas City has this as its slogan: "Wake up, sing up, preach up, pray up and pay up, but never give up or let up or back up or shut up until the cause of Christ in this church and in the world is built up."

Information from Paul Lee Tan, *Encyclopedia of 7,700 Illustrations* (Dallas, TX: Bible Communications, Inc., 1979), 1668–1670, 4544.

Beginning and Ending

Jesus' birth and death are like beautiful bookends. Great parallels exist between Christmas and the resurrection:

JESUS' BIRTH	JESUS' DEATH and RESURRECTION
Foretold by God to the psalmist, by the angel Gabriel to Mary, and in a dream to Joseph	*Foretold* by Jesus to his disciples
Firstborn son of the virgin Mary	*Firstborn* of God the Father, the *firstborn* of all who would become the "sons and daughters of God" through believing in Jesus
Born in a *borrowed cave*, a stable in Bethlehem	Buried in a *borrowed cave*, tomb of Joseph of Arimathea
Born in infamy, to an "unwed" mother	*Died in infamy,* crucified on a Roman cross
Blood and water were a natural accompaniment to birth	*Blood and water* flowed from Jesus' side at death
A *heavenly sign* at birth: a new star in the sky	A *heavenly sign* at death: the sun refused to shine
Angels appeared to say, "He is here"	*Angels* appeared to say, "He is not here"
Wrapped in swaddling cloths— *long strips* of cloth	Wrapped in *long strips* of cloth embedded with spices

JESUS' BIRTH	JESUS' DEATH and RESURRECTION
Laid in a *stone* manger—a stone hollowed out to hold water for flocks and herds	Laid in a *stone* tomb—a stone shelf hollowed out to hold a body
Born amidst the royal flocks of Bethlehem as the "*Lamb*" of God (flocks of Bethlehem produced the lambs offered as sacrifices)	Died as our Passover *Lamb*, the sacrifice for sin, at the precise time the Passover lamb was being sacrificed in the Temple
Mary was the first person to greet Jesus	*Mary* was the first person to greet Jesus after his resurrection
Birth was a divine sign: *God with us.*	Death made it possible: *Us with God.*

The Baptist preacher was talking to a children's Sunday school class about being good and going to heaven. When he was through with his talk, he decided to ask some questions so he could see how much information the children had retained.

"After you die, where do you want to go?" he asked.

"Heaven!" one little girl cried out.

"And what do you have to be to get there?" the preacher asked.

"Six feet under!" yelled one of the boys.

Wonders of the Deep

What an amazing world God has made! Consider these mysteries of the sea:

Swim or Sink

As white and mako sharks glide through the ocean their forward motion forces water through their mouths and gills, delivering oxygen to their muscles and other organs. These sharks must keep moving—if they stop, they slowly suffocate.

Whale of a Song

Male humpback whales sing the most during mating season. Their songs can be heard by other whales 100 miles away. Their low-frequency moans have rhythm, structure, and repeated "phrases" just as do human songs. Some whale songs last more than an hour. Whales swimming in one part of the ocean sing the same song, but individual whales vary the number of verses. Whales change their songs as the seasons change.

Don't Feel the Eel

The electric eel is one of almost 500 species of electric fish. A large electric eel can be nine feet long and weigh 50 pounds. The eel uses electric impulses to feel its way through dark waters.

When two electric eels meet, each stops generating electricity and then both change frequencies. That way, their electrical fields don't interfere with each other. An irritated eel may build up a charge of 500 volts, enough to knock a human being unconscious and light up a room full of light bulbs.

Thanksgiving's True Origin

Few Americans are aware that the Pilgrims, highly religious Protestants, were strong believers in the Old Testament. They kept the Old Testament laws diligently, including the statutes related to the celebration of biblical feasts. In fact, many of our first settlers advocated that Hebrew be named the official "second language" of the new nation they were hoping to establish.

One of the feasts that the early settlers celebrated was the Feast of Tabernacles, a feast held in early autumn and one to which any "foreigners" (non-Jews) were always invited. The first thanksgiving, in all probability, was a meal celebrating this biblical feast, held outdoors as is appropriate for Tabernacles celebration and including all neighbors in the general vicinity—in this case, Native Americans.

The Feast

The Feast of Tabernacles has also been called the Festival of Booths, Feast of Booths, and God's Festival. The Festival begins on the fifteenth day of the seventh month (Tishri), just five days after the Day of Atonement. The exact date varies on the Roman-based calendar, but it usually falls in late September or early October.

The children of Israel were commanded to celebrate the Feast of Tabernacles to commemorate the protection God gave them as they wandered in the wilderness for 40 years. The Israelites were not to forget how God had kept them safe, provided food daily, and kept even their shoes from wearing out during those hot months and years of living in tents or "tabernacling" on the desert. They were to celebrate God's protection, provision, providential guidance, and promises with great outpourings of thanksgiving and praise.

Instructions for Celebration

Moses was given explicit instructions for celebrating the Feast of Booths. See Leviticus 23 and Numbers 29.

- The people were to live in temporary shelters or "booths" for seven days. They were to eat, drink, sleep, and relax in their makeshift family tabernacles. The booths were to be one room, made with a lattice-like roof that provided more shade than sunlight.
- The people were to bring meal, burnt, and drink sacrifices as required during the other feasts. These sacrifices for the Feast of Tabernacles, however, were to be greater in number and accompanied by freewill offerings and vows.
- The people were to use boughs of four plants—hadar tree, palm tree, myrtle tree, and the willows of the brooks—for a wave offering.
- The first and last days of the weeklong celebration were called "holy days." The middle five days are considered "half-holidays" during which time some work could be done. In Israel today, this week is a school holiday, and many people close their businesses.

The last day is marked by a great banquet meal when the booth is dismantled and merriment spills over into the streets.

Information from Roberta Hromas, *Celebrate the Feast* (Torrance, CA: Ark Productions, 1982).

Sayings of Satan

Much is said *about* Satan in the Bible but only three passages of Scripture actually *quote* Satan or the devil. In Genesis 3:1–5 Satan in the form of a serpent tempts Adam and Eve. Satan accuses Job in Job 2:1-6, and in Matthew 4:1–11 Satan tempts Jesus.

In these three incidents recorded in Scripture, the only time that Satan addresses mankind *directly* is before Adam and Eve sinned and before the devil, himself, was cursed. In speaking to Adam and Eve, the devil focuses on what *God* has said, not on man. In the other two instances, Satan addresses God—God the Father regarding Job and God the Son regarding Jesus' mission on earth. Satan's battle has always been, and continues to be, against God and his supreme authority.

Knowing the devil may speak to God *about* us—rather than *to* us—our best recourse is always to speak to God *about* the devil rather than *to* him. Ask God to rebuke the devil on your behalf, to deliver you from evil, and to silence the devil's accusations against you.

CHILDREN AND CHURCH

Six-year-old Angie and her four-year-old brother, Joel, were sitting together in church. Joel giggled, sang, and talked out loud. Finally, his big sister had had enough. "You're not supposed to talk out loud in church."

"Why? Who's going to stop me?" Joel asked. Angie pointed to the back of the church and said, "See those two men standing by the door? They're hushers."

A Praise Bouquet

If you visit Israel in the fall during the Feast of Tabernacles or Festival of Booths, you are likely to notice men, women, and children carrying bundles of branches and fruit as they walk the streets. These are "Succoth bouquets." *Succoth* means "booths." The bouquets are officially called *lulav* and are described in Leviticus 23.

Here are the traditional items in the *lulav*:

- A branch of palm
- A citron—or *ethrog*, the fruit of the hadar tree (translated "goodly tree" in the King James Version)
- A branch of myrtle or *hadas*, known as the "thick tree"
- A branch from a willow tree, also known as *aravoth*

In Nehemiah's time—after the 10 northern tribes had returned to Jerusalem to rebuild the city's walls—new elements were added to the *lulav*: branches of olive and wild olive trees. These branches symbolized the righteous Gentiles dwelling together in harmony with the Jews. (Christians are regarded as "wild branches" grafted into Israel in Romans 11:17–24.)

The Lulav Symbolism

Every plant in the *lulav* bouquet is common in Israel, showing us that God will always provide what we need to serve him fully. Each of the species stays green and fresh for seven days after harvest. We, too, can know that we will have fresh, new revelations, energy, endurance, and direction from God.

Wave Offering

The four species were bound together and used at the time of daily sacrifice in the Temple, specifically as part of the "wave offering" to the Lord. Today, many believers in Protestant denominations lift their hands in praise to the Lord. They offer a living wave offering in keeping with the psalmist's declaration: "I will lift up my hands in Your name" (Psalm 63:4 NKJV).

From All Areas of Israel

Each of the species of the *lulav* is found in a different geographic area of Israel. The palms are found in valleys and the olives on the plains. The myrtle bushes are frequently found on mountainsides. The willows grow by brooks. The citron trees are in the fertile lowlands. (In some desert areas, all of the species can be found at an oasis.)

> **BEST-SELLER**
>
> Approximately 50 Bibles are sold every minute, making the Bible the world's best-selling book. It is also the world's most shoplifted book.

As Christian believers we are called to offer praise and worship to God as one global body of believers—from all parts of the earth, each person committed to the Lord Jesus and bundled together with other believers. Just as the different species each retain their own identity, so do believers of various nations, tribes, and ethnic backgrounds. Even so, in praise, we are united.

Source: Roberta Hromas, *Celebrate the Feast* (Torrance, CA: Art Productions, 1982), 57–61.

When Angels Spoke

The Bible identifies some 30 instances in which angels spoke to men and women. These encounters are as follows:

REFERENCE	PERSON(S) AND MESSAGE

Birth Announcements

Genesis 16:7–12	Hagar, foretelling birth of Ishmael
Genesis 18:9–14	Abraham, promise of Isaac's birth and rebuke of Sarah
Judges 13:3–18	Manoah and his wife, foretelling birth of Samson
Luke 1:13–20	Zacharias, foretelling birth of John the Baptist
Luke 1:26–37	Mary, announcing conception of Jesus
Matthew 1:20–21	Joseph, foretelling birth of Jesus
Luke 2:9–12	Shepherds, announcing birth of Jesus

Messages to Prophets

Judges 5:23	Deborah, curse on Meroz
Isaiah 6:3–7	Isaiah, crying "holy, holy, holy" as burning coal touches the lips of the prophet
Ezekiel 2:1; 3:3; 8:12–13; 10:1–22	Ezekiel, prophetic directives
Daniel 10:18–21; 12:7–13	Daniel, prophetic words and directives
Zechariah 1:9–19; 3–6	Zechariah, prophetic words to speak
Book of Revelation	John, revelations of Jesus Christ

Messages to Individual Men and Women

Genesis 21:17–18	Hagar, promise regarding Ishmael
Genesis 22:11–18	Abraham, promises regarding Isaac

REFERENCE	PERSON(S) AND MESSAGE
Genesis 19:15–22	Lot, deliverance from Sodom
Genesis 28 and 32	Jacob, face-to-face wrestling with God
Exodus 3:2–6	Moses, at burning bush
Numbers 22:32–35	Balaam, directions on way to encounter with Balak
Joshua 5:13–15	Joshua, prior to battle against Jericho
Judges 6:23	Gideon, call to deliver people from Midianites
1 Kings 19:5–7; 2 Kings 1:15	Elijah, giving directives about where to go
Matthew 2:13–20	Joseph, taking family from Bethlehem to Egypt
Matthew 28:5–7	Women at sepulchre about resurrection
Acts 5:19–20	Peter and John, opening prison doors
Acts 8:26	Philip, directions to go toward Gaza
Acts 10:3–6	Cornelius, order to send for Peter
Acts 11:13–14	Peter, unclean declared clean
Acts 12:7–8	Peter, release from chains in prison
Acts 27:24	Paul, promise he would speak before Caesar

Source: The System Bible Study (Chicago: System Bible Company, 1925).

ALMOST-HOLY LAUGHTER

A minister waited in line to have his car filled with gas just before a long holiday weekend. Finally, the attendant motioned him toward a vacant pump.

"Reverend," said the young man, "sorry about the delay. It seems as if everyone waits until the last minute to get ready for a long trip."

The minister chuckled, "I know what you mean. It's the same in my business."

Dig Deep

Roots have been defined as the underground digestive tracts of vegetation. A plant's root system provides a continual supply of water and minerals.

Providing food is only one of the functions of roots. The other primary job is to anchor the plant into the ground so it won't get blown over or pulled up. Other roots, such as turnip roots, act as a place to store food.

The depth of the root is often equal to the aboveground height of the plant. A foot-tall mature alfalfa plant can have a combined line of roots 30 feet long.

Corn Cables

In an annual plant such as corn, the primary root system may grow 4 to 8 feet deep. If the root system of a four-month-old corn plant extended in one line it would reach 400–600 feet. For a 10-acre field of corn, the total underground root length could be 5,000 miles long. Corn also has aboveground roots that extend like guy wires from the bottom of the stalk and help the plant to stand upright.

Neighborly Roots

Roots of large trees are known to grow 100 feet deep. The roots of the California redwoods are amazingly shallow, about 10 feet deep, but they spread out as far as 125 feet. The roots of individual redwoods frequently grow intertwined with the roots of their neighbors. By intertwining underground, the roots form a network that allows the trees to withstand great storms.

How deep are your roots?

A Literary Approach

The Bible has long been the world's best-selling book. Millions of homes have one or more Bibles. But reading the Bible is different from owning a Bible. There are three ways to read the Bible. Each approach is helpful in understanding the Bible, which is essential to maturing as a Christian.

As History. Some people read the Bible as history—the dramatic story of the ancient peoples and nations of the Near East.

As Philosophy and Theology. Some take a philosophical-theological approach to find the abstract ideas and concepts in Scripture.

As Literature. Still others may read the Bible from a devotional perspective—what God is saying to the reader in the passage and helping understand the spiritual life. Another way to get more out of reading the Bible is to read the Bible as literature, understanding the Bible from the variety of literary genres. The Bible is actually a "book of books"—66 books to be exact, and while each contributes to the whole, each book has its own contribution to make.

The first step in reading the Bible as literature is to identify the genre, or literary type, of the book being read. Different genres are read with different expectations, and they are interpreted by recognizing the relationship between what is said (the content) and how it is said (genre).

The books of the Bible are categorized into these types:

✠ Pentateuch, the Books of Moses: Genesis, Exodus, Leviticus, Numbers, Deuteronomy

- ✣ Historical: Joshua, Judges, Ruth, 1 & 2 Samuel, 1 & 2 Kings, 1 & 2 Chronicles, Ezra, Nehemiah, Esther
- ✣ Poetry: Psalms, Lamentations, Song of Solomon
- ✣ Wisdom: Job, Proverbs, Ecclesiastes
- ✣ Major Prophets: Isaiah, Jeremiah, Ezekiel, Daniel
- ✣ Minor Prophets: Hosea, Joel, Amos, Obadiah, Jonah, Micah, Nahum, Habakkuk, Zephaniah, Haggai, Zechariah, Malachi
- ✣ Gospels: Matthew, Mark, Luke, John
- ✣ Acts
- ✣ Pauline Epistles: Romans, 1 & 2 Corinthians, Galatians, Ephesians, Philippians, Colossians, 1 & 2 Thessalonians, 1 & 2 Timothy, Titus, Philemon
- ✣ General Epistles: Hebrews; James; 1 & 2 Peter; 1, 2, & 3 John; Jude
- ✣ Revelation

Genres of literature can be compared to the differences in reading various things: for example, a novel, the newspaper, a letter, a recipe, assembly instructions for a bicycle, or an advertisement. All of these communicate differently.

Beyond the types of literary genres, there are the variety of literary devices that are used in Scripture just as in many types of literature. These devices include hyperbole, euphemism, metaphor, simile, symbolism, allegory, personification, apostrophe, synecdoche, metonymy, satire, irony, and archetypes.

It's a 10!

In the Olympics, the number 10 is a perfect score. The FBI's 10 Most Wanted are the most dangerous criminals who are yet at large. The decimal system used worldwide is based on units of 10.

Here are 10 ways the number 10 is significant in the Bible:

1. There were 10 patriarchs before the Flood: Adam, Seth, Enos, Cainan, Mahalaleel, Jared, Enoch, Methuselah, Lamech, and Noah.
2. There were 10 plagues on the Egyptians: water turned to blood, frogs, gnats, flies, anthrax, boils, hail, locusts, darkness, death of firstborn.
3. Ten Commandments were given to Moses on Mt. Sinai: no other gods, no idols, no vain use of God's name, keep the Sabbath, honor father and mother, no murder, no adultery, no stealing, no false testimony, no coveting.
4. One-tenth is the tithe to be given to God (Genesis 14:20; 28:22; Leviticus 27:30; 2 Chronicles 31:5; Malachi 3:10).
5. The woman who lost a coin, started with 10 coins (Luke 15:8).
6. Ten lepers were healed (Luke 17:17).
7. Ten pounds, 10 servants, 10 cities (Luke 19:11–27).
8. Ten virgins: 5 wise and 5 foolish (Matthew 25:2).
9. Ten powers cannot separate the believer from the love of God: death, life, angels, principalities, powers,

things present, things to come, height, depth, any other creature (Romans 8:38–39).

10. Ten types of people do not show evidence of belonging in the kingdom of God: fornicators, idolaters, adulterers, effeminate, abusers of themselves with mankind, thieves, covetous, drunkards, revilers, or extortioners (1 Corinthians 6:10).

OUT OF THE MOUTHS OF BABES

Children listen carefully when their parents, Sunday school teacher, or pastor tell them a story from the Bible. But the words are sometimes hard and the facts sometimes get scrambled in their retelling.

An oft-quoted story tells of "Johnny" whose mother asked what he learned in Sunday school that morning.

"Well," says Johnny, "I learned that a guy named Moses was taking the Israelites out of Egypt when he realized they were being chased by chariots. The only way to escape was across the sea. So he loaded up his amphibious machines and a bunch of helicopters and took the Israelites to safety. But the Egyptians' chariots wouldn't float and so they all drowned."

"Johnny!" Mom replies in shock. "Surely your teacher didn't really tell you that!"

"No," replies the child, "But the way she told it, you'd never believe it!"

You Can Choose

Everyone has the power to choose. It is a right that cannot be taken from you; you can only give it away by letting others make your choices for you.

There are many things that are given to us and are not ours to choose: our parents, appearance, birthplace, natural abilities, and so forth. What is within our power to choose is our attitude and what we do with the things given us. Many people who have been born into the worst of circumstances have risen above the difficulties and made significant contributions to others. On the other hand, some people with privileged lives have not put those extraordinary opportunities to good use. What is the difference? The difference is choice—what you choose to do with what you have.

Here are some suggestions for making good choices:

1. First and foremost, pray about any decision you face. Ask God for wisdom and guidance; he will give it to you. He knows you best. Sometimes God supernaturally answers prayer with direct and specific guidance. Other times God wants us to use the gifts he has already given us, particularly a good mind and the ability to think things through. Ask the Lord to prevent you from making a decision that is not in his purpose for your life.

2. Get good information. Research and gather all the facts you can about a matter and become as informed as possible about all facets of the decision before making it.

3. Get good advice. Consult with others whose opinion you respect before making an important decision, especially on career and job choices or the choice of a spouse. Read the Bible for wisdom and guidance, especially the Book of Proverbs.

4. A good decision is just that—good. It promotes your well-being and the welfare of others. A decision to do something immoral is never in anyone's best interest.

5. Decisions affect other people, so try to assess what impact each option will have on others. Will it be helpful or harmful to others? Try to make a win-win decision for as many people as possible.

6. Not to decide is to decide. Some decisions can't be avoided. When no option seems to be a good one, we get paralyzed and fail to choose. Sort out all your options and, if possible, try to create some new options that could bring better results.

7. Learn from the mistakes of others.

8. Despite our best efforts, decisions don't always turn out the way we hoped. But take responsibility for the outcome and, if necessary, make lemonade out of lemons.

9. If you seek the Lord, sincerely desire to do his will, and act on the best you know to do, trust God. No situation is beyond hope.

The Rest of the Song

"Heaven Came Down and Glory Filled My Soul"

At the Bible Conference Grounds in Montrose, Pennsylvania, in 1961, John Peterson heard the words that inspired this well-known song. During a time of testimonies, an old gentleman stood and told about his conversion. He described that night as a time that seemed "like Heaven came down and glory filled my soul." Peterson sensed that phrase was a title to a song, so he wrote it down and completed the song later that week. It was immediately popular. Peterson has written over 1,000 songs and 34 cantatas that are known throughout the world.

The words to the chorus are these:

> *Heaven came down and glory filled my soul,*
> *When at the cross the Savior made me whole;*
> *My sins were washed away,*
> *And my night was turned to day.*
> *Heaven came down and glory filled my soul!*

"Just As I Am, Without One Plea"

One of the most famous of all altar-call hymns has this refrain:

Just as I am, without one plea
But that thy blood was shed for me,
And that thou bid'st me come to thee,
O Lamb of God, I come.

This well-known hymn of consecration was written in 1834 by Charlotte Elliott of Brighton, England. As a youth, she wrote humorous poems. In her early 30s, she contracted a serious illness that left her an invalid.

Miss Elliott wrote more than 200 hymns. She wrote this hymn when her brother and other family members were invited to a fund-raising bazaar to benefit St. Mary's Hall, a college in Brighton for the daughters of poor clergymen. Elliott was too ill to attend but instead wrote this hymn as a statement of her faith in the face of her disability.

The words were inspired by an evangelist, Dr. Cesar Malan, who told Miss Elliott to come to Christ "just as you are." Those words helped her to find Christ. The poem was published without her name on it. One day her doctor handed her a copy of the poem not knowing she was its author. The poem had been published and sold with the revenue going to the building fund. Her eyes filled with tears as she realized even with her physical limitations she had made a significant contribution to the building fund.

"Jesus Loves Me"

Most Christians know the words to this simple song:

Jesus loves me! This I know,
For the Bible tells me so.
Little ones to Him belong;
They are weak, but He is strong.
Yes, Jesus loves me!
Yes, Jesus loves me!
Yes, Jesus loves me!
The Bible tells me so.

Probably one of the best-known and best-loved songs, "Jesus Loves Me," was written by Anna Bartlett Warner, the daughter of a wealthy New York attorney. When Mr. Warner lost much of his wealth in the recession of 1837, Anna and her sister Susan began writing to boost the family income. It was in a novel the sisters coauthored, *Say and Seal,* that the words to "Jesus Loves Me" first appeared.

"Jesus Loves Me" is a favorite of children around the world. Missionaries teach this to new converts as one of the first hymns. It was a favorite of philosopher Francis Schaeffer, who appreciated the need for a simple message for intellectuals and children alike. Theologian Karl Barth also claimed "Jesus Loves Me" as a favorite hymn. The Irish missionary to India, Amy Carmichael, became a Christian after hearing this hymn at a children's mission in England.

Serious Fun

Laughter is good for you. It is healthy and healing. Even the Bible says that laughter is good medicine: "A cheerful heart is good medicine, but a crushed spirit dries up the bones" (Proverbs 17:22).

No Laughing Matter

Laughter has a number of health benefits:

- Laughter has been proven to act as a safety valve to reduce levels of certain stress hormones in the body that suppress the immune system and raise blood pressure.
- When people laugh, the body releases disease-fighting agents that stimulate the immune system.
- Researchers estimate that laughing 100 times is equal to 10 minutes of rowing or 15 minutes of biking.
- Laughter relieves muscle tension, lowers blood pressure, and stimulates blood flow increasing oxygenation of the blood.
- Laughter acts as a pain reliever by releasing endorphins into the bloodstream that act as natural painkillers.

Humor and laughter are good for physical health and emotional and mental well-being. Laughter releases negative emotions that are often held inside. These emotions can otherwise cause biochemical changes that affect our bodies adversely. One of the most emotionally healthy traits a person can have is the ability to laugh at oneself. It establishes a healthy perspective of our fallible humanity—warts and all.

Good Versus Bad Humor

Good humor is said to make fun of things people can change, such as petty attitudes, ignorance, or taking themselves too seriously. Bad humor targets things people cannot change, such as gender, race, or even physical handicaps. Humor also implies an acceptance of the incongruities of life—those things that remain a puzzlement: the sublime and the ridiculous, or the expected and the surprising.

Humor can help the Christian gain a healthy perspective and recognize the truth about oneself—strengths and weaknesses—and acknowledge God's sovereignty in all the details of life.

Humor gives us a different perspective on problems, helping us to distance ourselves from those challenges that weigh on our minds and bring pressure to our lives. Laughing at a situation increases our sense that things, and perhaps especially those things that are out of our control, will be all right, and we no longer see a situation as personally threatening.

Humor helps take the dreariness out of the routines of daily life. Shared laughter implies acceptance of people and brings them to a common bond. Allowing someone to make you laugh means you trust that person. Laughter is contagious. You are more likely to laugh in a group than when you are alone. It can be a constructive way to make difficult situations tolerable.

So . . . laugh a little today!

Making a Difference

The biggest obstacle to making changes or improvements in a community is our attitude of resignation. "What good can I do? I'm only one person." It's easy to think that if one person's efforts aren't enough to "fix it"—to right the wrong or eliminate a problem—that it is not worth the effort.

Fortunately, not everyone thinks that way. A person is only responsible for what he or she can do—but every person is responsible for doing that.

How can one person make a difference?

1. **The first place to plug in is right in your own neighborhood.** Is there an elderly person who needs help getting groceries? Is there a person who is ill who needs to get to a doctor's appointment? Reaching out to others on your street or block will invigorate your neighbors and neighborhood. Every neighbor and neighborhood profits from a neighborhood cleanup effort. Remove dead trees or eyesore trash, or turn an overgrown empty lot into a garden center. There are many ways to spruce up things around you.

2. **Call your local volunteer center** to find out what volunteer needs they have. They will be glad to hear from you. Every civic leader says that it is the volunteers in the community who make the community a good place to live.

3. **Most nonprofit agencies have a wish list** of things they need or work that volunteers can provide. Contact

them—a women's shelter, a home for runaway or delinquent children, a soup kitchen, or another place of your choice—to find out if there is something you can do.

4. **Churches rely on volunteer help.** Check with your church to find out its needs. Perhaps you could teach a Sunday school class or sing in the choir. If you have an idea for a new ministry, don't be afraid to speak up and to ask others to help you. Ministry is about loving others by seeing a need and meeting it.

5. **Are you an organizer?** If so, you may be energized to pull together a group of people to provide a service or meet a need. Depending on the interests and skills of the group, you can find a unique niche to fill and likely build friendships along the way. You could form a handyman's group to do odd jobs for senior citizens or single parents. Or organize a food or toy drive to help people in your community.

6. **A great way to make new acquaintances is to join an auxiliary group or service club.** Most hospitals depend on auxiliaries to recruit and organize volunteers to run the gift shop or information desk.

7. **Take a working vacation.** Use some of your vacation time to volunteer in your community. Offer to donate several consecutive days of full-time labor utilizing your existing job skills or learning new ones. Habitat for Humanity, an organization that builds homes for poor people, has a place for both kinds of volunteers—the novice and the expert.

8. **If you enjoy working with children, a local elemen-**

tary school can use some of your time. Children's reading programs, after-school activities, or a tutoring program would help out the school staff and teachers by providing one-on-one assistance to a young student.

9. **Working together on a community project** is a great way to strengthen your family. Involve every member of your family in some type of community outreach, such as a recycling effort that could raise funds for charity. Ask neighbors to save their recyclables— newspapers, plastic or glass throwaways, or tin cans. Pick them up and turn them in to raise money.

ALMOST-HOLY LAUGHTER

One Sunday after church Mom asked her very young daughter what the lesson was about. Daughter answered, "Don't be scared, you'll get your quilts." Needless to say, Mom was perplexed. Later in the day, the pastor stopped by for tea. Mom asked him what that morning's Sunday school lesson was about.

He said, "Be not afraid, thy comforter is coming." Now it made sense.

---

10. **Read up on the challenges facing mentally handicapped** persons and contact a local agency to spearhead an awareness effort in your community. Pull together persons who can help purchase a van to give rides to work, or help find and furnish adequate housing.

11. **Are you an animal lover?** If so, the local animal shelter would welcome your time and skills to help care for their population of lost or stray animals.

Jesus in My Heart

"Tomorrow morning," the surgeon began, "I'll open up your heart. . . ."

"You'll find Jesus there," the boy interrupted.

The surgeon looked up, then continued. "I'll open your heart to see how much damage has been done and then I'll sew your heart and chest back together and plan what to do next."

"You'll find Jesus in my heart. The Bible says he lives there. You'll find him in my heart!"

After the surgery was completed, the surgeon sat in his office recording his notes: "Damaged aorta, damaged pulmonary vein, widespread muscle degeneration. No hope for transplant, no hope for cure. Therapy: painkillers and bed rest. Prognosis: death within one year."

He stopped the recorder, but remained in his seat. "Why?" he asked aloud. "Why did you do this? You created him. You put him in pain. Why? He'll be dead in months. Why?"

The Lord answered, "The boy, my lamb, shall return to my flock—he has done his duty: I did not put my lamb with your flock to lose him, but to retrieve another lost lamb."

The surgeon wept.

Later, the surgeon sat beside the boy's bed. As the boy awoke he whispered, "Did you cut open my heart?"

"Yes," said the surgeon.

"What did you find?" asked the boy.

"I found Jesus."

One Hump or Two?

When you think of camels, you probably don't think of Perry, Oklahoma, but you'll find some of them there, living on a ranch and working as weed eaters. They serve the same purpose in Kansas.

Most camels—both the one-hump Arabian or dromedary and the two-hump Bactrian—are more frequently associated with the Middle East, the deserts of North Africa (Arabian), and the mountainous desert regions of Asia (Bactrian).

Camels also bring to mind the three Wise Men, who rode camels as they followed a star to Bethlehem to see the Christ child.

A man's property, especially his animals, was a measure of wealth in Old Testament times. Job had 3,000 camels before God allowed Satan to wipe them out. Later, when God restored Job's wealth, he had 6,000 camels.

Most people in Bible times did not need camels. Kings and other rulers made better use of them for traveling, transporting goods, and invading other lands.

From a distance, camels look strange but cute. Those who have been up close to one, however, will tell you about their abominable odor, their bad habit of spitting, and how quickly they kick if they are annoyed.

Suitable for Desert Life

When it comes to God's more unusual and adaptable creatures, the camel deserves a prize. Consider the following:

- Newborns are born with their eyes open. They weigh about 80 pounds, are four feet tall, and already have a tiny hump (or humps) and a short coat. They have to be ready for action immediately—following Mom and keeping up with the rest of the herd.
- After three or four months of its mother's milk, a baby camel is ready to eat plants.
- Camels are herbivores. They can spend up to 12 hours a day grazing. Because their upper lip is split and the skin inside their mouths is so tough, they can gobble up the shortest grasses and even eat plants with thorns. Camels have sharp teeth good for chewing—or for use as weapons.
- Like cows, camels chew their cud. They swallow their food almost whole and digest it later in their three-section stomach.
- Camels don't have eyes in the back of their head, but the range of their eyesight is remarkable. A third eyelid protects their eyes from blowing sand. They can smell water miles away, and they have an excellent sense of hearing.
- Special muscles allow camels to close their nostrils at will.
- The parts of a camel that touch the ground when he kneels down—his knees and breastbone—are callused to protect him from the hot sand.
- A camel's foot has two long toes and a sole with a pad that is hard, elastic, and very wide—up to seven inches across. A camel's feet are ideal for walking and not

sinking in sand. A Bactrian's feet are equally effective in snow and sand.

- How do camels survive the desert heat? They don't sweat a lot, but when they do, their hair is a good sweat-absorber.
- When food is scarce, camels can live off of the fat stored in their hump(s).
- Camels can survive a long time without water because their bodies are designed to help them conserve moisture and expel heat. When they drink, however, forget the two-liter bottles. Bring on a 20-gallon bucket.

Camels in Jesus' Teaching

The two most memorable Bible verses concerning camels are found in Matthew (19:24; 23:24). In the first, Jesus says it is easier for a camel to go through the eye of a needle than it is for a rich man to enter the kingdom of God. Jesus could have been referring to the extra-large needle—still not large enough—that was used to sew saddlebags for camels. These needles were threaded with rope!

In order to get into Jerusalem and other walled cities after dark, camels had to make their way through a small man-sized door fitted into the larger city gate. A camel's entry through this small doorway was not impossible, but very difficult. The camel had to be unloaded of its possessions and go through the gate on its knees. Jesus' may have meant that wealthy people depend too much on their riches and fail to humble themselves and depend on God the way they should to get into his kingdom.

The second verse accuses the Pharisees of "straining out a gnat and swallowing a camel." The Pharisees were good at accusing people of failing to follow the letter of the law, but not good at seeing the big picture: the purpose of the law, which was to lead the people to faithfulness and obedience to God and a better understanding of his love and mercy.

Camel Contributions

Aside from providing transportation, pulling plows, hauling cargo, and figuring prominently in the aforementioned Bible verses, camels had and continue to have other uses. They are a food source for both their meat, which tastes like veal, and their milk. Camel hair can be woven into cloth. Camel skin is good for making saddles and sandals.

Camels have been used in war by leaders such as Cyrus the Great. Horses do not like camels, which enabled Cyrus to defeat Croesus, king of Lydia, and his horse-mounted troops at the Battle of Sardis.

In the 1850s, the United States Army had a Camel Corps that was used to take supplies to forts in the western states.

And, no, those camels aren't the ancestors of the ones in Perry, Oklahoma.

The Perry camels were purchased partly because they can and will eat thorny plants and other ground cover that animals such as goats and llamas—their predecessors at the ranch—won't eat. The other reason this ranch couple bought camels is actually very simple: The husband was allergic to herbicides but not, apparently, to dromedaries.

The Fright of Famine

From the flood in Noah's time to the promise of a final earth-destroying fire in 2 Peter 3:10, the Bible is full of stories about "environmental challenges." One of the foremost of those environmental events is famine.

Some famines in the Bible were simply the result of a lack of rain or of invaders cutting off food supplies. But others, as Ezekiel 14:21 confirms, were classified as judgments of God.

Fast Famine Control

The city of Samaria once was under siege, overtaken by Ben-Hadad, king of Aram, and his army. Famine struck and food prices were sky-high. Some people, desperate for nourishment of any kind, resorted to cannibalism to survive (2 Kings 6:24–29).

For some unknown reason, Joram, king of Israel at that time, blamed Elisha for all the trouble his people were suffering—the siege, the famine, the price gouging. Elisha, being a prophet, knew that God was going to act within 24 hours of Joram's tirade against him.

Through an unusual set of circumstances, all three problems were solved right on schedule. The Arameans thought they heard the sound of approaching armies, so they abandoned their camp and ran. The Israelites appropriated everything that the army left behind, including food, so starvation became a distant memory and food prices fell to pre-famine levels.

Abram's Lie

It was a famine that showed us the all-too-human side of Abram (later called Abraham). He and his family left Canaan during a famine and moved to Egypt. When they arrived at their new home, Abram lied and told the Egyptians that Sarai (later called Sarah) was his sister and not his wife. He was afraid the Egyptians, seeing her beauty, would kill him to get to her. Abram's ruse resulted in lots of gifts from Pharaoh, and disease for Pharaoh and his household, since Pharaoh had taken Sarai with the intention of making her his wife. (See Genesis 12:10–17.) Abram and Sarai were asked to leave *immediately*, which they did, returning to Canaan.

The Story of Ruth and Naomi

A famine forced another Old Testament family to pull up stakes and move. Elimelech of Bethlehem took his wife, Naomi, and their two sons to Moab. One son, Mahlon, eventually married a Moabite woman named Ruth.

After Elimelech and his sons died in Moab, Naomi heard that the famine back home was over. She encouraged Ruth and her other daughter-in-law to go their own ways, but Ruth insisted on returning to Bethlehem with Naomi. It was in Israel that Ruth met Boaz, one of Naomi's relatives. Boaz and Ruth married and took their place in a special line. Their first child, Obed, was King David's grandfather, and an ancestor of the Messiah. (See the Book of Ruth.)

Other Bible Famines

The entire world was suffering through a famine during the time that Joseph was running the nation of Egypt. Fortunately for everyone, including the brothers who had sold him into slavery years before, Joseph had interpreted one of Pharaoh's dreams several years earlier and knew that the famine was coming. Seven years' worth of stockpiled grain, amassed on Joseph's orders, kept everyone fed through seven years of famine (Genesis 41:28–57).

The worst kind of famine was prophesied in Amos—"a famine of hearing the words of the Lord" (Amos 8:11 NIV). Amos tried to convince Israel to stop preying on the poor and repent before it was too late, but to no avail. The exile of Israel took place about 30 years after Amos wrote his book, and Jerusalem fell about 140 years later. The words of the Lord, taken for granted in good times, were not a part of the Israelites' diet in the ungodly nations that ground them underfoot.

In Revelation 6:8 the third horseman of the Apocalypse represents famine. And after famine comes the fourth horseman: death.

God's Love Remains

If Amos was ignored in the Old Testament, perhaps believers in the New Testament were more willing to listen to Paul when he talked about the effects of disasters such as famines. "Who shall separate us from the love of Christ?" he asked in Romans 8:35. "Shall trouble or hardship or persecution or famine or nakedness or danger or sword?"

Not on your life. And Paul, who endured more troubles than most of us will ever see, should know.

Climb Every Mountain

Many of the best-known stories of the Bible took place on mountains. Following are some of the "high points."

Mountains of Ararat—As the flood waters receded, Noah's ark came to rest here, and archeologists are still searching for it to this day (Genesis 8:4).

Mt. Carmel—Elijah battled 850 prophets of Baal and Asherah. God proved Himself faithful by sending fire from heaven to consume Elijah's sacrifice (1 Kings 18:16–39).

Mt. Ebal—God told the Israelites how they were to live, as well as what curses would fall on them if they disobeyed his commands (Deuteronomy 27:15–26; 28:15–68).

Mt. Gilboa—This is where King Saul's three sons were killed and Saul was mortally wounded (1 Samuel 31:1–6).

Mountains of Lebanon—When it was time to build the temple, Solomon used cedar from these famous mountains to build his palace (1 Kings 5:6).

Mt. Moriah—Abraham was prepared to sacrifice his beloved son Isaac on this mountain, but God provided a ram to take Isaac's place (Genesis 22:1–14).

Mount of Olives—After the resurrection, Jesus ascended into heaven from this mountain. It is also the predicted sight of his return (Matthew 26:30).

Mt. Pisgah—Moses was forbidden to enter the Promised Land, but God allowed him to catch a glimpse of it from this spot (Deuteronomy 3:27).

Mt. Sinai—God spoke to Moses, who recorded the Ten Commandments (Exodus 19:20–20:17).

Blest Be the Vine that Ties

Putting down roots is a familiar expression. It means finding a place that feels like home (or that you want to turn into your home), building or buying a house, and getting to know one's neighbors.

This concept was alive and well back in Old Testament times when one of the most vivid symbols of a settled-down lifestyle was the vine. If a man took the time and effort to plant a vineyard, his days as a wanderer were over.

Getting Started

Vineyards were oftentimes planted on hillsides and terraced when necessary to keep the soil from shifting. Owners would construct a hedge or a stone wall to keep animals out. Before planting, the ground had to be cleared of large boulders. All digging was done with a hoe or a spade.

To protect the vineyard, an owner would build a booth or a watchtower where a watchman actually lived in the summertime. Towers provided a bird's-eye view of the entire vineyard. They also indicated that the owner was planning to stay put for a while, and to enjoy many seasons of good harvests.

Waiting and Pruning

New vines were not expected to bear fruit immediately. They were cut back on a regular basis and only allowed to produce fruit at the end of their third year.

All vines need a little pruning occasionally to ensure healthy growth. Sometimes the branches get wild and have to be cut back severely. If a branch doesn't produce fruit it is cut off and burned. That's also what happens to branches that don't produce *good* grapes.

The branch that resides closest to the trunk or root of the vine usually produces the largest grapes, as well as the greatest quantity grapes.

In the Old Testament, Israel was described as a choice vine planted by God. Jesus said of the Christian life, "I am the vine, you are the branches" (John 15:5 NKJV).

Harvesting

Harvest time in the vineyards, beginning in September, was marked by celebrations, singing, and the shouts of those who trod on the grapes to make juice and wine. Grapes were also dried to yield raisins. Harvest was a family affair. Every seventh year, the vineyards and other fields enjoyed a Sabbath, a time of rest.

For a people with strict dietary laws, the fruit of the vine was tasty, precious, and valuable. Abigail used cakes of raisins, among other gifts, to convince King David not to kill her husband, Nabal, after he insulted the king. After the ark of the covenant was brought to Jerusalem and set up, David gave each person a cake of raisins in honor of the day.

> **A BIT OF CHURCH HUMOR**
>
> After the church service, a little boy told the pastor: "When I grow up, I'm going to give you some money."
>
> "Well, thank you," the pastor replied, "but why?"
>
> "Because my daddy says you're one of the poorest preachers we've ever had."

Imbibers

Most of the people who lived in Bible times embraced the vine and the nourishment it provided. The soil and climate of southern Israel were hospitable to vines, as was Canaan, the hill country of Judah, Syria, and the foothills of the Lebanon Mountains. Wine was an important drink that was also used as an antiseptic, a sedative, and a stimulant.

Teetotalers

Not everyone drank wine. Jonadab became head of his father's tribe, the Recabites, and established three firm rules: People had to live in tents. They couldn't plant crops of any kind since that would require staying in one place. They couldn't drink wine.

The fruit of the vine was banned from the Nazirites (for example, Samson). These "ones set apart" weren't allowed to drink wine, fermented drink, vinegar, or grape juice, or eat grapes, raisins, or anything that came from grapevines.

Lessons from the Vine

The Book of Proverbs uses the story of a vineyard to scold lazy people. The writer talks about walking past the field of a sluggard. There were thorns and weeds everywhere, he says, and the protective stone wall was in ruins. The lesson to be learned? If you sleep and relax too much, you'll lose your harvest and go broke. After all, vines can't tend themselves.

Top 10 Questions about Your Life

Every once in a while it is good to take time off to assess your life and to evaluate your priorities and progress toward goals. Make a practice of reflecting annually, perhaps at the end of the calendar year, at your birthday, or at a time of the year that is most convenient for you.

To get started, set aside a time and ask yourself these 10 questions:

1. What is most important to me?
2. Am I doing what I want to do? If not, why not and can I make a change?
3. Am I living out what I believe is most important?
4. Do I consider myself happy? If not, why not?
5. Are my relationships as good as I can make them?
6. Am I spending time in my relationship with God?
7. Am I giving back—to the family, church, community— for what I received?
8. What do I want to accomplish before I die?
9. Am I ready to die?
10. Am I growing or standing still?

You may have other questions to add to this list to help you discover what is most important as you evaluate your progress in life. Priorities you once regarded as important may change and no longer have the same significance. Now is a good time to make a course correction.

Tall Tales

Satan is called "the father of lies" (John 8:44 NIV), but many others have twisted the truth. Satan's lie in the garden of Eden led to the fall of the human race (Genesis 3:4). As a result, lying became a common practice among humans, and the Bible has many other stories about the lies people told . . . and the consequences.

- Afraid that Pharaoh would kill him to acquire his wife, Abram lied and said that Sarai was his sister (Genesis 12:10–20). The result? Pharaoh and his household were stricken with serious diseases.
- Does lying run in families? It might seem so, considering that Abram's son, Isaac, used the same ruse to try to protect himself from Abimelech, king of the Philistines (Genesis 26:1–11). He said that his wife Rebekah was his sister, in order to keep jealous men from killing him.
- Dead or alive? Jacob's sons implied that their brother Joseph had been killed by a wild animal, when in fact, they had sold him into slavery (Genesis 37:17–36).
- Ananias and his wife Sapphira lied about the amount of money they received for selling a piece of land. They held back a portion instead of giving it all to Peter for the needy. Both were struck dead (Acts 5:1–10).
- "I don't know Him," Peter said after Jesus' arrest. Three times he lied about knowing the Messiah (Matthew 26:69–75). Jesus later gave the disheartened Peter an opportunity for full restoration (John 21:14–19).

The Touch of God

Oil. Blood. Water. Spirit. What do they have in common?
They were used to anoint people and objects, to ordain and consecrate, to cleanse, and to heal.

First Mention

The first mention of anointing in the Bible appears in Genesis and involves a dream.

When Jacob was on his way to Paddan Aram to find a wife, he stopped for the night and slept on the ground, using a stone for a pillow. He had a dream in which God promised to keep the covenant he had made with Jacob's grandfather, Abraham. This covenant included God's promises to give Abraham countless descendants and to make them a blessing to others.

The next morning, Jacob was so moved by the dream that he set up his "pillow" as a pillar, poured oil on it, and called the place Bethel, which means "house of God."

Three Types of Anointing

The Bible describes three different types of anointing: ordinary, sacred or official, and medical.

Ordinary

Ordinary anointing involved personal hygiene—keeping the body clean. In Bible days, it was common for a host to offer this service to his guests. A servant would wash a guest's feet with water, and a guest's head would be anointed with oil. David lovingly refers to this latter custom in Psalm 23: "You anoint my head with oil," he says to God. Since so many people traveled by foot in those days, these practices were understandably soothing and refreshing.

Official

Official anointing is what Moses did to ordain Aaron and his sons for the priesthood, and to set aside items in the tabernacle for holy service. It is what the prophets did to indicate God's selection of kings such as Saul, David, Solomon, Hazael, and Jehu. The Spirit of God in the form of a dove anointed Jesus at his baptism and marked the official beginning of his ministry (John 1:32). Interestingly, two names for Jesus, *Messiah* and *Christ,* mean "the Anointed One."

Medical

The third form of anointing is one that many churches still practice today. The Roman

---

AN HOUR A DAY

One of the most famous Bible teachers and scholars of his day was Dr. Alexander Maclaren. Maclaren said that all he was in himself and his ministry he owed to a habit of spending an hour a day "alone with the Eternal." He spent this hour from nine to ten o'clock in the morning. At times, he allowed others to be in his study with him, but no word was allowed to be spoken.

Maclaren would sit in a well-worn armchair, his big Bible on his knees. Sometimes he read from the Bible's pages, not as a student, teacher, or preacher, but as a child might read a letter from a loving father. More frequently, he spent the time with his hand over his face in quiet prayer—listening far more than speaking, eager to discern what God might reveal to him.

Adapted from Paul Lee Tan, *Encyclopedia of 7,700 Illustrations* (Dallas, TX: Bible Communications, Inc., 1979), entry 4535.

Catholic and Eastern Orthodox churches anoint the seriously ill and the elderly with oil. The Greek Orthodox Church sometimes anoints a well person, in order to ward off illness. Some Protestants follow the instructions in James 5:14 and have the elders of the church anoint the ill with oil, in the name of the Lord, and pray for their healing.

The familiar story of the Good Samaritan is as much of a balm to our spirits today as it was to the victim in the story, and it involves this third type of anointing. When the Samaritan saw the half-dead man on the side of the road, he bandaged his wounds, anointing them with oil and wine. Nationality and political correctness were not on the Samaritan's agenda. Relieving suffering and giving comfort—anointing with love and compassion—were his only concern.

A Sacred Recipe

God gave Moses a specific recipe for sacred anointing oil in Exodus 30:22–33. It was made with precise amounts of liquid myrrh, cinnamon, cane, cassia, and olive oil. This oil was only to be used for anointing priests.

Anointing Today

Christians are anointed by God, the Bible says, in the official sense, meaning that once they have accepted his Son as their Savior, accepted the Bible as God's true Word, and agreed to be in God's service, they are "marked" by God and made holy. In another sense, we are also anointed or healed spiritually when we receive Christ. We can bring hope and healing balm to all those around us.

Short Prayers

Many Christians would name the prayer of Jabez as the best-known short prayer in the Bible: "Jabez cried out to the God of Israel, 'Oh, that you would bless me and enlarge my territory! Let your hand be with me, and keep me from harm so that I will be free from pain.' And God granted his request" (1 Chronicles 4:10 NIV).

Short, simple prayers pack a punch. Here are other short prayers.

The Sailors' Prayer

When the prophet Jonah was running away from God's command to go and preach to the sinful city of Nineveh, he hopped on a ship and soon found himself in deep water, literally and figuratively. A storm threatened to capsize the ship and kill everyone. Concerned for the others, Jonah said, "This storm is because of me. Throw me overboard."

The crew did not object. But before they tossed him, they prayed this prayer: "O Lord, please do not let us die for taking this man's life. Do not hold us accountable for killing an innocent man, for you, O Lord, have done as you pleased" (Jonah 1:14 NIV).

Once Jonah was thrown overboard, the sea calmed, the crew was converted, and Jonah was swallowed by a big fish that eventually expelled him up onto dry land (after a much longer prayer on Jonah's part).

Hezekiah's Prayer

Hezekiah was one of Israel's good kings. He became ill and was near death. When the prophet Isaiah told him he was going to die, Hezekiah prayed: "Remember, O Lord, how I have walked before you faithfully and with wholehearted devotion and have done what is good in your eyes " (2 Kings 20:3 NIV). Hezekiah made no outright request for more years, but God gave him 15 more years.

Hannah's Prayer

Hannah, one of Elkanah's two wives, was childless. She prayed: "O Lord Almighty, if you will only look upon your servant's misery and remember me and not forget your servant but give her a son, then I will give him to the Lord for all the days of his life, and no razor will ever be used on his head" (1 Samuel 1:11 NIV). God granted her request by giving her a son, Samuel, who became a prophet and priest. Hannah later had five more children.

The Disciples' Prayer

After the defection and death of Judas, the remaining eleven disciples were looking for a replacement, someone who had been present the entire time Jesus was among them prior to his crucifixion and resurrection. They narrowed their choices to Barsabbas and Matthias and prayed: "Lord, you know everyone's heart. Show us which of these two you have chosen to take over this apostolic ministry, which Judas left to go where he belongs" (Acts 1:24–25 NIV). They then cast lots, and Matthias was chosen.

Solomon's Prayer

When Solomon became king of Israel, he was about 20 years old. One night God came to him in a dream and asked what he would like to have. Solomon said, "Now, O Lord my God, you have made your servant king in place of my father David. But I am only a little child and do not know how to carry out my duties. Your servant is here among the people you have chosen, a great people, too numerous to count or number. So give your servant a discerning heart to govern your people and to distinguish between right and wrong. For who is able to govern this great people of yours?" (1 Kings 3:7–9 NIV).

God promised Solomon wisdom, riches, and honor. Then Solomon awoke. Even though this prayer was made and answered in a dream, Solomon received everything God had promised.

Jesus' Prayer

Shortly before his arrest, Jesus went to the garden of Gethsemane with three of his disciples to pray. Three times he prayed essentially the same prayer: "My Father, if it is possible, may this cup be taken from me. Yet not as I will, but as you will" (Matthew 26:39 NIV). God's plan for his Son did not change. Sometimes the answer to our prayers is "No."

What's one of the Bible's most powerful prayers? As Jesus hung on the cross he prayed for those who had crucified him, "Father, forgive them, for they do not know what they are doing" (Luke 23:34 NIV).

A Song in His Heart

If good looks had been a prerequisite for hymn writing, Isaac Watts would have been in big trouble.

Any biography of Watts is bound to include this description: He was just five feet tall, had what appeared to be an overly large head, and was most likely to be chosen last for any playground sports team.

In addition to his physical shortcomings, Watts had a father who was a Dissenter—one who disagreed with and refused to accept all the beliefs of the Anglican Church. The senior Watts was even imprisoned at one time for worshiping God in the way he thought best. Because of his parents' beliefs—which he shared—young Isaac, who was born in 1674 in Southampton, England, was forbidden to attend Oxford or Cambridge and did not have access to some of the better jobs of his day.

A Smart Boy

What Isaac did possess, and make the most of, was an incredible mind. He mastered Latin, Greek, French, and Hebrew, all by the age of 13. His habit of rhyming, even during conversation, drove his father crazy. But it was his gift for rhyming, and the love of God learned from his parents' example, that drove him to write 697 hymns and earned him the name, "the father of the English hymn."

Good or Bad Ending?

Most of the Bible's big names—Abraham, Isaac, Jacob, Joseph, Moses, and David—died quietly and in peace. Other Bible characters, however, met death in a different fashion.

Jehoram's Coming Out

When Jehoram became king of Judah, he did what many leaders of his time did: killed all his brothers to eliminate the competition.

Because he did evil, God struck him with an incurable disease in his bowels that, after two long, miserable years, actually caused his bowels to come out of his body. He died in great pain. (See 2 Chronicles 21:4, 18–19.)

Saul's End

During a battle with the Philistines, King Saul's three sons were killed and he was wounded. Not wanting the Philistines to finish him off, and unable to convince his armor-bearer to kill him, he fell on his own sword and died. When the Philistines found his body, they chopped off his head and hung it in the temple of their god, Dagon. (See 2 Samuel 31.)

Absalom's Death in Infamy

Absalom was not a model son. He was determined to take his father David's throne. Absalom stirred up the army of Israel to chase David and climbed aboard his mule to help.

It just wasn't Absalom's day. His trademark long hair got caught in an oak tree, and the mule took off, leaving him hang-

ing by his hair. Joab, one of David's men, found Absalom and stabbed him through the heart. Ten armor-bearers finished off the young man. Adding insult to injury, Absalom did not receive a dignified funeral. His body was thrown into a pit and covered with rocks. (See 2 Samuel 18:6–18.)

More Ignoble Deaths

Lot's wife became a pillar of salt when she disobeyed God's orders and turned to look back at the inferno that once had been Sodom and Gomorrah. (See Genesis 19:26.)

Ananias and Sapphira certainly didn't see their fate coming. After all, what's a little lie among friends? A lot, in God's eyes. Each of them fell down and died after lying to the apostles. (See Acts 5:1–11.)

Ahab would say his wife, Jezebel, had Naboth killed. Why should he, Ahab, be punished for taking the man's vineyard? Ahab repented of his complicity in the plot to steal the land, but he still died in battle. God's promise about his ending was still fulfilled: In the place where the dogs licked up the blood of the dead Naboth, the dogs licked up Ahab's blood—as it was being washed out of his chariot. (See 1 Kings 22:29–40.)

Nadab and Abihu, sons of high priest Aaron, offered unauthorized fire at the tent of meeting and were swallowed up by fire from God. (See Leviticus 10:1–3.)

Korah, Dathan, and Abiram were malcontents from the word go. They accused Moses and Aaron of acting self-righteous. In a showdown the earth opened up and swallowed Korah, Dathan, Abiram, their families, and all their possessions. (See Numbers 16.)

Ten Ways to Read the Bible

1. **Spend 10 minutes a day**. Sit quietly and read without interruption. Ten minutes is only about the length of time it takes to hear two songs and a commercial on the radio, or the time between commercials on television!

2. **Look for a new insight**. Read until you gain a new insight into God's plan and purpose for you and all mankind. The new insight may be new information, new understanding, new awareness, or new application of God's Word.

3. **Read a complete life story**. Read a complete life story, such as the life of Abraham, Isaac, Jacob, Joseph, David, Solomon, Esther, Ruth, Paul, Peter, or Joseph. Read all verses you can find that refer to the person, in both Old and New Testaments.

4. **Find key words**. Choose a word such as *cup*, *blessed*, *hope*. Then look up the word in a concordance. Write down the references, and over several days look up each reference. Next to the verse write the key concept that you draw from the passage or the verse that includes this key word. At the conclusion of your study, take a comprehensive look at all you have written. What has God's Word said to you on this topic?

5. **Keep at it until God convicts your heart**. Read until you feel the Lord convicting you in your heart to change something in your life, or until God compels you to pray with intensity for a particular person or for

a particular need.

6. **Read aloud.** Hearing the Bible causes extra senses and mental faculties to be drawn into the reading process.

7. **Read very slowly**. Stop to contemplate each word or phrase. Ask these things about every word: Why did the Lord place this detail, this adjective, this piece of information in his Word, and what does this mean to my life?

8. **Follow chain references**. Many Bibles have chain references built into the text. Take time to follow these chains—reading all verses related to your particular passage of study.

9. **Check out side-by-side versions**. In some versions, the Gospels are compared—Matthew, Mark, Luke, and John are interwoven so similar texts can be readily studied on the same two-page spread. In other versions, various translations of the Bible are compared.

10. **Enjoy a daily "buffet."** Read a portion of the Old Testament, a psalm, a chapter of Proverbs, a portion of the Gospels, and a portion of the remainder of the New Testament. In reading one psalm a day, you will complete Psalms every five months. In reading a chapter of Proverbs a day, you will complete the book every month.

Pray before you read: "Lord, help me to have eyes to see and ears to hear what you desire to tell me." Pray as you conclude your time of Bible reading: "Lord, help me to remember what I have read and to have the courage to do what you are asking me to do."

© 2000 Jan Dargatz, used by permission.

An Attitude of Gratitude

Why do struggles make some people *bitter* and other people *better*? Perhaps the latter have learned to appreciate and experience all of life—even the struggles—as a gift from God.

Choosing Gratitude

Gratitude is a choice. A rainy day, a move to a new city, a layoff at work—how we respond to situations is up to us. The same situation experienced by different people can bring despair or delight. It's all about having an attitude of gratitude.

Cultivating a Grateful Spirit

Gratitude can be learned. All you need to do is practice. Try these gratitude exercises for starters:

1. Be intentionally grateful—for little things and big things. Before going to sleep each night reflect on the good aspects of your day.
2. Count your blessings and write them down. When circumstances are difficult, read the list and remember God's faithfulness.
3. Express your gratitude to another person. The pleasure your words can give is another reason to be grateful!
4. Every day compile a list of 26 things to be grateful for—one for every letter of the alphabet! Or start with finding five things—one for each of the senses—something you see, hear, smell, taste, and feel.

Bulletin Bloopers

These are real bloopers that have appeared in church bulletins from a variety of denominations. Some of them have been around for awhile . . . but they're still good for a smile!

Don't let worry kill you—let the church help.

Remember in prayer the many who are sick of our community. Smile at someone who is hard to love. Say "hell" to someone who doesn't care much about you.

The associate minister unveiled the church's new tithing campaign slogan last Sunday: "I Upped My Pledge—Up Yours."

The ladies of the church have cast off clothing of every kind. They may be seen in the basement on Friday afternoon.

Scouts are saving aluminum cans, bottles, and other items to be recycled. Proceeds will be used to cripple children.

Bertha Belch, a missionary, will be speaking tonight. All are invited to come hear Bertha Belch all the way from Africa.

Announcement in the church bulletin for a National Prayer and *Fasting* Conference: "The cost for attending the Fasting and Prayer Conference includes meals."

Our youth basketball team is back in action Wednesday at 8 P.M. in the recreation hall. Come out and watch us kill Christ the King.

Miss Charlene Mason sang, "I will not pass this way again," giving obvious pleasure to the congregation.

Ladies, don't forget the rummage sale. It's a chance to get rid of those things not worth keeping around the house. Don't forget your husbands.

Next Sunday is the family hayride and bonfire at the Fowlers'. Bring your own hot dogs and guns. Friends are welcome! Everyone come for a fun time.

The peacemaking meeting scheduled for today has been canceled due to a conflict.

How Are We to Fear God?

The Bible promises many blessings if we "fear the Lord":

- Wisdom (Proverbs 9:10)
- Knowledge (Proverbs 1:7)
- Life and satisfaction (Proverbs 19:23)
- Riches, honor, and life (Proverbs 22:4)

What does it mean to *fear* the Lord? In the Bible, fear of the Lord is described as humble awe and obedience.

Humble Awe

Awe of the Lord is rooted in extreme reverence for God's position as our Creator and extreme humility that results from our recognizing that God has the right to judge the creation he has made. Those who fear the Lord acknowledge that God made it all, owns it all, governs it all, and alone is worthy of all adoration and worship. Humble awe also includes great awe that such a God of power and majesty loves his creation.

Obedience

To obey the Lord is not simply to obey him, but to do what he commands. Those who fear the Lord hate evil (Proverbs 8:13), depart from evil (Proverbs 16:6), and perfect holiness by cleansing themselves of all filthiness (2 Corinthians 7:1).

© 2001 Jan Dargatz, used by permission.

Are Dinosaurs in the Bible?

Does the Bible mention dinosaurs? Many believe it does. The word *dinosaur*, of course, does not appear in the Bible since that word was not a part of our vocabulary until the 1900s. The Bible does describe, however, creatures that we might recognize today as being dinosaurs.

Tannin

Tannin is a Hebrew word that refers to dragonlike animals and great sea creatures such as whales, giant squid, and marine reptiles. These references may be linked to dinosaurs.

Leviathan

One of the oldest books in the Bible is the Book of Job. Some scholars believe this book was written soon after the flood of Noah's time. In Job 41, a large, mysterious, sea creature is described. Given the name "Leviathan," it sounds amazingly like descriptions of the plesiosaurs:

1. "Can you pull in the leviathan with a fishhook or tie down his tongue with a rope? If you lay a hand on him, you will remember the struggle and never do it again! Any hope of subduing him is false; the mere sight of him is overpowering" (Job 41:1, 8–9 NIV).
2. "His back has rows of shields tightly sealed together; each is so close to the next that no air can pass between. They are joined fast to one another; they cling together and cannot be parted. His snorting throws out

flashes of light; his eyes are like the rays of dawn. Firebrands stream from his mouth; sparks of fire shoot out" (Job 41:15–19 NIV).

Some scholars believe this chapter in Job describes two creatures—the first, a seagoing creature (Job 41:1–11), and the latter a "king of the beasts" similar to an armored dinosaur (Job 41:12–34).

Notice these specific characteristics of the first "Leviathan" creature:

- watergoing (caught by hook, reed, or line)
- a strong jaw
- powerful and hard to catch
- tough skinned

The second creature has these specific characteristics:

- powerful, graceful limbs
- terrible teeth "all around"
- rows of scales, close together to form an impenetrable coat
- breathes fire
- eats small stones as if they are short grass (perhaps gastroliths)
- "tight" flesh (not saggy or fat)
- great strength
- capable of raising itself up (perhaps standing or walking on two legs)
- "crashes" (versus "splashes")

- cannot be killed with javelins, arrows, slings and stones, darts, or spears
- is capable of swimming (and when it does, causes a "boiling" of water)
- leaves behind a slick inky residue that shines "white"

A number of dinosaurs may have fit this description. If a dinosaur is being described, then Job gives us something no paleontologist has ever provided: a description of how these dinosaurs "behaved."

Behemoth

Another creature called "behemoth" is described in Job 40:15–24. This creature is much like a diplodocus: "Look at the behemoth, which I made along with you and which feeds on grass like an ox. What strength he has in his loins, what power in the muscles of his belly! His tail sways like a cedar; the sinews of his thighs are close-knit" (Job 40:15–17 niv).

Note the characteristics of this creature:

- It enjoys resting in the marsh under willow trees (lotus).
- Floods don't scare it (comfortable around water).
- It cannot be trapped.
- It is strong and large boned—a giant with a tail like the trunk of a tree.
- It has a large mouth, yet eats grass.
- It is gentle (other animals are comfortable around it).

Adapted from Phil Phillips, *Dinosaurs—The Bible, Barney, and Beyond* (Lancaster, PA: Starburst Publishers1994), 55–60.

What Would Jesus Drive?

Most people assume WWJD is for "What Would Jesus Do?"

But the initials might also stand for "What Would Jesus Drive?"

One theory is that Jesus would tool around in an old Plymouth because the Bible says, "God drove Adam and Eve out of the garden of Eden in a Fury."

But in Psalm 83, the Almighty clearly owns a Pontiac and a Geo. This passage urges the Lord to "pursue your enemies with your Tempest and terrify them with your Storm."

Perhaps God favors Dodge pickup trucks at times, because Moses' followers are warned not to go up a mountain "until the Ram's horn sounds a long blast."

Some scholars insist that Jesus drove a Honda but didn't like to talk about it. As proof, they cite a verse in John's Gospel where Christ tells the crowd, "For I did not speak of my own Accord."

Meanwhile, Moses rode on an old British motorcycle as evidenced by a Bible passage declaring that "the roar of Moses' Triumph is heard in the hills."

Joshua drove a Triumph sports car with a hole in its muffler: "Joshua's Triumph was heard throughout the land."

And, following the Master's lead, the apostles carpooled in a Honda: "The apostles were in one Accord."

Putting Things in Perspective

To help put things in proper perspective, take this quiz:

1. Name the five wealthiest people in the world.
2. Name the last five Heisman trophy winners.
3. Name the last five winners of the Miss America contest.
4. Name ten people who have won either a Nobel or Pulitzer Prize.
5. Name the last half dozen Academy Award winners for best actor and actress.
6. Name the last decade's worth of World Series winners.

Few people remember yesterday's headlines, even ones related to top achievers and those who are considered to be the best in their respective fields. Applause dies. Awards tarnish. Achievements are forgotten. Accolades and certificates are buried with their owners.

Now take this quiz:

1. List a few teachers who aided your journey through school.
2. Name three friends who have helped you through a difficult time.
3. Name five people who have taught you something worthwhile.
4. Name a few people who have made you feel appreciated and special.
5. Think of five people you enjoy spending time with.

6. Name half a dozen heroes whose stories have inspired you.

Is this quiz easier?

What's the lesson? The people who make a difference in your life are not the ones with the most credentials, money, fame, awards, or beauty. They are the ones who care.

FAST FOOT FACTS

Consider these interesting facts about the foot:
- The sole of your foot has 200,000 sweat pores per square inch.
- Your toenails never stop growing.
- Fourteen of your foot's 26 bones are in your toes.
- Your big toe has two parts, but the other four toes each have three.
- Your feet might look the same, but they're not exactly alike. One is usually a little larger than the other.
- Each person's footprints are unique. Even twins do not share the same print.
- When you're sick, your illness could show up in your toenails. Diseases such as diabetes, tuberculosis, and lung cancer can be indicated by changes in the condition of your toenails.
- Your big and little toes have their own muscles, but the middle three toes have to share.

Who Can Understand It?

For God so loved the world, that he gave his only begotten Son, that whosoever believeth in him should not perish, but have everlasting life. —John 3:16 NKJV

In the city of Chicago, one cold, dark night, a blizzard was setting in. A little boy was selling newspapers on the corner. The little boy was so cold that he found himself spending more time trying to keep warm than selling newspapers.

Finally, he walked up to a policeman and said, "Mister, you wouldn't happen to know where a poor boy could find a warm place to sleep tonight, would you? You see, I sleep in a box up around the corner and down the alley and it's awful cold tonight. Sure would be nice to have a warm place to stay."

The policeman looked down at the boy and said, "You go down the street to that big white house and knock on the door. When someone answers the door you just say John 3:16, and the person will let you in." So he walked to the house and up the steps. He knocked on the door, and a woman answered.

Magic Words

The boy looked into her eyes and said, "John 3:16." The woman replied with great kindness in her voice, "Come on in, son." She led him to a split bottom rocker in front of a big old fireplace ablaze with warmth, and she left the room as he sat down. The boy sat there for a while and thought to himself: *John 3:16—I don't understand it, but it sure makes a cold boy warm.*

PERSEVERING UNTIL RESULTS ARE SEEN

George Mueller, a well-known intercessor in the early 1900s, prayed specifically for a group of five personal friends to come to know Christ as their Savior. After 5 years, one of them came to Christ. At the end of 10 years, two more had accepted Jesus as their Savior. He prayed another 25 years before the fourth friend became saved. For the fifth man, Mueller prayed until he died—the man came to accept Christ a few months after Mueller's death. Mueller had prayed almost 52 years for this man's salvation.

Adapted from Paul Lee Tan, *Encyclopedia of 7,700 Illustrations* (Dallas, TX: Bible Communications, Inc., 1979), 4585.

Later the woman asked, "Are you hungry?"

He said, "Well, just a little. I haven't eaten in a couple of days, and I guess I could stand a little bit of food."

The woman sat him down to a table laden with food. He ate and ate. Then he thought to himself: *John 3:16—I sure don't understand it, but it sure makes a hungry boy full.*

Amazing Comforts

After the boy had eaten his fill, the kind woman took him upstairs to a bathroom that had a huge bathtub already filled with warm water. As he relaxed in the warm water, he reflected on his life and concluded that he hadn't had a *real* bath in a very long time. In fact, the only baths of the last several years had been ones he received when he stood in front of a nearby fire hydrant on the days the firemen flushed it out. The boy thought to himself: *John 3:16—I sure don't understand it, but it sure makes a dirty boy clean.*

He noticed as he got out of his bath that a clean towel and a clean pair of pajamas had been laid out for him. He quickly dried himself and put on the pajamas. Then the woman led him to a bedroom, where she tucked him in bed, pulled the covers up, and kissed him goodnight. As he lay in the darkness, he thought: *John 3:16—I don't understand it, but it sure makes a tired boy rest well.*

An Explanation

The next morning the woman came to his room, handed him clean clothes, and after he had dressed, she returned and led him back down to a kitchen table filled with breakfast foods. After he ate, she led him to the same split bottom rocker in front of the fireplace, but this time, she also sat down in a large chair nearby. She picked up a big old Bible and said gently as she looked intently into his young face, "Do you understand John 3:16?"

He replied, "No, ma'am, I don't. The first time I ever heard it was last night when the policeman down on the corner told me to say those words to you."

She opened the Bible to John 3:16 and began to explain to him about Jesus. Right there, he gave his heart and life to Jesus. After the woman had prayed with him, he thought: *John 3:16— I don't understand it, but it sure makes a lonely boy feel safe, secure, and loved.*

———————————

Author unknown

God's Mysterious Ways

A woman received a phone call that her daughter was very sick with a fever. She left work early and stopped by the pharmacy for some medication. As she returned to her car, she discovered she had locked her keys inside the car. She was frantic. She phoned her daughter's babysitter to tell her she'd be delayed. The babysitter suggested, "You might find a coat hanger and use it to open the door."

The woman found an old rusty coat hanger on the ground near her car. "I don't know how to use this," she said. So she bowed her head and asked God for help.

Just then, an old rusty car pulled up. The driver—a dirty, greasy, bearded man with a biker skull rag on his head—asked, "Need help?"

She thought, *God, is* this *who you have sent me?* Nevertheless, she was desperate and thankful for his help. She replied, "Yes, can you use this hanger to unlock my car?"

"Sure," he said. Within seconds he had it open.

She hugged the man and said through tears, "Thank you so much. You are a very nice man!"

Startled, the man stammered, "Lady, I ain't a nice man. I just got out of prison for car theft."

The woman spontaneously hugged him again and cried aloud, "Thank you, God, for sending me a professional!"

Trim Your Holidays with Meaning

So much is said at the holiday season about our need to regain the true meaning of Christmas. Here are 15 ways to do just that:

1. **Start a Christmas blessing book.** Purchase a blank book—from small, guest-book size to large scrap-book—to keep in your entryway. Ask friends who come by to write a blessing for your family. Make sure the entries are dated. You can add photos, holiday stickers, and other mementos of the season to the book (a good New Year's Day project). You'll enjoy reflecting on the blessings throughout the season, the year, and for years to come.

2. **Pray over your Christmas cards.** Store the Christmas cards you receive in a special basket. Then pick one card each day of the new year until you have reread all of the cards one by one. As you reread the card and any en-closed note or letter, say a prayer for the person or family who sent it.

3. **Keep an Advent diary.** Have a special diary for record-ing your holiday-related reflections. Take five minutes to write in it daily during the Advent season (the 24 days preceding Christmas).

4. **Hold your own silent night.** Set aside one day in the weeks leading up to Christmas as your own "Silent Night." No TV. Dim the lights and light some candles or build a fire in the fireplace. Take an hour or two to sit in quiet reflection, perhaps sharing with family

members or friends what you consider to be the spiritual highlights of the year that is drawing to a close.

5. **Light one black candle.** It may not sound very "Christmasy," but having one black candle in your home during the Christmas season can remind you of just how "dark" the world would be if Jesus had never come. As you light the candle each night in the weeks before Christmas, ask the Lord to cleanse you of your sins and to renew peace and joy in your heart. Thank the Lord for coming into the world to turn darkness into light.

6. **Spread warmth for the homeless.** Take warm socks, gloves, hats, or scarves to a homeless shelter. Let each person in your family wrap one bundle of warmth and carry it personally into the shelter.

7. **Fill appreciation stockings.** Rather than stuffing Christmas stockings with gift items, fill those stockings with words of appreciation. Cut out designs from old Christmas cards. On the back of each "picture," write one word or phrase that depicts something you like, admire, respect, love, enjoy, or find delightful in the person whose name is on the stocking. It can be something the person has done, said, or a character or personality trait. Stuff the stockings on Christmas Eve, allowing family members to contribute too. (Suggestion: Let each person read his stocking notes privately.)

8. **Have a quiet day.** Set aside one Saturday before Christmas for a "quiet day" retreat. You may want to go to a nearby church for several hours. Sit in quiet reflection,

taking time to read various passages of the Bible that relate to the prophecies of Jesus' birth. Reflect on how Jesus has fulfilled these prophecies not only in the world but also in your own life. Some churches sponsor official "quiet days"—seek out one and schedule your participation well in advance.

9. **Savor small morsels.** Don't load your holiday plate with a pile of sweets. Rather, choose one or two morsels. Savor each nibble. You'll not only feel less guilty later but also you'll *enjoy* each treat more. Savoring each taste of the holidays can lead to savoring each lighted candle you see and each carol or bell you hear.

10. **Make a moving manger scene.** Build a manger scene *slowly*. Put out the stable a week in advance of Christmas. Add the animals one by one over several nights. Meanwhile, start Mary and Joseph on their journey by placing those figures in another room. Each night move them closer to the manger. Do the same for any Wise Men. On Christmas eve, bring Mary and Joseph to the stable. On Christmas morning, add the baby Jesus to the scene along with the shepherds. Move the Wise Men so they arrive at the stable on January 6, also called Epiphany.

11. **Tape Christmas past.** As older relatives gather for the holidays, ask each to record a special memory from his or her childhood. Keep the atmosphere relaxed and invite your children and others to ask questions. Your tape of Christmas past may become a treasured heirloom.

12. **Burn prayer cones.** Gather pine cones throughout the year and keep them in a large basket. At Christmas time, give each member of the family several pine cones. Toss the pine cones into the fire one by one, voicing a special praise or prayer request to the Lord. Let each pine cone glow in beauty and rise in smoke to the Lord as a "prayer."

13. **Read the Story Aloud.** Gather children around you—your own children, grandchildren, nieces and nephews, or perhaps a Sunday school or neighborhood group of children—and read aloud the Christmas story, either from the Gospel of Luke or from a beautifully illustrated book.

14. **Recycle the sweets.** Do you receive too many home-made cookies and candies at Christmas? Keep a few small Christmas tins available and use the goodies you receive to form new collections of holiday treats to take to those who are homebound in your church, or who have lost a loved one in the previous year.

15. **Say, "I love you."** Make an intentional effort to hug each person who comes into your home and to say, "I love you" to that person. There's never too much expression of love at Christmastime!

Remarkable Puzzle

Can you find the names of 25 books of the Bible in this paragraph?

This is a most remarkable puzzle. Someone found it in the seat pocket on a flight from Los Angeles to Honolulu, keeping himself occupied for hours. One man from Illinois worked on this while fishing from his johnboat. Roy Clark studied it while playing his banjo. Elaine Victs mentioned it in her column once. One woman judges the job to be so involving, she brews a cup of tea to help calm her nerves. There will be some names that are really easy to spot . . . that's a fact. Some people will soon find themselves in a jam, especially since the book names are not necessarily capitalized. The truth is, from answers we get, we are forced to admit it usually takes a minister or scholar to see some of them at the worst. Something in our genes is responsible for the difficulty we have. Those able to find all of them will hear great lamentations from those who have to be shown. One revelation may help, books like Timothy and Samuel may occur without their numbers. And punctuation or spaces in the middle are normal. A chipper attitude will help you compete. Remember, there are 25 books of the Bible lurking somewhere in this paragraph.

See answer next page.

> **CHILDREN AND CHURCH**
>
> A Sunday school teacher asked her little children, as they were on the way to church service, "And why is it necessary to be quiet in church?"
>
> One bright little girl replied, "Because people are sleeping."

Remarkable Puzzle answer

This is **a mos**t re**mark**able puzzle. Someone found it in the seat pocket on a flight from Los Angeles to Honolu**lu**, **ke**eping himself occupied for hours. One man from Illinois worked on this while fishing from his **john**boat. Roy Clark studied it while playing his ban**jo**. **El**aine Victs mentioned it in her column once. One woman **judges** the **job** to be so involving, **she brews** a cup of tea to help calm her nerv**es**. **Ther**e will be some names that are really easy to spot . . . that's a f**act**. **S**ome people will soon find themselves in a **jam**, **es**pecially since the book names are not necessarily capitalized. The t**ruth** is, f**rom ans**wers we get, we are forced to admi**t it** **us**ually takes a minister or scholar to see some of the**m** **at the w**orst. Something in our **genes is** responsible for the difficulty we have. T**hose** **a**ble to find all of them will hear great **lamentations** from those who have to be shown. One **revelation** may help, books like **Timothy** and **Samuel** may occur without their **numbers**. And punctuation or spaces in the middle are nor**mal**. **A chi**pper attitude will help you com**pete**. **R**emember, there are 25 books of the Bible lur**king s**omewhere in this paragraph.

A BIT OF CHURCH HUMOR

Over the massive front doors of a church, these words were inscribed: "The Gate of Heaven."

Below that was a small cardboard sign, which read: "Please use other entrance."

• • •

A pastor once said that the best prayer he ever heard was: "Lord, please make me the kind of person my dog thinks I am."

A Prayer of Augustine

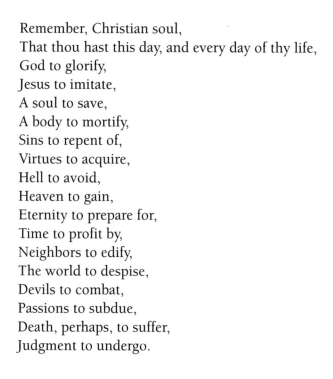

Remember, Christian soul,
That thou hast this day, and every day of thy life,
God to glorify,
Jesus to imitate,
A soul to save,
A body to mortify,
Sins to repent of,
Virtues to acquire,
Hell to avoid,
Heaven to gain,
Eternity to prepare for,
Time to profit by,
Neighbors to edify,
The world to despise,
Devils to combat,
Passions to subdue,
Death, perhaps, to suffer,
Judgment to undergo.

Source: St. Augustine's Prayer Book

A Shared Life

Children spell love, T-I-M-E. Here are 10 ways to build more time into your relationship with each of your children.

1. **Share the fun.** Play with your child every week. Sit down on the floor and play a game. Take your child to the park. Make sure you have a "fun" outing scheduled with each child each week.
2. **Share the work**. Build, make, sew, or repair something around the house with your child—it might be a bookcase for their room or a model airplane to hang as a mobile or a costume for a party.
3. **Share a signal.** Whether it is a hand sign such as "I love you" in the language of the deaf), a special whistle, or a special word—have a way of signaling "I love you" to your child across a crowded room, auditorium, or stadium. Let it be a sign that is private between you and your child.
4. **Share a memory box.** Build a special memory box for each child. Put in it things that are related to times you have spent with your child. Both Mom and Dad can have their own boxes. Periodically allow your child to see what is in his or her box and to reflect on good memories.
5. **Share books.** Read aloud to your child. As your child learns to read, ask your child to read aloud to you. No child is ever too old to hear a story read by Mom or

Dad—even teenagers enjoy this although they may not admit it. And no parent is ever too old to hear a story read by a child, even a parent in a nursing home. Shared books create a base of shared ideas on which to build conversations.

6. **Share hugs.** Be affectionate to your child—not in a way that embarrasses but in a way that says, "I sure do like you." That hug may be an arm clasped on a shoulder, a touch on the hand, or a pat on the knee.

7. **Share music.** Introduce your child to the music you enjoyed as a child or teen. And listen to your child's music with your child (even though you may not like it). If you dance, you may want to teach your child the dance steps that were popular in "your day." Try the dance steps of your child's world in return.

ALMOST-HOLY LAUGHTER

A minister parked his car in a no-parking zone in a large city because he was short of time and couldn't find a space with a meter. So he put a note under the windshield wiper that read: "I have circled the block 10 times. If I don't park here, I'll miss my appointment. FORGIVE US OUR TRESPASSES."

When he returned, he found a citation from a police officer along with this note: "I've circled this block for 10 years. If I don't give you a ticket, I'll lose my job. LEAD US NOT INTO TEMPTATION."

---

8. **Share ministry.** Take your child with you as you visit the sick in the hospital, take a casserole to an ailing or bereaved friend, build a home for a poor family, feed the homeless at a shelter, or stop by to visit a person who is homebound. Include your child in planning the visit or project. Be sure to include your child in the conversation during the visit.

9. **Share relationships.** Be generous in sharing your child with your trusted friends and other family members. Give your child "alone" time with longstanding friends, grandparents, aunts, and uncles. As your child builds a relationship with someone you love, your child sees you in a new light and grows in respect for you.

10. **Share prayer.** Spend time praying with your child and for your child. Pray for specific needs in your child's life. Pray also for those in leadership, including the leaders of our nation, the teachers and principal at your child's school, the pastors of your church, and others who are in authority positions. Pray for the peace of Jerusalem and for godly resolution of world conflicts and crisis situations. Be sure to include praise to God for creating your child and allowing you to love your child.

Bible Bird Symbols

A number of birds are used in early Christian paintings, banners, vestments, and ceremonies. Here are insights into several of these birds and what they symbolize:

Peacock

The peacock is a symbol of immortality and eternal life. According to legend, the peacock's flesh does not decay. Roman coins depicted empresses being carried to heaven by peacocks.

Dove

The dove is a symbol for the Spirit of God, and a symbol of the power of God in people's lives. At the baptism of Jesus, the Holy Spirit appeared as a descending dove, engulfing Jesus in a divine embrace (Matthew 3:16; Mark 1:10; Luke 3:22). Dove symbols are often shown in a descending pattern with a three-rayed nimbus of feathers, symbolizing divinity.

Seven doves are often arranged around a circle, symbolizing the seven gifts of the Spirit listed in Isaiah 11:2—wisdom, understanding, counsel, might, knowledge, fear of the Lord, plus piety (a seventh gift added by the Septuagint version). The letters *SS* are often put in the center of the circle—an abbreviation for *Sanctus Spiritus*, Latin for "Holy Spirit."

Owl

An owl is often included in scenes of the crucifixion. The owl symbolizes darkness and solitude. The allusion is drawn to Psalm 102:6: "I am like an owl of the desert" (KJV).

Pelican

A legend popular with early Christian writers says the pelican saves the life of its young by stabbing its breast with its beak and sprinkling them with its own blood so that predators think the young are dead. This bird became a symbol of Christ's sacrifice on the cross, the shedding of his blood for the sins of mankind, and for his resurrection.

Eagle

The eagle is one of the four living creatures around the throne of God (Revelation 4:7). As early as the second century, the eagle was associated with the four evangelists: Matthew, Mark, Luke, and John. It is also a symbol of royalty. The eagle is often placed atop the poles of banners as a sign of Christ's ultimate divinity as King of kings and Lord of lords.

Swallow

In ancient times people were puzzled about the disappearance and reappearance of swallows as they migrated. Many thought the swallow hibernated in the mud during the winter and re-emerged in spring as being "reborn from the earth." This legend led to the swallow being used as a symbol of resurrection. Along with the dove and eagle, ancient peoples thought the swallow carried souls to heaven.

Source: John Bradner, *Symbols of Church Seasons and Days* (Harrisburg, PA: Morehouse Publishing, 1977).

Deep Calls unto Deep

Walking along a sandy ocean beach, one might think that the ocean floor extends like an underwater desert with a sandy bottom. But that isn't so. The ocean floor is as varied and irregular as land features.

Not surprisingly, the deepest point in the world is in the ocean—the Challenger Deep in the Mariana Trench in the Pacific Ocean. It is 35,802 feet or 6.8 miles deep. At that depth, the water pressure is eight tons per square inch.

Deep Dives

The deepest recorded dive of a manned submersible was made by the Trieste. In 1960, it dove to 10,912 meters (35,802 feet).

In May of 2001, 26-year-old Audrey Mester-Ferreras set a women's record, diving 426.5 feet deep on a single breath of air. The current men's record is held by Francisco "Pipin" Ferreras, who dove 531.5 feet in Mexico in January 2000.

Longest and Largest

The underwater mountain range, Mid-Ocean Ridge, is the longest mountain range on Earth. It is 46,600 miles long and extends from the Arctic Ocean, through the middle of the Atlantic Ocean, and into the Pacific Ocean. It is four times the lengths of the Andes, Rockies, and Himalayas combined.

The Earth's largest waterfall is underwater. It is 2.2 miles long and is found beneath the Denmark Strait between Greenland and Iceland. The tallest waterfall on land is Venezuela's Angel Falls at 3,212 feet high.

A dormant volcano, the Mauna Kea in Hawaii, is the world's tallest mountain from base to peak. It rises some 33,465 feet from the sea floor. It is partly underwater and only the top 13,796 feet extend above sea level. By comparison, the world's highest elevation is Mt. Everest, with a peak at 29,035 feet.

A Dark, Lonely World

Most of the familiar marine life of the ocean is found near the water surface. The deepest parts of the ocean are not easily inhabitable because of the lack of sunlight, crushing water pressure, and frigid water temperatures. A deep water variety of squid, basket stars, seapigs (related to sea cucumbers), sea spiders, and the deep sea medusa (a relative of the jellyfish) are among the few species of marine life that are adapted to live in the deepest parts of the ocean.

Food is not readily available in the deepest parts of the ocean because there isn't any sunlight. Almost all of the animals at this depth are predatory, and must get food when they can. Much of the food comes from more shallow lighted depths, and simply filters down into the deeper reaches. At that depth, animals do not live in large groups because there isn't enough food to support them all.

The only light produced beyond the reach of sunlight is from bioluminescent marine life. Bioluminescence is light produced by a chemical reaction that originates in the marine organism.

Good Words to a Friend

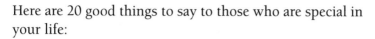

Here are 20 good things to say to those who are special in your life:

1. "I Believe in You."
2. "I Miss You."
3. "I Feel Blessed to Have You as a Friend."
4. "I'm Praying for You."
5. "You Did Great."
6. "Please Join Me."
7. "Please Forgive Me."
8. "What Can I Do to Help?"
9. "I Was Wrong."
10. "Thank You."
11. "I Really Like You."
12. "I'm Sorry You Are Hurting."
13. "I'm Glad You're Here."
14. "I Admire You."
15. "You Are Growing."
16. "You Have Options."
17. "I Don't Believe You Need that Crutch."
18. "This Won't Last Forever."
19. "I Forgive You."
20. "God Loves You."

Count These Blessings

Feeling down? There's nothing like counting your blessings to perk you up. Think on these blessings.

- Finding a $10 bill in the pocket of a coat you haven't worn since last winter
- A child's peanut-butter kisses
- Hearing someone defend your good name
- Light flooding through stained glass windows to fill a quiet sanctuary with an abundance of color
- Seeing the first crocuses of spring
- Looking back and feeling no regret
- Thinking of the word that has eluded you
- Balloons, and having enough air to blow them up
- A smile between friends

CHILDREN AND CHURCH

One particular four year old prayed, "And forgive us our trash baskets as we forgive those who put trash in our baskets."

• • •

A little boy was overheard praying: "Lord, if you can't make me a better boy, don't worry about it. I'm having a real good time like I am."

Bug Bites

Some of the smallest creatures are among the most amazing of God's creation. Here are some little-known facts about bugs.

- There are more kinds of insects on earth than any other kind of living creature—95 percent of all the animal species on the earth are insects.
- Insects eat more plants than all other creatures on earth. They are important in the breakdown of plant and animal matter. Without them, the world would be covered with dead plants and animals.
- The largest spider in the world, according to the *Guinness Book of World Records*, had over an 11-inch leg span, making it larger than the average dinner plate. The smallest spider is the *Patu marplesi* of Samoa, which is about the size of the period at the end of this sentence.
- The female Queen Alexandra birdwing butterfly of New Guinea is considered the world's largest butterfly with a wing span over 11 inches.
- A species of praying mantis has unusual mating habits. The female begins to eat the male while they are mating, when she reaches his abdomen the mating is completed. The father becomes a nourishing meal providing food for the eggs that become his children.

Talk About a Family!

Jacob had twelve sons by four women—certainly that made for a large and complicated family!

Leah was the woman that Jacob was "tricked" into marrying. (See Genesis 29:15–30.) In all, she bore six sons—half of the tribes of Israel—and was the many-great-grandmother of Jesus. Leah's handmaiden Zilpah bore Jacob two sons. Bilhah was the handmaiden of Jacob's other wife, Rachel. Bilhah bore him two sons. The woman Jacob loved, Rachel, was the last to bear him children—her sons were numbers eleven and twelve. She died giving birth to Benjamin.

Abraham—father of eight

Most people know that Abraham had two sons—one by Sarah (Isaac) and one by Sarah's handmaiden Hagar (Ishmael). After Sarah's death, Abraham took Keturah as a concubine. She bore him six sons: Zimran, Jokshan, Medan, Midian, Ishbak, and Shuah. Abraham gave gifts to each of these boys and sent them away to lands east of Canaan (Genesis 25:1–5).

Izban—a man with lots of weddings to arrange!

Perhaps the most complicated of all families in the Bible, however, is that of little-known Izban, the eleventh judge of Israel (he judged Israel for seven years). The Bible tells us, "He had thirty sons. And he gave away thirty daughters in marriage, and brought in thirty daughters from elsewhere for his sons" (Judges 12:8–10 NKJV). In all, he had sixty children! The Bible does not say how many wives bore those children.

And the Band Plays On

Red kettles at Christmas. Thrift stores and brass bands. Bonnets and doughnuts. For more than 100 years, the **Salvation Army** has prayed, preached, stirred up a little controversy, and left an indelible impression on millions of people the world over.

The Army grew out of a Christian mission established by William and Catherine Booth. Living and preaching in London's East End, they saw the squalor of urban life and the effects it had on the poor.

Target Audience

Influenced by the methods of an American revivalist named James Caughey, William embraced the concept of aggressive soul-winning. In what became the model for his Army, he preached on street corners, rented halls for meetings, and purposely sought out the types of people that the church wasn't reaching—the poor, the alcoholics, and the sexually promiscuous. His Christian Revival Association became the Salvation Army in 1879.

Why an army? During that era the military was popular, especially among men. The uniforms inspired respect. Booth decided that his Army should wear uniforms as well. (The Army uses military titles for its leaders and calls its members soldiers.)

Through the Stomach

Salvationists, whose primary goal has always been to evangelize, were savvy enough to recognize that the way to a sinner's heart, in many cases, was through his or her stomach. The Army that began as and remains to this day a church, became more and more involved in charitable work.

Like most nonprofit groups, the Salvation Army has had its detractors. This was especially true in the early days, when city fathers railed against and sometimes outlawed (as in New York City) the Army's street-corner meetings. Then came World War I, and everything changed.

World War I Advance

The Salvation Army had been given permission to carry out its work in France. Salvationists set up huts near the lines and dispensed hard-to-get (or expensive to purchase) toilet articles, sweets, and stationery items. What this small group of Salvationists (no more than 250) became famous for, however, was doughnuts.

A Salvation Army colonel and four women were driving around in September of 1917, looking for troops to comfort. They found a group, spent time with them, and proved so popular, the boys were loath to let them go. In exchange for their freedom, one of the women offered to bake something.

Doughy Success

With primitive kitchen supplies, her best bet was doughnuts, and the rest is history. In the minds of World War I veterans, and the families they wrote to back home, the Salvation Army would always be associated with this simple symbol of home and hearth, and with the kindness they showed to homesick men.

Red Kettles

The Christmas kettle first appeared in 1891. A Salvationist in San Francisco needed to raise money to fund a Christmas dinner for the poor. A crab pot hanging from a tripod, positioned on a street corner, seemed to him like a good receptacle for any loose change that passersby might like to toss in.

Soon after, those kettles, painted red, were springing up everywhere at Christmastime. The slogan for this campaign? "Keep the Pot Boiling."

Marching On

Today, the Salvation Army has 50 territories that cover 100 nations. Activities and services offered by Salvationists include homeless shelters, alcoholism treatment, programs to rescue throwaway children, Boys and Girls Clubs, disaster relief, counseling, health education, agricultural projects, literacy classes, drilling of wells, employment assistance, and nurses training.

> ### ALMOST-HOLY LAUGHTER
>
> People want the front of the bus, the back of the church, and the center of attention.
>
> • • •
>
> Somebody once figured out that we have 35 million laws trying to enforce 10 commandments.

This "infantry" of the Christian church, as Salvationist Henry Gariepy calls it, remains at war: first of all, against sin and its devastating effects, and second, against any circumstance that prevents God's created ones from achieving wholeness.

You Are Invited

The invitation to live life with Jesus Christ is always open and extended to every individual. All a person has to do is respond with a "yes." Read some invitations in Scripture:

- "Behold, I stand at the door, and knock: if any man hear my voice, and open the door, I will come in to him, and will sup with him, and he with me" (Revelation 3:20).
- "But without faith it is impossible to please him: for he that cometh to God must believe that he is, and that he is a rewarder of them that diligently seek him" (Hebrews 11:6).
- "Come now, and let us reason together, saith the Lord: though your sins be as scarlet, they shall be as white as snow; though they be red like crimson, they shall be as wool" (Isaiah 1:18).
- "Ho, every one that thirsteth, come ye to the waters, and he that hath no money; come ye, buy, and eat; yea, come, buy wine and milk without money and without price" (Isaiah 55:1).
- "Come unto me, all ye that labour and are heavy laden, and I will give you rest" (Matthew 11:28).
- "Let us therefore come boldly unto the throne of grace, that we may obtain mercy, and find grace to help in time of need" (Hebrews 4:16).
- "And sent his servant at supper time to say to them that were bidden, Come; for all things are now ready" (Luke 14:17).

And God Said, "It Is Good."

God created the heavens and the earth. And the earth was without form, and void, and darkness was upon the face of the deep.

And Satan said, "It doesn't get any better than this."

And God said, "Let there be light," and there was light.

And God said, "Let the earth bring forth grass, the herb yielding seed, and the fruit tree yielding fruit," and God saw that it was good.

And Satan said, "There goes the neighborhood."

And God said, "Let us make Man in our image, after our likeness, and let them have dominion over the fish of the sea, and over the fowl of the air and over the cattle, and over all the earth, and over every creeping thing that creepeth upon the earth."

And so God created Man in his own image; male and female created he them.

And God looked upon Man and Woman and saw that they were lean and fit.

And God populated the earth with broccoli and cauliflower and spinach, green and yellow vegetables of all kinds, so Man and Woman would live long and healthy lives.

And Satan said, "I know how I can get back in this game." And Satan created McDonald's. And McDonald's brought forth the 99¢ double cheeseburger.

And Satan said to Man, "You want fries with that?" And Man said, "Supersize them." And Man gained five pounds.

And God created the healthful yogurt that Woman might keep her figure that Man found so fair.

And Satan brought forth chocolate. And Woman gained five pounds.

And God said, "Try my crispy fresh salad."

And Satan brought forth Ben and Jerry's. And Woman gained 10 pounds.

And God said, "I have sent thee heart-healthy vegetables and olive oil with which to cook them."

And Satan brought forth chicken-fried steak so big it needed its own platter. And Man gained 10 pounds and his bad cholesterol went through the roof.

And God brought forth running shoes and Man resolved to lose those extra pounds.

And Satan brought forth cable TV with remote control so Man would not have to toil to change channels between ESPN and ESPN2. And Man gained another 20 pounds.

And God said, "You're running up the score, Devil."

And God brought forth the potato, a vegetable naturally low in fat and brimming with nutrition.

And Satan peeled off the healthful skin and sliced the starchy center into chips and deep-fat fried them. And he created sour cream dip also. And Man clutched his remote control and ate the potato chips swaddled in cholesterol.

And Satan saw and said, "It is good." And Man went into cardiac arrest.

And God sighed and created quadruple bypass surgery.

And Satan created HMOs.

What's So Revealing about Revelation?

Martin Luther is reported to have had little patience for the Book of Revelation. He agreed with St. Jerome who said that Revelation has "as many mysteries as it has words." After suffering through the ecclesiastical battles of the Reformation, Luther gained an appreciation for Revelation whose primary theme is "the lamb who was slain has begun his reign." Luther took much encouragement from the prophesied triumph of good over evil in the last days of the church.

Revelation is one of the hardest books of the Bible to understand; there may be as many interpretations as there are biblical scholars. It's unlikely that two people will agree on every aspect of Revelation, but that doesn't mean we shouldn't study it.

Apocalyptic Literature

The word *apocalyptic* means "unveiling." Revelation is written in apocalyptic style with strong symbolism, mysterious numbers, and powerful images. The book presents a message of the Lord to seven contemporary churches in chapters 1 to 3, and an account of the apostle John's vision while in exile on the island of Patmos. The vision, chapters 4 to 22, is of the future events that are to come—an unveiling—ending with the triumph of the reign of God.

Apocalyptic literature from the Jewish and early Christian world has three primary characteristics:

1. **Recognition of a dualism of powers**—God and Satan, good and evil. Dualism of powers is not the contrast of

two equal powers of good and evil, but the dualism of the created beings who have rebelled against their Creator.

2. **Belief in two distinct ages**—this age and the age to come. This age is under the influence of the evil rebellion; the age to come is the age when all rebellion will be over and salvation will be complete. Apocalyptic literature also emphasizes that the new age comes only with the catastrophic end of the present age.

3. **Belief in two worlds**—the visible and the invisible. We live in two worlds at the same time: the visible physical world and the invisible spiritual realm. What happens in the visible world is connected to what happens in the unseen world and vice versa. The spiritual world gives insight into the meanings and causes of things in the world that we inhabit every day.

Ultimate End

Apocalyptic literature unveils a picture of the ultimate end of history and of final judgment. Since it is beyond anything we have yet experienced, it is not surprising that it is expressed in highly symbolic language and images as in the Book of Revelation.

The main point to remember in reading Revelation is that the world will one day end and God will triumph; our part is to live in such a way that we are ready at all times for his coming.

Martyrs

The word *martyr* comes from the Greek word for "witness." It means

- one who chooses to suffer death rather than deny Jesus Christ as the Son of God and Savior of mankind;
- one who bears testimony to the truth of what he has seen or heard or knows;
- one who endures severe or constant suffering for their Christian witness;
- one who sacrifices something very important to further the kingdom of God.

A Regent University study estimated that 156,000 Christians were martyred around the world in 1998, and 164,000 Christians were martyred in 1999.

Links in the Chain

Through the centuries, millions upon millions of Christians have been martyred for the sake of the Gospel. One Christian prisoner in Cuba was asked to sign a statement of charges against fellow Christians. He knew his signature would lead to their arrest, so he said, "The chain keeps me from signing this."

The communist officer in charge of the proceeding protested, "But you are not in chains!"

"I am," said the Christian. "I am bound by the chain of witnesses who throughout the centuries gave their lives for Jesus Christ. I am a link in this chain. I will not break it."

Worthy to Pray

Have you ever felt unworthy to pray for your friends—or for that matter, strangers or enemies? Take comfort in this prayer from a godly man who lived almost 1,000 years ago. Try reading it aloud.

My good Lord,
I long to pray to you for my friends,
But I am held back by my sins.
Since I stand in such need of grace myself,
How can I dare ask for grace for others?
I anxiously seek intercession on my own behalf.
Yet even so I shall be so bold
As to intercede for others.
You commend me to pray for my friends,
And love prompts me to do so.
So I pray to you, good and gracious God,
For those who love me for your sake
And whom I love in you.
If my prayer does not deserve to be answered,
Please love them for their own sakes,
For you are the source of all love.
And make them love you with all their hearts
So that they will speak and do
Only that which pleases you.
My prayer is but a cold affair, Lord,
Because my love burns with such a small flame.
Yet you who are rich in mercy
Will bestow your grace not according to my prayers
But according to the infinite warmth of your love.

Source: Anselm of Canterbury c.1033–1109

There Was a Rabbi, a Priest, and a Minister

A PRIEST AND A RABBI operated a church and a synagogue across the street from each other. Since their schedules overlapped, they decided to pool their money and buy a car together.

After the purchase, they drove it back and parked it on the street between them.

A few minutes later, the rabbi looked out his window and saw the priest sprinkling water on their new car. It didn't need a wash, so the rabbi hurried out and asked the priest, "What are you doing?"

"I'm blessing it," the priest replied.

The rabbi went back into the synagogue. He reappeared a moment later with a hacksaw, walked over to the back of the car, and cut off two inches of the tailpipe.

A PRIEST, A MINISTER, AND A RABBI were playing their usual Thursday round of golf when they began discussing the weekly collections. Specifically, they started to compare how they each determined what portion of the collection to keep for themselves and what portion to give to the Lord.

The priest explained, "I draw a circle around myself and toss the money in the air. Whatever lands in the circle I keep for myself. Whatever lands outside the circle, I give to God."

The minister said, "Yes, I use a similar method, except that whatever lands inside the circle I give to God, and whatever lands outside the circle I keep for my personal needs."

The rabbi then proclaimed, "Brothers, we are in agreement on this! I use the same method, as well. Except that when I toss the money in the air, I figure that whatever God wants he can keep."

A MINISTER, A PRIEST, AND A RABBI went out for a hike one hot afternoon. They were sweating profusely when they came upon a small lake with a sandy beach. Since it was a secluded area, they left all their clothes on a log, ran down the beach to the lake, and jumped in the water for a long swim.

Refreshed, they were partway back up the beach to where they had left their clothes when a group of women from town came along. Unable to get to their clothes in time, the minister and the priest covered their privates, but the rabbi covered his face while they all ran to take cover in the bushes.

After the women wandered on and the men got dressed, the minister and the priest asked the rabbi why he covered his face rather than his privates.

The rabbi replied, "I don't know about you, but in *my* congregation, it's my face they would recognize."

> Someone has well said that there are only two kinds of people in the world—those who wake up in the morning and say, "Good morning, Lord," and those who wake up in the morning and say, "Good Lord, it's morning."

Jesus Speaks Your Language

In the past 22 years, over four billion people in 236 countries have heard "Jesus" speak in their own language. Through the inspiration and efforts of Dr. Bill Bright, founder of Campus Crusade for Christ, **the JESUS film** became a reality in 1978. The film is the story of the life of Jesus taken right out of the Gospel of Luke. It was Dr. Bright's dream that the film would be translated and re-recorded into the languages of the world.

Teamwork

The *JESUS* film is the work of a team of 500 scholars and leaders from a variety of secular and Christian organizations. They set five criteria for the film to meet:

1. The film must be as archaeologically, historically, and theologically accurate as humanly possible.
2. The presentation must be unbiased, acceptable to all as a true depiction of Christ's life.
3. The film story must appeal to all ages.
4. The script must be easily translatable into virtually any language on earth.
5. The film must be of theater quality and effective with both urban and rural audiences worldwide.

As a result of seeing the film, more than 146 million people have indicated decisions to accept Christ as personal Savior and Lord. That works out to an average of one person every two seconds who indicates a decision to receive Christ as Savior after seeing the film. The film is distributed through the JESUS Film Project and by more than 1,500 Christian agencies who use the film in worldwide evangelism.

Accessible to Nearly All

The film has been translated into 685 languages, and over 200 additional translations are in process. Technicians complete a new translation of the film every four days. JESUS Film Project director, Paul Eshleman, said he estimates that with the current available translations over 90 percent of the world population could listen to the film in their native language. That doesn't mean the project is over. The film is now available in 28 of Nigeria's 435 languages, and the team continues to do more translations for increasingly remote locations. Besides the 14,000 film prints in circulation, there are an additional 31 million videocassettes in circulation, making the story of Jesus even more accessible.

The film has been viewed on either national television stations or through satellite transmissions in 174 countries. Still other viewers have accessed its message by watching it on the internet or on video.

Fight Stopper

Eshleman stated that the film has been shown in nations where there are hostile tribes or warring factions, such as El Salvador, Cambodia, and Ethiopia. For many people it has led to the realization that they cannot follow Jesus and continue to fight one another.

Handwriting on the Wall

Everyday conversation is filled with references that come from the Bible. Here are common expressions that are rooted in the Bible.

"Am I my brother's keeper?" This was Cain's response to God when God asked Cain his brother's whereabouts after he killed Abel (Genesis 4:9). This question is used when there is an unwillingness to take responsibility for another's well-being.

"Apple of the eye." God calls the Israel the apple of his eye (Deuteronomy 32:10). This phrase is used to refer to something cherished and precious. It comes from the concept that the eye's pupil was apple-shaped and essential to sight, and therefore precious.

"Baptism by fire." In Luke 3:16, John the Baptist spoke about Jesus, saying, "He shall baptize you with the Holy Ghost and with fire." This phrase refers to a severe or painful experience that is usually life changing.

"Camel through a needle's eye." This figure of speech is found in the Gospels and makes the point that it is easier for a camel to go through a needle's eye than for those who put their trust in their wealth to see their need of Christ (Matthew 19:24; Mark 10:25; Luke 18:25).

"Cast one's bread upon the waters." This expression is found in Ecclesiastes 11:1: "Cast thy bread upon the waters: for thou shalt find it after many days." In modern usage it means to invest time, money, or effort without expecting immediate return or reward.

"Den of lions." Daniel was thrown into a den of lions to be killed (Dan. 6). This phrase is used to refer to a naïve person facing hostile situations or sophisticated individuals with almost no chance of survival.

"Eye for an eye." This phrase is found in the Mosaic law in Deuteronomy 19:21: "And thine eye shall not pity; but life shall go for life, eye for eye, tooth for tooth, hand for hand, foot for foot." This phrase is used to mean revenge or repayment in kind.

"Forbidden fruit." God commanded Adam and Eve not to eat the fruit of the tree of knowledge of good and evil in the garden of Eden. The story is found in Genesis 2:17–3:6. The phrase means anything that is tempting but forbidden, often referring to illicit love.

"Go the second mile." In the Sermon on the Mount, Jesus said: "And whosoever shall compel thee to go a mile, go with him twain" (Matthew 5:41). In ancient culture, Romans could compel a Jew to carry something for a mile. Jesus said his followers should offer to go farther. The phrase is used now when someone gives more than is expected or required.

"Handwriting on the wall." This expression comes from Daniel 5:5–31 when a mysterious hand appeared and wrote words on the wall during a feast held by King Belshazzar. Daniel was called to interpret the words and told the king of his coming downfall. The phrase implies obvious signs of coming disaster.

"Job's comforters." In Job's misery, his three friends tried to explain his great losses. They told him that God sent the misfortune to punish Job's secret sins. The phrase refers to people who try to offer comfort, but actually make a person feel worse.

"Leopard cannot change its spots." Jeremiah 13:23 reads: "Can the Ethiopian change his skin, or the leopard his spots? Then may ye also do good, that are accustomed to do evil." People cannot change their basic nature.

"Like manna from heaven." In the Bible, this refers to the miraculous supply of food for the people of Israel on their sojourn from Egypt to the Holy Land. The phrase has come to be used for an unexpected good or advantage, particularly financial.

BUG BITES

• Juicy caterpillars are good bird fare so they disguise themselves to hide from hungry predators. Some caterpillars disguise themselves to look like bird droppings or twigs, and some match the colors of leaves.

• Cicadas are below ground as nymphs for 17 years then emerge above ground, turn into adults, lay eggs, and die within a few weeks. The 17-year cycle then begins all over again. The male cicada may be the loudest insect known. His mating call can be heard about a quarter of a mile away.

• A cockroach can live for nine days without its head.

• Dragonflies fly at speeds up to 30 miles per hour.

• In the United States alone, it is estimated that insects cause as much as $5 billion in damages to crops each year.

• The heaviest insects are the Goliath beetles. One species is over four inches in length and three-and-one-half ounces in weight—almost a quarter of a pound.

"Man does not live by bread alone." This is Jesus' response to Satan when he was tempted to turn stones into food (Matthew 4:4). This expression refers to the fact that people have spiritual needs as well as physical and material needs.

"Nothing new under the sun." This phrase is from Ecclesiastes 1:9: "The thing that hath been, it is that which shall be; and that which is done is that which shall be done: and there is no new thing under the sun." This has a cynical outlook meaning nothing new will ever happen.

"Pearl of great price." Taken from a parable of Jesus in Matthew 13, this phrase refers to a trader who sold everything he owned to purchase the much more valuable pearl. It has come to mean anything of enormous value.

"Salt of the earth." This metaphor dates from biblical times when Jesus referred to his followers as "salt of the earth," meaning people who added "flavor" to life. It is used to mean those people who are considered the best or noblest of the kind.

"Scapegoat." On the Day of Atonement, the high priest of Israel chose two goats. One goat was sacrificed to the Lord. The priest laid his hands on remaining goat and confessed the sins of Israel, symbolically transferring the people's sins onto the goat. This goat was sent into the desert as the scapegoat. (See Leviticus 16:7–10, 21–22.) The word means an innocent person who suffers for the wrongdoing of another.

"Walk on water." Jesus walked on the water of the Sea of Galilee to his disciples who were in a boat during a storm. When Jesus climbing into the boat, the wind became calm. (See Matthew 14:22–33.) The phrase refers to the high regard some people have of others who successfully face difficult tasks.

Healing Remedies

Healing remedies mentioned in the Bible include the use of medicines. The first medicines were most likely introduced to the Hebrews by the Egyptians who were more advanced in their use of medicines.

Oil

Oil was one of the most frequently used medicines, generally applied with the idea of soothing and calming. Often oil was mixed with wine, which was the medicine given by the Good Samaritan to the man he found wounded on the road to Jericho.

Honey

Honey was also frequently used as an ointment, which was put on open wounds. It was also used to soothe sore throats, as is common today.

Poultices and Herbs

A fig poultice was used to treat anthrax, which was a cure given by Isaiah for the boil that afflicted King Hezekiah. Purple aloes mixed with wine was another good remedy.

Herbs and plants recommended for stomach pains were rosemary, hyssop, rue, polygonum, bignonia, and certain kinds of palm. Barley soaked in curdled milk was given as a remedy for irregular heartbeats. A drink of maidenhair fern used to cure a case of tapeworms.

Poultices of fish brine were applied to ease rheumatism. The mandrake plant and root were regarded as having many healing properties, including stimulating fertility.

Bleeding and Thermal Waters

Bleeding was a procedure recommended every month for persons up to the age of 40. Eye diseases were treated with eye salves—some based upon the ingredient antimony.

Then as now, thermal waters were recognized for their healing benefits. Surgery was primitive due to lack of knowledge of anatomy and physiology. But small operations such as cauterization and lancing of abscesses were routine. Toothaches were treated with garlic and pains in the gums with salt or yeast.

Rites of Purification

Ritual purifications described in Leviticus (chapters 12, 13, 15, 21) and observed by temple priests had medical significance. Rites were performed for these events and conditions: postchildbirth, leprosy, sexually transmitted diseases, male sexual function, sexual intercourse, menstruation, and touching dead bodies.

Mosaic law detailed in the Pentateuch regarding public hygiene, water supply, sewage disposal, selection of food, and infectious disease promoted health and helped prevent the spread of disease. Quarantine, separating patients with contagious diseases from the rest of the community, was practiced.

In many respects, biblical practices of health and medicine were more up-to-date and effective than would have been anticipated from the ancients before modern medical science.

Spending More Time with God

In the life of a Christian, the most important "task," or privilege, is spending time with God. Down through the centuries, heroes of the faith have stressed the need to "enter God's presence" on a daily basis, and usually several times a day.

In centuries past believers did not have the distractions that assault this generation, such as TV, videocassettes, or the internet. But we have some benefits that earlier generations did not have, such as electric lights and great quantities of Christian books and Bibles at reasonable prices. Here are some practical tips for carving out precious pieces of your day for visits with God:

- **Make up your mind.** The first step is deciding that time with God is a priority.
- **Lengthen your day.** Get up early or stay up late. A morning person can set the alarm for an earlier hour, while a night owl can have devotions late in the evening.
- **Use the buddy system.** Accountability can give you an edge. Let someone who cares about you know what your daily plan is so that he or she can ask if you've kept your commitment.
- **Substitute the godly for the secular.** Instead of spending extra time reading popular fiction, spend more time reading the Bible.
- **Write God a letter.** Sit in a quiet place and pour your heart out on paper. Don't hold back. Tell God how much

you love and need him, what you're struggling with or angry about, how you've been hurt, and what gives you joy. No postage required.

- **Pray at the wheel.** Before you drive off to work or arrive home at the end of your day, stop and pray. Thank God for your vehicle and pray for safety as you drive. Pray for the attitudes of other drivers. Pray again to thank God when you arrive at your destination. Do the same as you ride buses, trains, subways, or planes.

- **Stay alert in church.** How often minds drift during the sermon! Those familiar hymns become rote rather than our heart's cry to God. Ask God to speak to you through the sermon. Look at familiar songs with a fresh eye; make them your prayer. As you wait for the service to begin, close your eyes and thank God for the freedom to worship him, which many around the world do not have.

- **Say grace.** If you eat three meals a day, you have three opportunities to make a connection with God. Thank him for nourishing your body as well as your spirit.

- **Keep the Sabbath.** The fourth commandment is not merely a nice idea; it's a necessity for optimum performance. The Sabbath, observed by Christians on Sunday, is to be set aside for rest, to focus on the Creator, and to restore our souls for the busy week ahead. Use the day to meet God through prayer, Bible study, and fellowship with other believers.

Slow Down and Fast

Most Christians know that fasting often accompanied prayer in Bible times, but few know the reason for fasting, how to fast, or why to fast.

Reasons for Fasting

The prophet Isaiah gave these reasons: Do it to loosen the bands of wickedness, get rid of heavy burdens, and be set free so that you can be a witness to others.

Fasting in the Bible

Fasting takes on a greater significance when you remember that Jesus prepared for his public ministry by completing a 40-day fast in the desert.

Jesus' fast brings to mind another 40-day fast—the first one mentioned in the Old Testament. Moses went to Mt. Sinai and spent 40 days and nights with God, during which he recopied the 10 Commandments on two new tablets (to replace the ones he had broken).

Another Old Testament fast took place in conjunction with the Day of Atonement—the one time in the Bible that God told people to fast. On the tenth day of the seventh month, the high priest went into the Holy of Holies to make atonement for sins—his and the nation's.

Focusing on God

Fasting is about focusing on God, being drawn to him in a way that doesn't happen when you are caught up in your daily rou-

tine. Fasting makes you more aware of your dependence on him. Today, Christians fast and pray for God's help with problems, healing, wisdom for the nations and their leaders, help in breaking addictions, ability to serve others, protection, and revival.

How to Fast

The Bible doesn't provide any solid rules on how to fast. In fact, Christians are not required to fast.

A typical fast can last anywhere from one to forty days. Some who fast abstain from all forms of nourishment, while others do a liquids-only fast. Some fast just one meal, and others decide not to eat a certain group of foods—perhaps favorite foods.

In the early church Christians fasted twice a week. They chose Wednesdays and Fridays as their fast days because the Pharisees fasted on Tuesdays and Thursdays.

In American history the Pilgrims fasted for one day before leaving the Mayflower to begin a new life in the New World. Abraham Lincoln called for a national day of prayer and fasting during the Civil War.

Benefit to the Body

Aside from the obvious spiritual benefits, fasting can be good for the body. It can rid the system of harmful elements introduced by the less-than-nutritious foods we often eat, give the digestive system a rest, and help fight infections.

Note: Those with medical conditions, and pregnant women, should always consult their physician to see if it's safe to fast.

Faith Trumps Adversity

Being a Christian in China is at once dangerous and glorious. Stories of God's miraculous works in this nation of more than 1.3 billion people—the world's largest—filter out of the country, but Christians in the West know little of China's back-to-basics faith.

House Churches

Like the New Testament church, China has been evangelized largely through house churches. There are "official" churches sanctioned by the government and run by what is known as the Three-Self Patriotic Movement, but true believers steer clear, since TSPM forbids evangelism, sharing the gospel with those who are under 18, and talking about healing.

Christians involved in house churches put their lives at risk, since the government has been ruthless in attempting to wipe them out. Each house church has a pastor or leader who might or might not have formal training. Access to books, tapes, and other teaching materials is limited. There is always the risk that the leader will be arrested and tortured in an effort to get names of other Christians.

Young Evangelists and Few Bibles

China also has evangelists who bravely travel through the provinces at their own expense to share the good news. *Charisma* magazine says that a typical Chinese evangelist is female and between 18 and 22 years of age.

Bibles are still a precious commodity—scarcest of all in rural areas where a worker's annual wage is about $100 per year and a Bible is a luxury. Even when Bibles are available, illiteracy and lack of good, solid teaching cause problems. With cults springing up and heresy becoming more widespread, the people need teachers who can help them spot the lies.

A Growing Body

The number of people in house churches is about 80 million, *Charisma* said, and about 25,000 converts embrace the faith each day. On the flip side, the magazine said, well over 20,000 people go to their graves every day in China with no knowledge of Jesus Christ.

Perception of Threat

The government sees Christianity as an ideological rival for the Chinese people's loyalty, and an antirevolutionary movement. In fact, house church leaders encourage their members to work hard and follow the law. Christianity was once, and perhaps still is considered, an attempt by Western nations to impose their culture on the Chinese. Because of decades of restrictions and closed doors, however, any vestiges of Western influence are mostly gone, and Chinese Christians have made Christianity their own, uniquely Chinese faith.

No one knows how many Chinese Christians are imprisoned. What *is* known is that while they are incarcerated, many are severely beaten, sometimes to the point of death. Yet, while they suffer, they remain focused on their faith and frequently lead other prisoners and even guards to the Lord.

Manasseh Comes to His Senses, Just in Time

Many Bible characters "did evil in God's sight," failed to repent, and were obliterated in one way or the other.

Then there are those who went their own merry way for years and realized, just in time, that they'd made a *big* mistake. In this latter category we find King Manasseh of Judah who, with a reign of 55 years (696–642), was on the throne longer than any other king of Judah.

Not a Chip off the Old Block

"Like father, like son" does not entirely apply here. Manasseh's father, King Hezekiah, was responsible for a great reformation in his nation. Then along came Manasseh, who got an early start by ascending to the throne at the tender age of 12. It didn't take him long to undo all of his father's good work.

The Bible describes him as a man "worse than the heathen" and the person responsible for the destruction of Jerusalem and the exile of Judah (2 Chronicles 33:9).

In abandoning God's law, Manasseh caused his subjects great harm by effectively removing the law from their minds. When a king makes it clear that he considers God to be irrelevant, his subjects are likely to follow suit.

Charges of Evil

In 2 Kings 21:1–9, we find the list of Manasseh's destructive behavior:

- He rebuilt the high places. These were lofty areas used as shrines for worship of false gods. When the Israelites

entered Canaan, God told them to destroy these places.

- He built altars to Baal (a sun god) and made an Asherah pole (Asherah was a goddess of fertility). Adding further insult, he put the Asherah pole in God's holy Temple.
- He built altars to the stars in God's Temple and bowed down to them.
- He sacrificed his own sons.
- He practiced sorcery and divination.
- He consulted mediums and spiritists.

Destruction Foretold

Did anyone speak up about Manasseh's reign of evil? Of course. Through the prophets, God told of the destruction that was coming to Jerusalem and Judah because of all the sin. "I will wipe Jerusalem as a man wipeth a dish" was God's message (2 Kings 21:13).

As 2 Kings 21 ends, it appears Manasseh did not change his evil ways, and simply died. But in 2 Chronicles 33, we find the rest of the story.

An Ending Better than His Beginning

Members of the Assyrian army captured Manasseh, put a hook in his nose, and took him to Babylon. Manasseh finally humbled himself before God. God was moved to the point of taking him back to Jerusalem and restoring him to the throne.

Upon his return to Jerusalem, Manasseh rebuilt the outer wall of the City of David, got rid of the foreign gods, removed the ungodly altars he had built, restored the altar of the Lord, and told his people to serve God.

The Reward Is Worth the Cost
of Commitment

How many missionaries choose to deprive themselves of comforts *before* they go to foreign fields as a way of learning to rely solely on God?

Hudson Taylor was such a man. Born in 1832, he became a Christian at 15 and was shortly thereafter impressed to go to China to serve God. After reading a book on medical missions, he decided to get medical and surgical training before going overseas.

Pumping Faith Instead of Iron

Rather than enjoy London's comforts while he could, he rented a cheap room, began tithing and exercising, gave away most of his books and clothing, and lived on a meager diet of oatmeal and rice. In this way, he said, he was able to give more than two-thirds of his income to help others.

At one point, both his father and the Chinese Evangelization Society offered to provide him with monetary support, but without admitting how he was living, he turned them both down. He had decided that if he was going to be a missionary, he'd better get his faith in God in the proper shape.

Steady through All

Taylor arrived in China on March 1, 1853, and entered war-torn Shanghai. The years ahead were not much easier than those early days. Lack of money, learning a difficult language, adjusting to a culture so unlike England's, a shortage of missionaries to share the work, loss of personal belongings, and the death of loved ones were some of the many burdens he had to bear. Rather than allow these troubles to discourage him, Taylor stayed the course.

Mission Founded

After spending many years in ministry to people in towns along China's rivers, however, his ill health forced him to return to England. It was there in 1865 that he founded the China Inland Mission. The interior of China was about to experience the shock waves of God's grace.

"While in the field," Taylor said in his book, *A Retrospect*, "the pressure of claims immediately around me was so great that I could not think much of the still greater needs of the regions further inland!"

Moving Inland

As Taylor prayed, relying always on God to round up the workers, the mission grew and grew. By the time he died in 1905, the work of the China Inland Mission was being conducted by 849 missionaries at 205 mission stations. Chinese Christians who were part of the Mission numbered 125,000.

Beginning in 1927, the Mission made a practice of transferring leadership in Christian churches to Chinese Christians. It can be said that Taylor helped lay the groundwork for something that ensured the continuation of the Christian faith in China, despite wars, rebellions, and the government's attempts to erase it.

Top 10 Pieces of Good Advice

10. Avoid troublemakers (Romans 16:17).
 9. Reconcile with the person you've argued with (Matthew 5:24).
 8. Be thankful (Colossians 3:15).
 7. Don't worry about anything (Philippians 4:6).
 6. Don't get drunk (Ephesians 5:18).
 5. Don't be lazy (Hebrews 6:12).
 4. Do unto others as you would have others do unto you (Matthew 7:12).
 3. Give generously (2 Corinthians 9:6–7).
 2. Follow the law (Romans 13:1).
 1. Love your enemies and pray for people who persecute you (Matthew 5:44–46).

CHILDREN AND CHURCH

A woman had been teaching her three-year-old daughter the Lord's Prayer. For several evenings at bedtime, the little girl would repeat after her mother the lines from the prayer. Finally, she decided to go solo. Her mother listened with pride as she carefully enunciated each word, right up to the end of the prayer: "Lead us not into temptation," she prayed, "but deliver us some E-mail.

Amen."

The Original Home School

Did children in ancient Israel complain about going to school? Hardly. At home, they were *at school!*

Archaeologists have determined that as far back as Abraham's day, children had writing lessons, studied the multiplication and division tables, and conjugated verbs. More advanced students tackled square and cube roots and practical geometry.

Under Mosaic law, the parents were the primary instructors. They were assisted by the priests and Levites who read the law to all the people every seventh year during the Feast of Tabernacles.

Today, adults shake their heads and worry about what their children are picking up "on the streets." In ancient Israel, the street was the place to be if you wanted to learn about business transactions and negotiations.

> A father was approached by his small son, who told him proudly, "I know what the Bible means!"
> His father smiled and said, "So, son, what does the Bible mean?"
>   B - BASIC
>   I - INSTRUCTIONS
>   B - BEFORE
>   L - LEAVING
>   E - EARTH

God made it clear that the law was the most important element of any child or adult's education. As he told Moses in Deuteronomy 31:12, it wasn't just for the Israelites; it was also for the aliens living in their towns. God wanted *everyone* to hear and learn the law. Why? So that they would develop a reverence and respect for God and make up their minds to follow the law.

What's in a Word?

When people look at a best-selling Christian novelist like **Frank Peretti**, they may envy him. After all, he's sold more than 9 million copies of his books, which include *This Present Darkness, Piercing the Darkness, Prophet, The Oath, The Visitation*, and several for children known as the Cooper Kids Adventure series.

Peretti is also a pilot and a former minister with many hobbies including carpentry, hiking, banjo playing, bicycling, and sculpting.

He's been compared to John Grisham and Stephen King. In an article for *Christianity Today*, Elizabeth Cody Newenhuyse said Peretti "made it acceptable for Christians to read a tale of the supernatural." The religion editor at *Publishers Weekly* described him as "the grand old man of the (Christian thriller) genre."

Has it been smooth sailing all the way? Not exactly.

Painful Words

In his first nonfiction book, Peretti tells "the story behind the story"—the trauma he endured as a child because of a condition called cystic hygroma.

The Wounded Spirit describes Peretti's difficult birth, the cyst that formed on his neck shortly after his birth, and the grueling surgery (one of many) and awful complication that resulted from it: a swollen, oozing tongue that hung outside his mouth and caused constant drooling.

School can be tough for a child, especially a preacher's kid who is small for his age. For a child who has a highly visible, extremely unpleasant condition like Peretti had, school was torture.

Unconditional Love

The worst experiences, Peretti said, came in junior high and his first two years of high school in the shower room after gym class. The harsh hateful words and cruel taunts of the other boys cut deep. Peretti says his parents' unconditional love and his faith kept him going.

In the worst possible way, this future writer learned the power of words: the kind that destroy and, eventually, the kind that save. One day on his way to gym class, Peretti passed a gym teacher who asked, "How you doing? You feeling okay?"

Powerful Words

Peretti was amazed that someone in authority had actually noticed him and showed concern. It gave him the courage to write a letter to his gym teacher about the other boys' attacks on him. His teacher passed the letter to the school's counselor, who excused Peretti from gym class for the rest of his high school career.

Peretti's books talk about different types of bullies and battles. His first two novels explore spiritual warfare and feature angels fighting demons—good conquering evil. *The Oath* is the story of a man whose faith is put to the test when he faces evil.

Peretti's childhood struggles might be over, but their impact has had a definite influence on his writing. In *The Wounded Spirit* he said, "Having been hurt by words, I have a better appreciation for what words can do."

An Answer in Timbuktu

Stephen Saint is the missionary pilot son of a pioneer missionary pilot, Nate Saint, one of five missionaries killed in Ecuador in the 1950s by stone-age Auca Indians. Stephen Saint has written:

"For years, I'd thought Timbuktu was just a made-up name for 'the ends of the earth.' When I found out it was a real place in Africa, I developed an inexplicable fascination for it. In 1986 on a fact-finding trip to West Africa for Missionary Aviation Fellowship that fascination became an irresistible urge. Timbuktu wasn't on my itinerary, but I knew I had to go there."

Saint hitched a ride from Bamako, Mali, 500 miles away, on a small plane chartered by UNICEF. He knew he would need to find his own way back.

Stranded

Saint recounts, "The pilot said, 'Try the marketplace.' Someone there might have a truck. But be careful. . . . Westerners don't last long in the desert if the truck breaks down, which often happens.'"

Suddenly Saint had a powerful desire to talk to his father, who had known what it was like to be a foreigner in a strange land. However, his father, Nate Saint, had died in the jungles of Ecuador when Stephen was a month shy of his fifth birthday. He had only a few fleeting memories of his dad. In place of memories, a question had lingered in Stephen's mind through the years: Did his father have to die? He wondered if there was a *purpose* to the murders.

A Cry to God

"God," Saint found himself praying in the marketplace, "I'm in trouble here. Please keep me safe and show me a way to get back. Please reveal Yourself and Your love to me the way you did to my father."

No bolt of lightning came from the blue, but he remembered that just before he'd started for Timbuktu, a fellow worker had said, "There's a famous mosque in Timbuktu . . but there's also a tiny Christian church, which virtually no one visits. Look it up if you get the chance."

Saint asked a group of children, "Where is Eglise Evangelique Chretienne?"

The youngsters led him to a young, handsome man with dark skin and flowing robes. Saint learned his name was Nouh. He led Saint to a compound on the edge of town where an American missionary lived.

The Lure of a Bic Pen

With the missionary translating for him, Saint asked Nouh, "How did you come to have faith?"

Nouh answered: "This compound has always had a beautiful garden. One day when I was a small boy, a friend and I decided to steal some carrots. It was a dangerous task. We'd been told that Toubabs [white men] eat nomadic children. Despite our agility and considerable experience, I was caught by the former missionary here. Mr. Marshall didn't eat me; instead, he gave me the carrots and some cards that had God's promises from the Bible written on them. He told me if I learned them, he'd give me an ink pen!"

"You learned them?" Saint asked.

"Oh, yes!" he exclaimed. "Only government men and the headmaster of the school had a Bic pen! But when I showed off my pen at school, the teacher knew I must have spoken with a Toubab, which is strictly forbidden. He severely beat me."

Outcast

When Nouh's parents found out he had portions of such a despised book defiling their house, they threw him out and forbade anyone to take him in. He was not allowed in school.

But something had happened: Nouh had come to believe that what the Bible said was true. Nouh's mother became desperate. Her reputation as well as her family's was in jeopardy. Finally she decided to kill her son. She obtained poison from a sorcerer and poisoned Nouh's food at a family feast. Nouh ate the food and wasn't affected. His brother, who unwittingly stole a morsel of meat from the deadly dish, became violently ill and remains partially paralyzed. Seeing God's intervention, the family and the town's people were afraid to make further attempts on his life, but condemned him as an outcast.

Why Risk Life?

"It couldn't have been easy for you as a teenager to take a stand that made you despised by the whole community," Saint said. "Where did your courage come from?"

Buoyed by Jungle Story

"Mr. Marshall couldn't take me in without putting my life in jeopardy. So he gave me some books about other Christians who'd suffered for their faith. My favorite was about five young men who willingly risked their lives to take God's good news to stone-age Indians in the jungles of South America." Nuoh's eyes widened as he continued, "I've lived all my life in the desert. How frightening the jungle must be! The book said these men let themselves be speared to death, even though they had guns and could have killed their attackers!"

The missionary translator said, "I remember the story. As a matter of fact, one of those men had your last name."

"Yes," Saint said quietly, "the pilot was my father."

"Your father?" Nouh cried. "The story is true?"

"Yes," Saint said, "it's true."

A Mutual Giving of "Gifts"

The missionary and Nouh talked with Saint through the afternoon. When they accompanied Saint back to the airfield that night, they found there was room for Saint on the UNICEF plane.

Saint recalls: "As Nouh and I hugged each other, it seemed incredible that God loved us so much that He'd arranged for us to meet 'at the ends of the earth.' Nouh and I had gifts for each other that no one else could give. I gave him the assurance that the story that had given him courage was true. He, in turn, gave me the assurance that God had used Dad's death for good. Dad, by dying, had helped give Nouh a faith worth dying for. And Nouh, in return, had helped give Dad's faith back to me."

Source: Adapted from Stephen Saint, "To the Ends of the Earth." Copyright © 1998 Hopewell United Methodist Church.

10 Proverbial Questions

The Book of Proverbs has a number of verses that can readily be rephrased as questions a person is wise to ask about a potential spouse:

- Does your potential spouse truly know how to comfort you when you are discouraged? Or does your potential spouse try to "gloss over" your discouragement or make light of your disappointments? (See Proverbs 26:20.)
- Does your potential spouse like to quarrel? Like to pick a fight? Find lots to criticize? (See Proverbs 21:9.)
- Does your potential spouse have a bad temper—quick anger, frequent anger, or vehemently expressed anger? (See Proverbs 21:19.)
- Does your potential spouse seek God's wisdom and godly counsel? (See Proverbs 19:20–21.)
- Does your potential spouse refrain from the use of chemical substances that alter behavior (drugs and excessive alcohol)? (See Proverbs 20:1.)
- Does he or she forgive quickly? (See Proverbs 19:11.)
- Does your potential spouse encourage you to be your best, develop a godly character, and pursue the highest ethical standards? (See Proverbs 27:17.)
- Does your potential spouse refrain from lying or using perverse or foolish language? (See Proverbs 19:1.)
- Does he or she trust God? (See Proverbs 3:5–6.)
- Does your potential spouse live a life of integrity? (See Proverbs 20:6–7.)

Keep on Trucking

Sometimes a person in dire straits gets visited by a hero—a human being who shows up at just the right moment with exactly what that person needs to solve a problem. The solution can be as simple as a can of gas for an empty tank, a jack to fix a flat tire, a cell phone to make an emergency call, or a dollar to make up the difference at the grocery store when the old wallet turns out to be thinner than expected.

These heroes are everywhere, performing acts of kindness every day. Volumes will no doubt be written about their selflessness after the September 11, 2001, tragedy in New York, Pennsylvania, and Washington, D.C. On that day, ordinary people became heroes to many whose world had just gone black.

Tennessee Responds

Kindness spread quickly from those epicenters of disaster. It made its way all across America, inspiring regular people who weren't famous to do amazingly kind things.

The residents of East Tennessee knew that they wanted to help some of those heroes in the New York City fire department, especially after learning that more than 300 firefighters lost their lives on September 11. Lives cannot be replaced, they reasoned, but the dozens of fire-fighting and emergency vehicles that were lost *could* be. And so, the *Knoxville News-Sentinel* and six other corporate sponsors launched a drive to raise money for a new fire truck. They called it the "Freedom Engine Campaign."

As the people of Tennessee learned, fire trucks are not cheap.

The original goal, according to one News-Sentinel manager, was to raise between $300,000 and $700,000. That would be enough to buy a pumper truck. By the time the campaign ended in November, it appeared that Tennesseans had exceeded their wildest dreams, raising more than $900,000—enough to cover the cost of a top-drawer, fully-equipped ladder truck.

A Little Helps a Lot

How did they raise so much money in such a short time? According to the *News-Sentinel*, most of the donations came not from the corporate sponsors but from schools, churches, and civic groups. Everyone wanted to help.

Some of the early childhood centers, elementary schools, middle schools, high schools, and even private piano students in the area had collected about $9,796.01 by November 11—just two short months after the tragedy.

About $156,000 was raised through a telethon and an auction.

South Carolina Repays a Favor

Another fire truck story comes from Columbia, South Carolina. This story made the *Today* show and *People* magazine.

New York Helps Columbia

The Carolina story actually began in 1867, shortly after the Civil War. In a gesture of extreme kindness—considering that the North and the South had just done their best to annihilate each other on the battlefields—the New York Fireman's Association responded to Columbia's pleas for assistance and collected $2,500 to help the beleaguered city put its fire-fighting operation back together.

In a tragic turn of events, the ship carrying an NYFA-purchased fire truck was wrecked before it got to South Carolina. Undaunted, the NYFA again raised $2,500 and bought a second truck, which arrived safely.

According to *People*, the president of Columbia's fire company, Capt. J. J. Mackey, "pledged that New York City's kindness would 'forever remain green in our memory.'"

Principal Gets an Idea

In the aftermath of the September 11 tragedy, White Knoll Middle School principal Nancy Turner and her students decided to help New York City after the World Trade Center attacks by raising money to buy a new pumper truck. Turner told Columbia fire chief John Jansen about their plans, and this native New Yorker informed the principal that what they were actually doing was returning a 134-year-old favor.

Like the people of Tennessee, the students of White Knoll proved themselves equal to the challenge of raising huge sums of money, bringing in more than $325,000 by mid-November. The entire community rallied behind them, lining up for car washes, overpaying for T-shirts and buttons featuring American flag imprints, buying untold numbers of baked goods, and anteing up when collections for the truck were taken at college football games.

Urim and Thummin?

The story is told of a young pastor in the Church of England who was greatly helped in his understanding of the Scriptures by frequent conversations with an uneducated cobbler who was, nevertheless, well acquainted with the Word of God.

One day as a young theologian friend visited the pastor, the pastor told him about the remarkable knowledge of the Bible that the cobbler possessed. The young theologian had recently completed an advanced study and presented papers before colleagues. Perhaps he felt challenged by the possibility that a common laborer could impress his friend when he had expected to receive that praise.

In a spirit of pride, he expressed a desire to meet the cobbler, saying he felt sure he could ask some questions that he would be quite unable to answer.

Upon being introduced to the man in his little shop, the theologian asked, "Can you tell me what Urim and the Thummim were?"

The cobbler replied, "I don't know exactly; I understand that the words apply to something that was on the breastplate of the high priest. I know the words mean 'Lights and Perfection,' and that through the Urim and Thummim the high priest was able to discern the mind of the Lord. But I find that I can get the mind of the Lord by just changing a few letters.

"I take this blessed Book, and by 'usin' and 'thummin' I get the mind of the Lord that way."

Which New Testament Book?

Circle the book in the New Testament where you will find the event, subject, or verse. Answers follow.

1. "For God so loved the world, that he gave his only begotten Son, that whosoever believeth in him should not perish, but have everlasting life."
   a. Jude
   b. Revelation
   c. Galatians
   d. John

2. "Put on the whole armor."
   a. 1 Samuel
   b. Joshua
   c. Ephesians
   d. Daniel

3. "Jesus wept."
   a. Matthew
   b. Mark
   c. Luke
   d. John

4. The fruit of the Spirit
   a. Proverbs
   b. Galatians
   c. Colossians
   d. Genesis

5. "Our Father, which art in heaven."
   a. Revelation
   b. Psalms
   c. 1 Corinthians
   d. Matthew

6. "For with God nothing will be impossible."
   a. Job
   b. Luke
   c. Jonah
   d. Romans

7. "I am the Bread of Life."
   - a. John
   - b. 1 Corinthians
   - c. 2 Peter
   - d. Exodus

8. Jesus ascends to heaven
   - a. Matthew
   - b. Romans
   - c. Acts
   - d. Revelation

9. "There is therefore now no condemnation to those who are in Christ Jesus."
   - a. Exodus
   - b. Revelation
   - c. Romans
   - d. Esther

10. "Love is of God."
    - a. 1 John
    - b. Titus
    - c. Ephesians
    - d. Jude

11. "If it be possible, as much as lieth in you, live peaceably with all men."
    - a. Exodus
    - b. Matthew
    - c. Romans
    - d. Song of Solomon

Answers
1.d 2.c 3.d 4.b 5.d 6.b 7.a 8.c 9.c 10.a 11.c

Prayers around the World

As the following prayers so beautifully illustrate, people all over the world, facing a variety of challenges, opportunities, dangers, and blessings, have their own special way of expressing themselves to God.

I Have No Words to Thank You—*From Kikuyu, Kenya*

O my Father, Great Elder,
I have no words to thank you,
But with your deep wisdom
I am sure that you can see
How I value your glorious gifts.
O my Father, when I look upon your greatness,
I am confounded with awe.
O Great Elder,
Ruler of all things earthly and heavenly,
I am your warrior,
Ready to act in accordance with your will.

Be Good to Me—Breton Fisherman's Prayer, *France*

Dear God, be good to me. The sea is so wide,
and my boat is so small.

You Have Helped My Life to Grow Like a Tree—*From Nigeria*

God in heaven, you have helped my life to grow like a tree. Now something has happened. Satan, like a bird, has carried in one twig of his own choosing after another. Before I knew it he had built a dwelling place and was living in it. Tonight, my Father, I am throwing out both the bird and the nest.

A Child's Prayer—*From England*

Make me, dear Lord, polite and kind
To everyone, I pray;
And may I ask you how you find
Yourself, dear Lord, today?

Drive Away Darkness—*From the Philippines*

As our tropical sun gives forth its light, so let the rays from your face enter every nook of my being and drive away all darkness within.

Prayer of a Muslim Convert

O God, I am Mustafah, the tailor, and I work at the shop of Muhammed Ali. The whole day long I sit and pull the needle and the thread through the cloth. O God, you are the needle and I am the thread. I am attached to you and I follow you. When the thread tries to slip away from the needle it becomes tangled up and must be cut so that it can be put back in the right place. O God, help me to follow you wherever you may lead me. For I am really only Mustafah, the tailor, and I work at the shop of Muhammed Ali on the great square.

Humor in All Denominations

Don't like the way one of the following jokes reads? Just insert your own favorite denomination in place of the one mentioned!

One sunny day a Catholic, a Baptist, and a Methodist were going fishing. Right after they left, the Catholic realized that he had left his supplies on the shore. So, he got out of the boat, walked on the water to the shore, got his supplies, walked back across the water, and got into the boat.

Then, of course, the Baptist realized that they didn't have enough bait. So, he got out of the boat, walked on the water to the shore, went to a nearby bait shop and bought a pack of bait, walked back across the water, and got into the boat.

Having watched his two friends make short work of the lake, the Methodist was feeling pretty confident. Then he looked at his wrist, realized that his watch wasn't working, decided there was no time like the present to buy a new one, got out of the boat, and promptly sank straight to the bottom of the lake.

At that point, the Catholic and the Baptist were feeling pretty guilty. They looked at each other and said, "Oops! I guess we should have told him where the rocks are!"

One Sunday morning, the nondenominational pastor noticed little Alex was staring up at the large plaque that hung in the foyer of the church auditorium. The plaque was covered with names, and small American flags were mounted on either side of it.

The seven year old had been staring at the plaque for some time, so the pastor walked up, stood beside the boy, and said quietly, "Good morning, Alex."

"Good morning, pastor," said Alex, still gazing intently at the plaque. "Can I ask you a question?"

"Of course," the pastor said with a smile, intrigued by the boy's serious demeanor.

"What is this?" Alex asked, pointing to the plaque.

"Well, son, it's a memorial to all the young men and women who died in the service."

Soberly, the pastor and the child stood together, both staring at the plaque.

Little Alex's voice was shaking and barely audible when he finally asked, "Which service, the 8:30 or the 11 o'clock?"

A little girl was getting more and more restless in church one morning as the Holiness preacher's sermon dragged on and on. Finally, she leaned over to her mother and whispered, "Mommy, if we give him the money now, will he let us go?"

A boy was watching his father, an Orthodox priest, write a sermon. "How do you know what to say?" the boy asked his father.

"Why, God tells me," the father assured his son.

"Oh," the boy said. "Then why do you keep crossing things out?"

Dragons—Real or Fiction?

Dragons have long been a staple in fantasy stories and science fiction movies. Could they have been real creatures that existed at some time on the earth?

The Book of Job describes a creature with dragonlike characteristics:

His sneezings flash forth light,
And his eyes are like the eyelids of the morning.
Out of his mouth go burning lights;
Sparks of fire shoot out.
Smoke goes out of his nostrils,
As from a boiling pot and burning rushes.
His breath kindles coals.
And a flame goes out of his mouth. (Job 41:18–21 NKJV)

World Facts

Before dismissing this as a mythical creature, consider these facts:

- Ancient legends around the world tell of dragonlike creatures, including specific stories and illustrations in Africa, India, Europe, the Middle East, and Asia. The word *dragon* actually comes from Europe. Many of these legends are dated about the same time in history, even though communication or travel among these various areas did not exist at the time the stories originated.
- The foremost land of the dragon is China where the dragon is still considered a major symbol of power among the Chinese people. For centuries, the dragon

symbol was used exclusively by the emperor. Old Chinese legends tell of dragons being chased into the sea when rice paddies were made, of families keeping dragons as pets, and of dragons pulling royal chariots.

- Dragons are described as being real until the 1500s, although writers of that time call them extremely rare and relatively small. In fact, a scientist named Ulysses Aldrovandus claimed to have seen a small dragon in northern Italy in 1572. A farmer had killed it by knocking it on the head when it hissed at his oxen. The scientist measured the body, made a drawing of it, and had it mounted for a museum. It had a long neck, very long tail, and a fat body—a description that fits numerous ancient reptilelike creatures, but none known today.

- Some creatures alive today exhibit properties associated with dragons. The lightning bug has a tail that glows in the dark as the result of an electrochemical reaction. Electric eels can emit enough volts to kill a man. The bombadeer beetle holds chemicals in separate pouches near its mouth. When frightened or attacked, this beetle is capable of mixing those chemicals to emit a spark that has a scorching temperature of 212 degrees Fahrenheit! Surely it is not an improbability to think that a larger creature was capable of producing chemical heat and light—a creature now extinct.

Adapted from Phil Phillips, *Dinosaurs—The Bible, Barney, and Beyond* (Lancaster, PA: Starburst Publishers, 1994), 60–63.

THE LITTLE INSPIRATIONAL **227** BATHROOM BIBLE BOOK

Top 10 Tips from Queen Esther

1. **Don't get too sure of yourself or your position.**
   Queen Vashti, the beautiful wife of King Xerxes,
   snubbed the king by refusing to come to his banquet
   so that he could show her off. Big mistake. She lost
   her crown.

2. **Be nice to your relatives.** When Esther lost her
   parents, her cousin Mordecai took her in and raised
   her. When King Xerxes was looking for a new queen,
   Mordecai made sure she was one of the candidates.

3. **Know when to keep quiet.** Mordecai did not tell
   anyone that Esther was Jewish. There were no laws
   (that we know of) against a Jewish woman becoming
   queen, but Mordecai knew there were some preju-
   diced people in the king's court. Revealing this
   information also could have prevented Esther from
   doing what she needed to do later.

4. **Accept good advice.** Esther listened to the wise
   counsel of the king's eunuch before her first meeting
   with the king, and it paid off. The king liked her best
   and made her his queen.

5. **Don't just stand there; do something!** Mordecai
   overheard two officers discussing a plot to assassi-
   nate the king. He gave the information to Esther,
   who told the king, and the plot was thwarted.

6. **Give credit where credit is due.** Esther told the king
   that Mordecai had uncovered the assassination plot. It
   cost her nothing to do the right thing. Later, her truth-

fulness paid off for Mordecai: He was honored by the king.

7. **Don't let pride and prejudice rule your life.** Haman, newly elevated to a position of power, was insulted when Mordecai refused to pay homage to him. Upon discovering that Mordecai was a Jew, Haman allowed his prejudice to send him over the edge. He convinced the king to issue an edict calling for the destruction of the Jews. Later, of course, Haman was the one who lost his life.

8. **Trust those who have proven themselves trustworthy.** When Mordecai asked Esther to go to the king on behalf of the Jews, she was afraid. But she trusted Mordecai, who had never steered her wrong. She trusted the king, whom she knew adored her (and whose life she had saved by telling him of the assassination plot). She also trusted God to watch out for her, and asked the Jews to fast and pray for her.

9. **Pick your moment.** Rather than blurt out her request at her first meeting with the king, Esther invited him to a banquet and then to another banquet. By the end of the second meal, he was ready to give her anything.

10. **Know when to speak up for your cause.** When the time was right, Esther told the king that she was Jewish and asked him to spare her people. The king agreed. He ordered that Haman, who had hatched the plot, be hanged. Then the king gave Esther Haman's entire estate.

Compassion Lands Workers in Jail

The world watched as **Heather Mercer** and **Dayna Curry**, two American humanitarian aid workers, were captured by the Taliban in Afghanistan and imprisoned for being Christians. The charge against them? An attempt to convert Muslims to Christ.

Here is a quick profile of Mercer and Curry—their work, imprisonment, and release.

- **For whom were they working?** Shelter Now International (SNI). This relief organization has headquarters in Oshkosh, Wisconsin, with support offices in Australia and Spain. SNI had been working with Afghans since shortly after the 1979 invasion of their nation by the Soviet Union.

- **Did they know each other prior to going to Afghanistan?** No. Curry is from Tennessee and Mercer from Virginia. Both, however, were graduates of Baylor University in Waco, Texas. Mercer went to Afghanistan in March 2001. Curry was already there, having joined Shelter Now two years earlier.

- **Who else was with them?** Curry and Mercer were part of a team that included two Australians (Peter Bunch and Diana Thomas) and four Germans (Georg Taubmann, head of the group, Katrin Jelinek, Margrit Stebner, and Silke Durrkopf).

- **What was their mission?** To respond quickly and with compassion to those who as a result of war, persecution or natural disaster are homeless and in desperate need of shelter, and in doing so, to be instruments of God's love for all people and especially the poor. In the 1980s, SNI set up a multipurpose Geodesic Dome Project and used it to provide housing for widows and disabled refugees in Peshawar, Pakistan. SNI helped thousands of Afghans with emergency shelter, food, and training so they might work to support their families.

- **When were they arrested?** August 5, 2001.
- **What evidence was used to accuse the team of attempting to convert Muslims to Christianity?** Christian literature found in the SNI offices in Kabul.
- **Were Westerners the only ones arrested?** No. Sixteen Afghans who worked with SNI in Kabul, including cooks, gardeners, and house guards, were also arrested.
- **Did family members go to Afghanistan?** Members of the Mercer and Curry families went to Afghanistan to help arrange for legal counsel and to support the two women. When all United States officials left Afghanistan after the September 11 terrorist attacks on the United States, the two women's family members had to leave.
- **Were they mistreated in the prison?** Mercer and Curry say "no," although they have also said they heard other prisoners being beaten and tortured. They reported they were fed adequately, and that they spent much of their time praying and singing.
- **When did Mercer and Curry regain their freedom?** November 15—just over 100 days after their arrest. The team was abandoned in a Ghazni prison as members of

the Taliban fled to Kandahar under heavy pressure from U.S. military forces and Afghanistan's Northern Alliance. Northern Alliance forces and Ghazni residents found and released the eight Westerners from the jail, and three American special forces helicopters arrived soon after to take them to safety in Pakistan. The Americans returned to American soil on November 25.

- **What happened to the Afghan coworkers?** All reportedly made their way to safety.
- **Why did the Taliban leave these prisoners behind rather than take them as hostages for later negotiations?** Nobody knows why. The families of Mercer and Curry believe the answer lies in prayer. Curry's mother, Nancy Cassell, said on October 30: "If our God can part the Red Sea, keep Daniel safe in the lions' den, bring down the walls of Jericho, and so many other things, as well as rising from the grave, then he can protect eight of his flock sitting in a Kabul jail waiting for him to bring about another miracle."

After meeting with Mercer and Curry at the White House, President George Bush was quoted by the Associated Press as saying, "It's a wonderful story about prayer, about a faith that can sustain people in good times and in bad times."

Curry said she and her fellow prisoners believe the "millions" around the world who offered up prayers on their behalf were the ones who ultimately secured their freedom.

Down with the Status Quo

Martin Luther wasn't looking to start a new denomination in 1517 when he began raising questions about the Roman Catholic Church. All he wanted to do was foster a . . . "reformation."

What Upset Luther?

Among other things, Luther was upset that the pope and many priests in Rome were ignoring their vows of poverty and celibacy. He was also upset that Pope Leo X, devised a new indulgence to pay for the construction of St. Peter's Cathedral in Rome.

An Unlikely Reformer

Martin Luther was born in 1483 in Eisleben, Germany. His parents were disciplinarians who firmly believed in "spare the rod, spoil the child."

School was more of the same. The teachers, Luther once said, were "tyrants and executioners." It's not surprising that after viewing all the authority figures in his life, Luther thought that God, too, was looking for a good excuse to punish him. It's also not surprising that Luther felt totally unworthy and insignificant, or that he worked overtime to win God's favor.

Struck by Lightning

Luther initially pursued a course of study to become a lawyer, but then one day, as he was walking down the road, he was nearly struck by a bolt of lightning. The power of it knocked him to the ground. According to some scholars, this experience resulted in Luther's decision to enter a monastery, which he did in 1505. (Others scholars say Luther's constant preoccupation with death drove him into the monastery.)

Even after becoming part of the Order of Augustinian Eremites, studying the Bible, taking his vows, and being ordained a priest, Luther continued to feel a heavy weight of guilt for his sin. He sought to make pilgrimages to assuage his guilt. During a trip to Rome in 1510, Luther had just climbed the 28 steps of the chapel of Sancta Sanctorum—on his knees—when he suddenly "knew" deep within that salvation did not come from tithing or making pilgrimages to shrines. Five years later, after much study in the Book of Romans, Luther further concluded that only God's grace saves the sinner, and grace is received only by faith.

Open Confrontation

In 1517, Luther posted his famous 95 Theses. People all over Germany read Luther's work and began to question the church's position and policies. The pope ordered Luther to renounce his statements. Luther refused. A stalemate resulted.

In 1520, Luther wrote three treatises that pointed to the need for a major reform of the Roman Catholic Church. He criticized aspects of all of the church's sacraments and wrote, "All believers are priests."

On October 11, 1520, the pope sent Luther a "Bull"—a papal proclamation that, along with listing several punishments, gave him 60 days to recant.

On day 60, Luther burned the Bull—in public. Excommunication followed.

Kidnapped for Safekeeping

The pope set another "command performance" date in April of 1521. In response, the princes of Germany "kidnapped" Luther and took him to a castle near Eisenach.

Even while in hiding, Luther continued to be the subject of debate. The 1521 Edict of Worms declared him an outcast. Anyone who followed Luther's teachings, the pope said, would suffer his same fate.

Meanwhile, back at the castle, Luther was translating the New Testament from the original Greek into a more user-friendly German than had been available to the people up to that time. By 1534, he had completed the translation of the Old Testament from the original Hebrew.

Not without Bloodshed

Overzealous reformers, including peasants, used violence to bring about change, both in the church and in their towns. Luther criticized them and even returned to Wittenberg to try to stop the violence, but to no avail. The church blamed him for the rebels' actions. Blood flowed as the government put down the revolt.

Over the years, hundreds of churches in Europe took the name *Lutheran*. Luther, however, never approved of having his name used for this new denominational trend.

It was at this time that the word *Protestant* also came into use. Followers of Luther's teachings, not allowed to pursue their faith in Catholic provinces of Germany, spoke up and became known as Protestants.

And the rest, as they say, is history.

Prayer Tips

Imagine that you are out in the desert, minding your own business, keeping an eye on a flock of sheep. You wander over to this mountain, and suddenly you see something strange—a bush on fire that doesn't burn up.

You go to see what's happening, and as you get closer, a voice comes out of nowhere and calls your name.

The next thing you know, you're hearing God tell you that he has chosen *you* to rescue his people from slavery.

Is this a bad dream? Are you hallucinating? Or are you someone whose heart is tuned toward God?

Your name doesn't have to be Moses for you to hear God's voice. And you don't need to see a burning bush to know that God is with you. To hear him and sense his presence, you just need to be ready to listen.

Holy Spirit Help

God has given us the ability to hear his voice. The Holy Spirit, who came to live inside us after Jesus returned to heaven, knows everything that God is thinking. When we become Christians, we receive the Holy Spirit, which means that we have access to what he knows about God. We also have the mind of Christ, as Paul says in 1 Corinthians 2:16. All this tells us that we can be on God's wavelength. He's not speaking some foreign language we'll never be able to interpret. He can speak to us, and we can understand him!

Five Tips

Here are some tips for a healthy prayer life.

1. Make it your first and last words of the day.
2. Find a quiet place to pray.
3. Set a time to start and stop.
4. Read the Bible before you pray.
5. Praise God before petitioning.

Say "amen," but don't get up. Keep your eyes closed. Stay focused on the Lord. Try to clear your mind of distractions, such as the grocery list, chores that are undone, and your plans for the weekend. Just sit and listen. Wait for God to speak to you.

God's Response

Will you hear an audible voice in response to your prayers? Not necessarily. Some people do, but most say they receive thoughts or impressions that could only have come from God. You might feel that God is telling you to pray for someone or some situation that you hadn't thought of or didn't know about. If you've been under stress, you might feel waves of peace.

When you know God has spoken to you, whether through an audible voice or with a thought or by pointing you to a specific Bible verse, write it down. Keep records. That will encourage you to keep listening.

Extra! Extra! Read All about It! Part 2

Prison Break Under Investigation

Questions have arisen concerning the management of Roman prisons following the escape last week of a notorious inmate.

Simon Peter, regarded as the ringleader of a growing group of people called "Christians," had been seized by King Herod's men and incarcerated. This followed closely on the heels of Herod's order that James, another of the Christians, be put to death.

Herod's detractors say he feels threatened by the people who practice this new offshoot of Judaism. A spokesman for Herod said that the king is merely trying to "clean up the streets" and "extend an olive branch" to the Jews.

At the prison, Peter was guarded by four squads of soldiers—a total of 16 men. He was scheduled to go on trial right after the Jewish celebration of Passover. The night before the trial, however, there was a major breakdown in prison security, allowing Peter to escape.

The soldiers and sentries who stood guard that night could not explain how the escape was pulled off. They won't get a second chance to come up with answers since all have been executed, on Herod's orders.

A friend of Peter's, speaking on condition of anonymity, described what had happened to this apostle of the late Jesus Christ, who was crucified several years ago. (Jesus' followers claim he rose from the dead.)

"Peter was asleep," said Nico. "They had him in chains and surrounded by guards. He said somebody shone a light in his face, and when he opened his eyes, he saw this man—Peter figured out later that it was an angel—who told him to get up and get dressed and get out of there. Well, you didn't have to tell him twice!"

"Peter," Nico said, "thought he was seeing a vision. He followed this angel past a bunch of guards; I don't know if they were asleep or if they were just 'temporarily blinded.'"

Nico also said that he and

other members of the Christian "church" had been praying for Peter all along.

"We just trusted God to get him out of prison—alive," Nico said, with an earnest look on his face.   ,

A servant girl named Rhoda, who works for Mary, the mother of John (also called Mark), said she was the one who answered the door when Peter unexpectedly showed up at the house that night.

"I didn't let him in at first," Rhoda said a little sheepishly. "I was in shock! So was everybody else. Nobody believed me when I said he was there."

Peter has reportedly left Judea for parts unknown.

Those wishing to apply for jobs at the prison should check with the Employment Office. (Read the official report of this story in Acts 12:1–19.)

Conspirator Converts to New Religion

Saul of Tarsus, a former ally of the high priest, has announced his conversion to a new faith.

Raised in Jerusalem, son of a Pharisee, member of the tribe of Benjamin, taught by the esteemed and intellectual Rabbi Gamaliel, and possessing important family connections, Paul appears to have turned his back on a promising career to join adherents of an upstart religion called the Way. This "Way" involves following the teachings of Jesus Christ of Nazareth, the Jew who was crucified and, reportedly, rose from the dead and subsequently appeared to many of his disciples.

This turnaround by Saul has been met with a great deal of suspicion and skepticism by both his former colleagues and members of the Way.

"Saul was standing right there when that Stephen-fellow was stoned," said one insider. "He sure wasn't upset about what happened to the guy. In fact, after that, he acted like he was more determined than ever to stamp out this so-called church."

A spokesman for the high priest confirmed that before his recent trip to Damascus, Saul asked the priest for letters to the synagogues that would give him permission to arrest any Jewish followers of Jesus.

A neighbor of Damascus resident and Jesus follower Ananias says that Ananias had a meeting recently with Saul.

"He didn't want to go," the neighbor said. "He knew all about Saul and why he had come to Damascus. Heads were going to roll by the time Saul was through. But Ananias is really into this 'follow Jesus'

stuff. When the Lord told him to go see Saul, he went."

Another source said that Saul was actually "struck blind" on the road into Damascus. Saul said that Jesus himself spoke to him and told him to go on into Damascus and that a man named Ananias would come pray for him so he would get his sight back.

Once he could see again, Saul astonished those who knew him by going to the synagogues and preaching that Jesus is the Son of God.

"It has to be a hoax," one man said. "He came here to wipe out the converts, not join their ranks."

Sources say that the Jews hatched a plan to kill Saul, but his new friends helped him escape from the city late one night.

A construction crew has been dispatched to the wall to make repairs.

The Jesus disciples in Jerusalem reportedly did not buy Saul's conversion story—at first. A longtime convert named Barnabas convinced them of Saul's sincerity.

The Grecian Jews, while denying that they felt threatened by Saul's preaching, also attempted to kill him.

The new convert, who has left the area, continues to create havoc in other cities.

"Saul's days are numbered" has become the popular refrain. (Read more about this in Acts 8:1; 9:1–30.)

Recognize God's Voice

If you think you feel or hear God telling you something, how do you know it's God?

Jesus described himself as the Good Shepherd. He said that his lambs know his voice (John 10:4). We are his lambs. His voice is authoritative, but it isn't cold or cruel. Measure what you hear or feel against Scripture. God won't tell us to do something that goes against his Word or against the person we know him to be.

Spend Time with God

The closer you are to him and the more time you spend with him, the better you'll be able to recognize his voice.

God won't repeatedly dredge up the past, although he might point out something in your life that needs correcting. (Satan, however, delights in bringing up your faults.)

God will encourage you to improve your relationships with others. (Satan won't; he loves a good family feud.)

God will focus on changing *you*, not your circumstances. He will give you the kind of guidance that will make you more like him. As Psalms 37:23 says, "the steps of a good man are ordered by the Lord."

Obey Him

Learning to hear God's voice can take some time. We also need to be willing to do what he tells us when he gives us instructions. We do well to follow the example of the prophet Samuel, who said to God, "Speak, for your servant is listening" (1 Samuel 3:8–10).

Coals of Fire

"If your enemy is hungry, feed him; if he is thirsty, give him a drink: for in so doing you will heap coals of fire on his head." (Proverbs 25:21–22 NKJV)

Many assume this statement means that kindness shown to a persecutor causes that person to feel a burning sense of shame and repentance, but two other interpretations are possible:

1. An Act of Worship to God

"Coals of fire" may refer to the hot coals placed on the incense altar in the tabernacle or the Temple. The coals caused the incense to release its fragrance in smoke rising to the Lord. Throughout the history of Israel this image represented prayer that was acceptable and pleasing to the Lord (Leviticus 16:12).

In showing kindness to enemies, we make life an act of prayer and worship. Our kindness rises like incense to God, from whom we receive eternal reward.

2. Stopping the Spread of Vengeance

In the Old Testament, coals of fire were taken from the altar of the tabernacle, placed in a censer, and rushed to the edge of a plague (the farthest limit to which the plague had spread). There, the incense smoke created a barrier that separated the unaffected from the inflicted, effectively stopping the plague from spreading. (See Numbers 16:46–48.)

When we show kindness to a persecutor, we put a stop to the spread of vengeance. In our failure to retaliate, we destroy the contagious virus of evil response.

Stress-Busting Strategies

We have seen the enemy, and its name is *stress*! We all need moments when we can stop, relax, and send our minds or bodies "on vacation." Here are 14 suggestions for alleviating stress:

1. **Yawn really big.**
2. **Stand up straight.** Poor posture is linked to about 80 percent of back pain. Slouching also reduces lung capacity by about 30 percent. Back pain and shallow breathing are directly related to physical stress!
3. **Do nothing.** Forget about appearing lazy. Take a cue from kids: Children don't feel guilt when they aren't productive. Veronique Vienne says in her book, *The Art of Doing Nothing* (Clarkson Potter Publishers, 1998), "For a child, doing nothing doesn't mean being inactive, it means doing something that doesn't have a name."
4. **Get a good night's sleep.** A National Sleep Foundation poll found that 56 percent of adults in the United States have insomnia several nights a week. At its worst, lack of sleep contributes to accidents. It also makes the immune system less effective.
5. **Start each day with prayer.**
6. **Eat a healthy breakfast** that includes some protein.
7. **Do aerobic exercise regularly.**
8. **Take short breaks.** As you're tackling assignments, take a couple of minutes every half hour or so to stand

up, walk around, roll your shoulders to release tension, and focus on something else—perhaps a sun-drenched beach or a cozy fireplace in a ski lodge.

9. **Drink plenty of water** to kick up your energy level. The lower the water intake, the thicker the blood—which puts more stress on the heart.

10. **Have a small mid-morning snack** that's low in fat and calories and an equally healthy lunch and mid-afternoon snack.

11. **Before the workday ends, clear your mind of job-related clutter** by putting your unfinished work in an imaginary box on your desk. Put the lid on the box and put the box in a safe. Lock the safe and leave the key on your desk. If you start to think about work at home, remember—you don't have the key!

12. **Carve out some quiet time** immediately after getting home. Go someplace where you can be alone. Sink into a hammock, a lawn chair, a recliner, or a bed, close your eyes, and do this non-exercise: Tense the muscles in your toes, and then relax them. Repeat this process in your feet, ankles, calves, knees, thighs, stomach, chest, back, fingers, hands, forearms, elbows, upper arms and shoulders, neck, face, and head.

13. **Replace TV time with "people" time.** Instead, call a friend or play a game with your family—do something that involves "fun" with other people.

14. **Take vitamins**—especially vitamin C, B-complex, and vitamin E—and other antioxidants. These vitamins help fight off the negative effects of stress.

The Day of Kings

Before Christmas became a day to celebrate, there was, and still is, Epiphany. In some churches, in fact, Epiphany is treated like Christmas Day.

Epiphany, from the Greek word *epiphaneia*, means "manifestation" or "to appear." As a religious term, it refers to the appearance of an invisible divine being (Jesus Christ) in a visible form.

It was the Eastern Church—generally composed of Eastern Orthodox, Oriental Orthodox, and eastern-rite churches affiliated with the Roman Catholic Church—that first celebrated Epiphany. Its purpose was to celebrate the Nativity of Jesus; it was also a day to baptize those who believed in him. Oriental Christians still celebrate the Nativity on Epiphany. The Eastern churches actually call the day *Theophany*, which means "manifestation of God."

When the calendar issue was finally settled and Christ's birth was set as December 25, the church in Rome put Epiphany on January 6. Epiphany, then as now, marks the end of the Christmas season. The days between Christmas and Epiphany are called "the twelve days of Christmas."

A Musical Catechism

Those 12 days were made popular by a song written in England sometime during the period of 1558 to 1829. That was when Catholics were forbidden to practice their faith. In order to teach Catholic children the catechism without getting into trouble with the government, the "12 Days of Christmas" was created.

Each day in the song refers to a gift, and the gift is a coded term for one of the church's teachings.

- The "true love" is God, and "me" is every baptized person.
- The partridge is Jesus Christ.
- Two turtle doves are the Old and New Testaments.
- Three French hens are the Trinity, or the theological virtues of faith, hope, and charity.
- Four calling birds are the four Gospels.
- Five golden rings are the Pentateuch—the first five books of the Old Testament (Genesis, Exodus, Leviticus, Numbers, Deuteronomy).
- Six geese a-laying are the six days of Creation.
- Seven swans a-swimming are the seven gifts of the Holy Spirit (Romans 12:6–8).
- Eight maids a-milking are the eight beatitudes (Matthew 5:3–10).
- Nine ladies dancing are the nine fruit of the Holy Spirit (Galatians 5:22–23).
- Ten lords a-leaping are the 10 Commandments.
- Eleven pipers piping are the 11 faithful apostles.
- Twelve drummers drumming are the 12 points of doctrine in the Apostle's Creed.

> Dogs are mentioned 14 times in the Bible, and lions 55 times, but domestic cats are not mentioned at all.

What Light through Yonder Window Breaks?

"I don't do windows."

You might not like washing them, but you probably enjoy looking at the stained-glass variety. Perhaps you even have some modern examples of this centuries-old art of "painting with light" in your house.

The history of stained glass windows is a little murky. No one knows exactly when the first one was created, only that it was long ago. In their writings, some early church fathers that lived around A.D. 240 to 400, talked about "colored glass windows" in basilicas.

It is said that Pope Gregory the Great had something to do with the designs that future artists chose for their windows. In the 6th century, the pope had urged churches to put scriptural scenes on their walls so that illiterate people could "read" the stories of the Bible. Those mosaics and frescoes, some of which survive, no doubt influenced stained glass artists. Much later, during the Romanesque period of the 12th century, the explosion in church construction made stained glass a popular art form.

Blown Glass

The process of making the windows was described for the first time by a monk named Theophilus in a book he had written about crafts around A.D. 1110. Being a stained glass artist in those days did not mean that you were the one who made the glass. For that, you needed the skills of a glassblower.

The glassblower would blow a bubble of glass, "roll" it into a tubular shape, create a cylinder by cutting off each end, and form a sheet of glass by making a top-to-bottom slit down one side of the still-hot cylinder. The sheet cooled—not too quickly—in a kiln. While the glass was still in liquid form, color was added using metallic oxides. The five colors available in the 1100s were ruby, blue, purple, yellow, and green. Because of the way churches were designed in that era, windows were few, so the light passing through those five deep colors was dazzling in a way that could not be matched by later churches with more plentiful windows that featured lighter colors.

Grozing Iron

The artist's design was drawn on a wooden board or table. After the artist picked out the appropriate colors, the glazier used a red-hot iron to cut pieces of glass from each sheet. With the help of something called a grozing iron, the edges of the different pieces of glass could be altered for a good fit.

Details of the artist's design were added to the glass with a paint of glassy enamel. After the enamel was permanently affixed to the glass by the heat of the kiln, the pieces were put together by surrounding and connecting them with strips of lead. The joints were soldered, the glazier applied a waterproofing putty, and the window was done.

At first, the strips of lead were simply in the way. Eventually, however, the artists decided to make them part of their designs.

A Revival in Usage

The glass of the 12th and 13th centuries wasn't perfect, but it had a quality that made it more attractive and more interesting than later versions. At least, that's what the Gothic Revivalists of the 1800s thought. By that time, the popularity of stained glass was on the decline.

A Frenchman named E. Viollet-Le-Duc and an Englishman named Charles Winston turned the tide. Winston was influential because he wrote a book on stained glass. He also raised the quality of the glass. In 1863, W. E. Chance went a step further, following Winston's lead and creating "antique" glass reminiscent of stained glass in its glory days.

More Advances

One of the best things to come out of the 12th century was windows that told a story. The 13th century brought the grisaille window—clear glass using a single color of paint.

The 14th century introduced new colors and an exciting innovation: painting with silver salts to create a beautiful yellow that could be used for crowns and halos.

Popular Subjects

The subjects depicted on the windows did not change much over the centuries. Bible figures remained popular and were joined by images representing the four seasons, the months of the year, shields, and coats of arms. Most stained glass windows were, of course, in churches, and members of the church hierarchy or other church patrons paid for them.

In some cases the windows were the result of a royal commission. That was the case with the windows at King's College Chapel in Cambridge, England. Installed between 1515 and 1531, they were started during the reign of Henry VII and finished when Henry VIII was on the throne. The 41 windows contain narratives of the life of Mary and of the life, passion, and resurrection of Christ and acts of the apostles. Many of the scenes are done in pairs, with an Old Testament-themed window, which serves as an "interpreter," appearing above a corresponding New Testament-themed window.

Windows Grow

As churches grew larger in the 14th and 15th centuries, thanks to advances in architecture and construction methods, so did their windows—including rose windows. Rose windows are round and usually geometric in design. In some ways they resemble kaleidoscopes. Common themes for these windows included creation, the last judgment, Israel's kings, and prophets of the Old Testament.

From the 12th through the 14th centuries, stained glass was about creating an atmosphere that inspired awe and brought people closer to God. In the 15th century, stained glass artists were influenced by artists who used canvases and easels. Piecing together colored glass to form a picture gave way to painting entire pictures on white glass. Stained glass then became more "fashionable" and in many ways, less inspirational. Improvements in the production of the glass continued during the 16th through 20th centuries, but the passion seemed to be gone until the Gothic Revivalists did their part to bring it back.

Down, but Not Out

Most people are familiar with the crack that a baseball makes when it hits the bat, and the sound brings pleasure.

For fans of **Dave Dravecky**, a similar sound was anything but pleasant. When he pitched during the San Francisco Giants-Montreal Expos game on August 15, 1989, his arm broke with an audible crack.

Dravecky was born in Boardman, Ohio, on Valentine's Day 1956. After graduating from college and playing in the minors, he became a major league baseball player with the San Diego Padres in 1982.

Dream Career

For many years he had a dream career. He was with the Padres when they took the 1984 National League Championship and went on to the World Series. After a trade to the Giants in 1987, he was back in the National League Championship series.

In 1988 Dave Dravecky's world came crashing down.

In the fall of 1987, he noticed a small lump on his upper left arm—his pitching arm. An MRI showed no cause for concern. By the fall of 1988, however, a second MRI indicated a tumor. A biopsy brought a diagnosis of cancer.

Nightmare Discovery

After surgery to remove the tumor—along with half of his deltoid muscle—Dravecky went through rehabilitation and miraculously returned to the mound in August 1989. His first game back was a win. A week later, his arm broke as he was pitching during the Montreal game, a break heard round the ballpark and by all those watching on TV or listening on radio.

Another break happened in October in a freak accident on the field during a victory celebration. Dravecky discovered the cancer was back. The prognosis forced him to retire.

In 1990, he had more surgery followed by radiation. A staph infection in 1991 kept him flat on his back. The worst followed shortly: the amputation of his left arm, shoulder blade, and left side of his collarbone.

Searching for New Meaning

Fortunately for Dravecky, he and his wife, Janice, had become Christians several years earlier while he was playing minor league ball in Amarillo, Texas. His roommate, Byron Ballard, helped him understand that God cared about every aspect of his life. In his 1990 book, *Comeback* (Zondervan), Dravecky said it like this: "God is personal. That lesson, learned in Amarillo, changed our lives forever. . . . Life isn't fair, at least in the short run, but the Bible taught me not to confuse life with God."

With baseball out of the question, Dravecky had to find a new meaning for his life. He and Jan were raising their two children, Tiffany and Jonathan. They were living in Ohio close to family, friends, and their church.

Dravecky had written *Comeback* before the amputation. It chronicled his life up to the point of his retirement. (The book won an Angel Award in 1991 in recognition of its "excellence" and "high moral, spiritual, social impact.") At the end of that book, Dravecky wrote, "I'm clearly not done with adversity.

My future is as unknown as before." He was right on both points.

Dravecky's next book, written with his wife, was perhaps even tougher to put on paper.

When You Can't Come Back (Zondervan, 1992) puts the family's pain out there for all the world to see. It's a book of hope, however, because it affirms that God can bring you through any crisis—even the severe depression that both Dave and Jan suffered after his retirement.

In *The Worth of a Man* (Zondervan, 1996), Dravecky talks about ministering to the patients at the hospital shortly after he had his arm amputated. He had also returned to the speaking circuit, sharing messages about God's love and compassion all over the country. Then one day, four months after the surgery, he finally had to admit that he was seriously depressed and the bad feelings weren't going away. He recognized that he needed help and went into counseling with his wife for more than a year.

Reaching Out with Hope

That could be the end of the story, but it's not. Dave and Jan and their family moved to Colorado Springs, Colorado, in 1993 and founded the nonprofit Dave Dravecky's Outreach of Hope. Dravecky never dreamed he would wind up ministering to cancer patients. From a young age, playing baseball was all he wanted to do.

Sometimes you can come back from life-changing surgery and sometimes you can't. As Dravecky would tell you, it's what you do with your life when you realize you can't come back that really matters . . . for all eternity.

Reading, Writing, and Bible Verses

Sunday school.

Is it hopelessly archaic? More relevant than ever? A missionary outreach?

Whatever your view or your understanding, there are probably lots of things about Sunday school that you didn't know.

Prison Prevention Program

It was started in Gloucester, England, in 1780 by a newspaper publisher named Robert Raikes. He saw a lot of "hooligans" on the streets on Sundays, up to no good. Since child labor laws hadn't come into vogue, many lower-class children were working six days a week. He decided to find a better way for them to use their minds and energy. He was also hoping to keep them from winding up in prison someday.

Sunday school was Raikes' solution. The first classes had the blessing of a minister but weren't held in a church. They were conducted in the homes of the teachers, and proved popular.

News Spreads

It didn't hurt that Raikes was a newspaper publisher. His stories about Sunday school were of great interest and caused other cities in Great Britain to follow his lead. Soon, there were Sunday schools across England.

Europe and North America were next to catch the fever. In the United States Sunday school started as, and remained, a Protestant endeavor. The first classes began in 1791, organized by the Philadelphia First Day Society of Pennsylvania.

As in England, the goal in America was to get children off the streets on Sundays. But there was more to it than that. With evangelistic fervor, the organizers also wanted to reach the children of poor and disadvantaged families with the gospel.

The Three R's and Manners Too

The first teachers in Philadelphia were schoolteachers, hired to teach on Sundays. In addition to the Bible and reading, writing, and arithmetic, they taught good manners and good behavior, hoping to instill respect for the Sabbath. Records from the 1800s also indicate that memorization of Bible verses was a popular activity. Some children could recite as many as 100 verses at a time.

Why were the three Rs taught in Sunday school? Free public schools had not yet come into existence. When they did, they did not eliminate Sunday schools. The genius of the Sunday school organizers was that they were able to change with the times. They fully supported the free schools and changed their mission to one of strictly Christian education. Some Sunday schools in the West and in rural areas, however, continued to act as primary schools, since most free schools were in urban areas and on the East Coast.

If anything, Sunday school was more important than ever after free schools opened. It was the only place for Protestant children to get a truly Christian education, since public schools presented a one-size-fits-all view of theology.

Classes for Poor Adults

Sunday schools did not limit themselves to the education of children. Although popularity waxed and waned, they also offered classes for adults, sometimes on weekday evenings. The focus was mostly on literacy. Free blacks in the North were quick to avail themselves of the opportunity to get an education. Sunday school was also offered in the South—in some cases, to slaves—but it was not truly accepted. There was the fear that if slaves became educated, they would revolt.

Sunday schools underwent another major change in 1820. That's when middle-class children began to attend. Poor children started feeling less welcome. In some Sunday schools, there were even separate classes for the two social classes.

CHILDREN AND CHURCH

A 10 year old, under the tutelage of her grandmother, was becoming quite knowledgeable about the Bible. Then, one day, she floored her grandmother by asking, "Which virgin was the mother of Jesus? The virgin Mary or the King James virgin?"

A Shift in Staffing

Another change was in the teaching staffs. In the early days professionals had been hired and paid. Eventually, most of the teachers were female volunteers under age 30 who were recent converts eager to serve God and share their faith.

It became harder and harder to recruit new teachers. America was becoming a mobile society. Many women married and stopped teaching. Churches then began using youth Bible classes as training grounds for new teachers. Getting men to teach was still tough because Christian teenage boys had no role models in the "profession" to follow.

Greater Support Services

Speaking of professions, Sunday school itself became more professional as time went by. Publishers developed national magazines and created curriculums, and institutes and conventions were held for teachers. That was another strength of the Sunday school movement: its ability to become a national, unified institution.

Although evangelism of children remained a primary objective, Sunday schools enlarged their reach by exposing the children to missions projects at home and abroad, giving the children the chance to contribute to the support of missionaries.

Still Popular

Has Sunday school lost its momentum in the 20th and 21st centuries? Not at all. Adult education has become a major division of many churches. More than ever, child and adult classes are being called upon to tackle missions projects—like helping to build Habitat for Humanity houses, collecting canned goods for food banks, or doing work projects in Appalachia or in other impoverished places. Sunday school is still a place to sharpen witnessing skills, study the Bible seriously, and operate prayer chains.

If you wonder just how viable Sunday school is in this century, do a keyword search on the internet. In late 2000, one search engine listed more than 1,900,000 sites and related articles.

Pint-Size Humor

A mother took her three-year-old daughter to church for the first time. The church lights were lowered and the choir came down the aisle, carrying lighted candles. All was as quiet as the proverbial church mouse until the little girl jumped up and started singing in a loud voice, "Happy birthday to you, happy birthday to you!"

A Sunday school teacher was carefully explaining the story of Elijah the prophet and the false prophets of Baal. She told the children how Elijah built the altar, put a stack of wood on it, cut a steer into pieces, and put the wood and the steer on the altar. "And then," the teacher announced, "Elijah commanded the people of God to fill four barrels with water and pour the water all over the entire altar. He told them to do this four times.

"Now," said the teacher, satisfied that she had done a good job of explaining this story, "can anyone in the class tell me why God would tell Elijah to pour water all over the steer on the altar?"

A little girl raised her hand and with great enthusiasm said, "To make the gravy!"

There was a little boy who knelt by his bed every night to say his prayers. His mother always knelt beside him, drawing great comfort from this family ritual. One night, however, the little

boy was obviously tired of saying the same words over and over, because he made some changes that went like this:

"Now I lay me down to sleep, I pray the Lord my soul to keep. If I should die before I wake . . . can I have breakfast with you in the morning?"

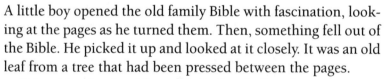

A little girl from Minneapolis came home from Sunday school with a big frown on her face.

"I'm not going back there any more," she announced to her mother. "I don't like the Bible they keep teaching us from."

"Why not?" asked her astonished mother.

"Because," said the little girl, "their Bible is always talking about St. Paul, and it never once mentions Minneapolis."

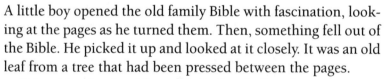

A little boy opened the old family Bible with fascination, looking at the pages as he turned them. Then, something fell out of the Bible. He picked it up and looked at it closely. It was an old leaf from a tree that had been pressed between the pages.

"Mom! Look what I found!" the boy hollered.

"What is it, dear?" his mother asked.

With astonishment in his voice, the boy answered, "It's Adam's suit!"

Positively Transformed

When it comes to the **Rebecca St. James** phenomenon, it's truly a family affair.

The Grammy Award-winning recording artist, known for her CDs (*Rebecca St. James, God, Christmas, Pray,* and *Transform*), two devotional books for teens, columns in *Campus Life* magazine, altar calls and Q&A sessions at her concerts, and sponsorship of a child through Compassion International, is the oldest of seven children. When she takes her God-inspired music out on tour for 200 dates a year, she's accompanied by her parents, David and Helen Smallbone (that's St. James's real last name) and her five brothers and sister—and they all have a piece of the action.

Still in her early 20s, St. James has been in music since being in a high school rock band and then going out on tour with Christian singing sensation Carman when she was 13. At that time the family was still living in their native Australia where her father was a Christian concert promoter. After losing a huge sum of money on one of those concerts, David accepted a job in Nashville, Tennessee, in 1991.

Early Lessons

When the job fell through shortly after their arrival, the family began living hand to mouth and learned valuable lessons about putting all of their faith in God. Those are lessons that the eldest child has not forgotten. She remembers how prayers for the bare necessities would be answered almost instantly. "I think that showed me the reality of God," St. James told Passageway.org.

Early Success

St. James signed a record deal with ForeFront Records in 1994 and recorded the pop-flavored CD *Rebecca St. James* when she was 16. Her fourth CD, *Pray*, won a Grammy for Best Rock Gospel Album. She was named Christian and Gospel Artist of 2000 by Amazon.com for her *Transform* CD. In 2001, she was voted most influential woman in Christian music by the Christian website Crosswalk.com. Her music is featured on the soundtrack of the *Left Behind* movie, in which she also made a cameo appearance.

The singer-songwriter, who starts her interviews with prayer, admits that with every CD, there's something that pushes her to do an even better job. Those who follow her music will tell you that *Transform* is light years removed from *Rebecca St. James*.

Lyrics Centered on God

One thing that won't change, however, is St. James's commitment to keep the lyrics centered on God. This young woman takes her position in the upper echelons of contemporary Christian music seriously.

In her website bio (www.rsjames.com), St. James says that being a big sister at home has prepared her well to be a "big sister" to her generation, and she's happy to wear that hat. In interview after interview, she shares her heartfelt concern for teens and young adults who are falling for the lies of this age.

Waiting Game

Although she's famous for her music, St. James is also an evangelist. She's not embarrassed to admit that she's still a virgin and that she intends to wait for marriage before having sex. This is a common theme when she talks to other young people.

One of the songs on *Transform*, titled "Wait for Me," is a love song to her future (as yet unknown) husband, and promotes living a life of purity. While encouraging sexual abstinence, St. James knows there are Christian teens who did not wait. For them, she says to become "recycled virgins," to put the past behind them, and to commit to purity from this day forward.

> Enjoy the little things in life, for one day you may look back and realize they were the big things.

Family Togetherness

After all these years on the road, she still enjoys having her family by her side. It's an unusual arrangement, but it works for them. Because of the tour schedule, all seven children have been homeschooled by their mother.

As her dad has said, their situation is actually more normal than most, because the family is able to spend large blocks of time together.

All that togetherness sure hasn't hurt the career or the ministry of Rebecca St. James.

Under the Watchful Eye of Jesus

A burglar broke into a house one night and turned on his flashlight to look for valuable items to steal.

As he was picking up a CD player, a voice came out of the darkness and said, "Jesus is watching you."

The burglar jumped, turned off his flashlight, and waited. Nothing.

Turning the light back on, he proceeded to disconnect the stereo. Again, a voice came out of the darkness and said, "Jesus is watching you."

Throwing caution to the wind, he searched for the source of the voice. His light came to rest on a parrot in a cage.

"Was that you?" he demanded of the bird.

"Yes," the parrot confessed. "I'm trying to warn you."

> **BUG BITES**
>
> • Tropical cockroaches are among the fastest land insects, moving at a speed equal to 50 body lengths per second. That speed would be the same as a human sprinter running the 100-yard dash in one second, or 200 miles per hour.
>
> • A centipede in southern Europe has the record of having the most legs with 177 pairs of legs.

The burglar laughed. "Warn me? Who are you?"

"Moses," the bird said.

"Moses?" the burglar laughed again. "What kind of idiot would name a parrot Moses?"

The parrot answered, "Probably the same kind of idiot who would name a Rottweiler Jesus."

Heavenly Post

One day God looked at the earth and was appalled at all the evil he saw. He decided to send a female angel down to determine how bad it really was.

After a few weeks, the angel came back and confirmed his worst fears. "Ninety-five percent of the people are bad-awful, and only five percent are good," she said.

To be fair, God decided he should send a male angel down and get his take on the situation.

When the male angel returned a few weeks later, he confirmed the female angel's assessment: ninety-five percent bad, five percent good.

God knew something had to be done, and so he sent a letter to the five percent who were good, to encourage them to keep up the good work as well as to give them something to help keep them going.

Do you know what the letter said?

Oh, so you didn't get one either?

> **PRAYER FROM HAWAII**
>
> Father of all mankind, make the roof of my house wide enough for all opinions, oil the door of my house so it opens easily to friend and stranger and set such a table in my house that my whole family may speak kindly and freely around it. Amen.

What Planet Is She On?

The fascinating thing about **Madeleine L'Engle**, besides that she uses her great-grandmother's last name instead of her parents' or late husband's name, is the questions her writings bring to mind. Even if you have read only one or two of her books, such as *A Wrinkle in Time* (Farrar, Straus and Giroux, 1962) or *A Circle of Quiet* (1972), you are likely to have questions.

Is she a Christian? Are her books supposed to convert you? If she believes in God, how can she write so honestly about sex? Are her "children's books" really for children, or are they for adults?

An Unorthodox Childhood

L'Engle, a native New Yorker, was born on November 29, 1918. She was the only child of a couple that had waited almost 20 years for her arrival. Rather than doting on her, they left her mostly to her own devices. She spent a lot of time in her room, reading, and writing. She completed her first story when she was five.

After her father had a serious bout of pneumonia, the family moved to a run-down chateau in France with no running water. L'Engle spent her teen years in boarding schools both in Europe and the United States. Her father died when she was 17. Unlike elementary school, which was a bad fit, high school brought out the best in her. She later graduated from Smith College and returned to New York.

Acting Career

Although writing is as essential as breathing to L'Engle, acting initially paid her bills. Her first novel, *The Small Rain* (Farrar, Straus and Giroux), was published in 1945. During rehearsals for *The Cherry Orchard,* she met her future husband, Hugh Franklin. They were married in 1946.

L'Engle's second novel, *Ilsa*, was published in 1946, followed by four more novels. It is the next book, however, for which she is best known.

Acclaim at Last

When L'Engle finished writing *A Wrinkle in Time*, she had no idea what was in store for this story of time and space travel. It took two-and-a-half years for the book to find a publisher. "I knew it was the best thing I'd ever done," L'Engle said in an interview. That was confirmed when the book won the prestigious Newberry award in 1963, and it continues to be confirmed at the cash register. Over 6 million copies have been snatched up, not just by children but by adults who love a good story with compelling characters.

Spiritual Struggles

L'Engle calls herself "a writer who is struggling to be a Christian." She embraces, more and more each day, she says, the practices of daily prayer, Scripture reading, and devotions.

Although she was raised in the Episcopal church, she is ecumenical in her outlook. God, she believes, does not belong to a specific denomination . . . but to all of us.

Lord, Make Me an Instrument

When you walk into some 21st-century churches and see string or brass ensembles, handbell choirs, or something just short of a full orchestra, it's hard to believe that as recently as 1850, most American churches did not even own an organ. The lack of one was due in part to their cost, but the main reason for their absence was that they ran counter to church doctrine.

Just Grow Up!

Early church fathers pointed to the Old Testament to explain why instruments were bad. When God's people were under the law, they explained, they needed something like musical instruments to "baby" them along in their faith. Once Jesus Christ came, these fathers—among them Clement of Alexandria—argued that our relationship with God "grew up" and we didn't need to be coddled anymore.

John Calvin took a similar approach in the 16th century when he lobbied against the use of musical instruments. In the New Testament, he said, there are absolutely no instructions for the use of these tools in a worship service. If the New Testament doesn't order us to use them, Calvin reasoned, we shouldn't.

Just Say Yes

Martin Luther (1483–1546) disagreed strongly. He took the approach, if the New Testament doesn't tell us we *can't* use musical instruments, it's okay to do so. The only thing to concern ourselves with is the type of music we use. It should be simple and direct and designed to help us keep our focus on God.

Here are some of the other facts and tidbits that have fueled various arguments and issues about the use of instruments in worship:

After the Temple was destroyed in A.D. 70, the Pharisees made sure musical instruments were not part of worship.

- The apostle Paul admonished Christians not to become like a "resounding gong" and a "clanging cymbal" (1 Corinthians 13 NIV).

- The Book of Revelation mentions musical instruments more times than all the rest of the books of the New Testament put together. In many cases, those instruments are being used on joyful occasions.

- D. L. Moody, who was probably the greatest evangelist of the 19th century, had a song leader who used a reed organ. One Scottish deacon called that organ, "a devilish pump machine that wheezes out blasphemously."

- Brass instruments were played while Christians were martyred in the Coliseum at Rome.

CHILDREN AND CHURCH

The preacher was wired for sound with a lapel mike, and as he preached, he moved briskly about the platform, jerking the mike cord as he went. Then he moved to one side, getting wound up in the cord and nearly tripping before jerking it again. After several circles and jerks, a little girl in the third pew leaned toward her mother and whispered, "If he gets loose, will he hurt us?"

- St. Augustine (A.D. 354–430) once said that music can be too sensuous and can lead us into sin.
- Thomas Aquinas (1225–1274) said that before long, tunes would eclipse words and we'd forget what we were singing and to whom.
- Both John Huss (1373–1415) and Ulrich Zwingli (1484–1531) encouraged their followers to have nothing to do with musical instruments—they both considered organs "a worldly distraction."
- The Council of Trent (1562) banished music "in which, whether by the organ or in the singing, there is mixed up any thing lascivious or impure."
- The Puritans considered musical instruments to be an example of "excess," which they sought to remove from their lives.
- The British Parliament passed two ordinances in 1644 that expressly called for "speedy demolishing of all organs." After the Reformation in 1660, however, the Church of England allowed churches to raise funds to purchase organs and other instruments.
- The Church of Scotland destroyed all but one of its church organs by 1727.

So what's *your* opinion about instruments used in worship?

Monk's the Word

A man was driving down the road when his car broke down near a monastery. He went to the monastery, knocked on the door, and asked if he could spend the night. The monks said sure. They even fed him dinner and fixed his car.

As the man was drifting off to sleep that night, he heard a strange sound. The next morning, he asked the monks what the sound was. "We can't tell you," they said. "You're not a monk."

Disappointed, the man thanked them for their hospitality and left.

Several years later, the same thing happened again—car breaks down, man goes to monastery, monks fix car, man hears strange noise.

"What was that noise?" he asked again.

Again, "We can't tell you. You're not a monk."

"I have to know," the man said. "I'll do whatever it takes. How do I become a monk?"

The monks told him, "You have to travel the earth and tell us how many blades of grass there are, and the exact number of sand pebbles. When you bring back these numbers, you can be a monk."

Forty-five years later, the man returned to the monastery. "I have your answers," he said. "There are 145,236,284,232 blades of grass and 231,281,219,999,129,382 sand pebbles on the earth."

"Congratulations!" the monks said. "You are now a monk. We will take you to the source of the sound."

Leading the man to a wooden door, the head monk said, "The sound is behind this door."

The man turned the knob, but the door was locked. "Where is the key?" he asked.

The monks gave him the key and he unlocked the door, only to find another door made of stone. The monks gave him another key, which he used to open the stone door, and behind it was a door made of ruby. Another key, another door, this time made of sapphire. Then there were four more doors, made of emerald, silver, topaz, and amethyst.

Finally, the monks said, "Here's the key to the last door." The man, hugely relieved, opened the door and was amazed to see the source of the strange sound.

But we can't tell you what it was, because you're not a monk.

ONE SMALL STEP OR ONE GIANT LEAP

The human foot has been described by Leonardo da Vinci as "a masterpiece of engineering and a work of art." It is also a workhorse.

The foot has 26 bones, 19 muscles, and 107 ligaments. Although most people don't often do this, the toes can be used to pick up things. Some people can write or draw with their feet. Feet turn into paddles when we swim.

Pull Up a Chair and Visit Mitford

Few things in life are more comforting than curling up on a sofa with a novel that can transport you to a different world.

For millions of readers the world they choose for their escape is the one inhabited by Father Tim, Cynthia, Dooley, Puny, Esther, Uncle Billy, Aunt Rose, Miss Louella, and Barnabas—main characters in the *Mitford* series.

Extraordinarily Ordinary

The Mitford books—*At Home in Mitford; A Light in the Window; These High, Green Hills; Out to Canaan; A New Song;* and *A Common Life*—depict a wholesome world of love, compassion, laughter, and joy. The books also deal with hard-hitting issues, such as child abuse, diabetes, alcoholism, bitterness, Alzheimer's disease, poverty, and broken hearts. No one is perfect in Mitford, and neither is the town. Perhaps the closest thing to perfection in this fictional world is Esther Bolick's scrumptious orange marmalade cake!

A Preacher or an Author?

Author Jan Karon grew up on a farm where she and her sister were raised by their grandparents. At age six, she wanted to be a preacher. At ten, after writing her first novel, she wanted to be an author. As a writer whose chief character is a priest, she now enjoys both professions!

Karon married young, was divorced a few years later, and as a single mother in need of work, took a receptionist's job at an

ad agency. Not content simply to type and file, she brashly wrote ad ideas and gave them to her boss. Soon she became a full-fledged advertising writer, and after winning awards, a creative vice president. After 30 years of life in the fast lane, however, she still wanted to become a writer of fiction.

Writer's Block

At age 42, Karon returned to the faith of her childhood. That's when God let her know it was time to get out of advertising and pursuing fiction writing.

Moving in with her brother and his family in the town of Blowing Rock, North Carolina, Karon sat down to write her first novel and experienced not only writer's block, but a total lack of anything to say. Feeling doomed, she cried out to God.

Hometown Serial

Within a matter of days, Karon had a vision of sorts. In her mind's eye, she saw a priest walking down the street, accompanied by a huge dog. The Mitford series was first published in the *Blowing Rock Rocket*, her hometown newspaper, which serialized her first novel over two years of issues. At the end of two years, Karon sought a publisher for her manuscript. Lion published *At Home in Mitford* in 1994. Karon hit the road to do most of her own promotion. Today the series has sold over 3 million copies.

Did You Hear the One About . . .

A salesman from the local newspaper stopped at the village's only grocery store to sell some advertising. "No thanks," said the owner. "This store's been here for 80 years, and we've never bought any advertising."

This salesman was quick on his feet. "Excuse me," he said, "but what is that building up on the hill?"

"That's the village church," the owner said.

"Has it been here long?" asked the salesman.

"About 300 years," said the owner.

"Well," the salesman pointed out, "they still ring the bell."

A man walked out of the sanctuary one Sunday morning and met another church member in the hallway.

"Has the pastor finished his sermon yet?" the member asked.

"Yes," the man said. "He finished it pretty soon after he got started, but he hasn't stopped talking."

A country pastor was walking through a field late one evening when he fell into a hole. Unable to climb out, he began to shout for help. A worker from a nearby farm happened by, heard him, and asked who he was.

"I'm the pastor of the local church," the pastor replied.

"Well, then," the worker said, "you don't need to make such a fuss. You won't be needed until Sunday, and this is only Wednesday night."

A father took his son to the Capitol in Washington, D.C., so he could see government in action. They were watching from the gallery when the House came to order.

"Why did the minister pray for all those men, Daddy?" the boy asked.

"He didn't," his father said. "He looked them over and he prayed for the country."

Before the service one Sunday, the pastor spoke to the church organist.

"When I get through with my sermon, I'll ask those of the congregation who want to give $1,000 toward the mortgage on the church to stand up. In the meantime, you play some appropriate music."

"What do you mean, appropriate?" asked the organist.

The pastor replied, "Play 'The Star-Spangled Banner.'"

> ### SAY NO TO BRAUN
>
> Hebrew men didn't need a razor. They were not allowed to cut the edges of their beards. Cutting one's beard was a symbol of great grief. Forget a trip to the barber too. Having one's beard cut off by another person meant shame and dishonor.

Excerpted from Herbert V. Prochnow, *The Public Speaker's Treasure Chest* (New York: Harper and Brothers Publishers, 1942).

Sluggards!

One of the most popular themes of the Book of Proverbs is the problem of laziness. Consider these statements:

- A sluggard sent out on an assignment is like vinegar to the teeth and smoke to the eyes —totally irritating! (Proverbs 10:26).
- A sluggard ends up doing slave labor—they never succeed in advancement or promotion (Proverbs 12:24).
- A sluggard's path is blocked by thorns—he sabotages his own success (Proverbs 15:19).
- The sluggard puts his hand into a dish of food and then doesn't even bring it back to his mouth—he doesn't follow through with what will benefit him (Proverbs 19:24).
- A sluggard doesn't plow in season so he has nothing to harvest (Proverbs 20:4).
- A sluggard's cravings kill him because his hands refuse to work (Proverbs 21:25).
- A sluggard uses ridiculous excuses for not going out to work, even saying, "There's a lion outside!" or "I will be murdered in the streets" (Proverbs 22:13).
- The vineyard of a sluggard is filled with thorns, the ground covered with weeds, the stone wall in ruins—he loses because he doesn't keep his life in "repair" (Proverbs 24:30–31).
- A sluggard turns in his bed like a door swinging on its hinges—he is aimless and unproductive, not to mention annoying! (Proverbs 26:14).

Ten Reasons They Didn't Believe

The top 10 reasons why the teachers of the law did not believe Jesus was the Messiah:

10. His mother wasn't even married when she got pregnant.
9. When was the last time a king was born in a stable?
8. He looks so ordinary!
7. He gets hungry and thirsty and tired just like we do.
6. Look at the riffraff he hangs around with.
5. We've read all the prophets' writings, and if we say it's not him, it's not him!
4. Those aren't miracles he's performing; they're just coincidences.
3. His own friends ran out on him when he got into trouble—one of them even denied knowing him! Would you do that to the Son of God?
2. When you cut him, he bleeds.
1. He died on that cross and, yes, people claim they saw him "resurrected," but *we* haven't seen any physical, scientifically-reliable proof that he came back. You expect us to take that on faith?

> **A BIT OF CHURCH HUMOR**
>
> A student was asked to list the 10 Commandments in any order.
>
> His answer?
>
> "3, 6, 1, 8, 4, 5, 9, 2, 10, 7"

You Gotta Have Heart . . . and Smarts

Singer-songwriter **Margaret Becker** is one tough lady to pin down, musically speaking. Pop? Rock? Jazz? Unlike some artists who have a "sound," Becker is a free spirit, willing to enter uncharted territory with each new CD.

This Long Island, New York, native first hit it big in 1987 with the release of the *Never for Nothing* CD and its spin-off number-one hit, "Fight for God." Since then there have been lots more CDs, more than a dozen number-one hits, four Grammy Award nominations (the first in 1989), three Dove awards and thirteen Dove Award nominations, a magazine column, two books, and scriptwriting. She also received the Episcopal Diocese Award (Delaware diocese) for her work "to end world hunger and to promote interfaith understanding."

Committed to Others

Becker is committed to the fighting hunger. In 1995, she served her second tour of duty as World Vision's 30-Hour Famine national spokesperson. The project involves thousands of teenagers from across the nation who fast for 30 hours, raise funds through sponsors, and spend their fasting time doing things like helping in soup kitchens.

Becker's involvement with World Vision continues today. She sponsors children in countries like Niger.

During one of her tours in the 1990s, Becker threw her support behind Habitat for Humanity, discussing the organization's work with her audiences. At the tour's first performance, about $7,000 was raised to help build a house.

Hard Work

What Becker has managed to accomplish might seem like a natural progression, but the beginning *and* the years since have been marked with hard work, moments of disillusionment and discouragement, and just plain exhaustion.

In an interview with *American Songwriter* magazine, Becker said that after arriving in Nashville in 1985, she spent the first year writing 8 hours a day, 7 days a week. Her songwriting style, she will tell you, hasn't really changed much. Her first act is coming up with a title, followed by a thorough search of the thesaurus and occasional glimpses at a rhyming dictionary. Her approach is like that of a literary critic examining a new book: What's it all about? What *should* this song say? Who will it reach?

Define Success

Managers tell their clients to strike while they're hot, but Becker has a different take on success. In 2001, Becker described the effects of a brief sabbatical she took in early 1995.

"As I examined my life, I realized that I was halfway living in that life because I was allowing other people to define what success was as it applied to me." Success, she said, is very individual.

"As you're starting out," she told an audience of college students, "I challenge you: Define what success is *for you*."

Margaret Becker will tell you it's not about awards and designer shoes. Success is about being consistent as a Christian, keeping things simple, learning to trust God, and recognizing his grace.

An Unsolved Mystery

Quick! Name all the angels mentioned in the Bible.

Most people readily name Gabriel, who foretold the birth of Jesus to Mary and who rolled the stone back from Jesus' tomb. Many name Michael, who fights against Satan in the heavens. Other than these two angels, all other references are to groups or categories of angels except one "mystery angel." He makes frequent appearances in the Old Testament but is called only "the angel of the Lord."

Angel of the Lord

This angel always appears when something awe-inspiring and of great importance is about to happen. This angel is a messenger, someone who, similar to John the Baptist before Jesus' ministry began, prepares the way for God to both appear and act.

Some Bible scholars describe this angel as a manifestation, a form of God himself, and yet not exactly like him. We know the angel can't be God, because the angel frequently appeared to men, and the Bible says that no one may see God's face and live.

Others suggest that the angel is Jesus Christ. Billy Graham doesn't question the belief that the angel is a "preincarnation manifestation" of Jesus, in other words, an appearance by Jesus prior to his life on earth. We know Jesus existed before he came to earth in human form. It's interesting to note that after Jesus was born, the angel of the Lord makes no more appearances in Scripture.

Angel Encounters of the Closest Kind

Who had an encounter with the angel? The list is long.

- The angel of the Lord came to Abraham to tell him that his descendants would be as numerous as the stars in the sky. This angel later called from heaven to tell Abraham not to sacrifice Isaac (Genesis 22).
- The angel appeared to Moses from the burning bush (Exodus 3).
- The angel saved Jerusalem by killing 185,000 Assyrians who were planning an attack (2 Kings 19:35).
- When Balaam disobeyed God, the angel stood in the road with a sword, scaring Balaam's donkey and convincing Balaam to do things God's way (Numbers 22).
- When Hagar, pregnant with Abraham's child, ran away, the angel found her and told her to go back, that she would have a son Ishmael, and that she would have innumerable descendants (Genesis 16:7).
- He told the infertile wife of Manoah that she would have a son, Samson, who was not to cut his hair. When the angel appeared a second time, Manoah asked the angel what his name was, so that they could honor him when their child arrived. "It is beyond understanding," the angel said (Judges 13).

The angel of the Lord is beyond our full understanding, but he certainly left plenty of calling cards.

A Kind Word or Deed

Out of the concept "random acts of violence" grew a new idea called "random acts of kindness." Looking at bookstore shelves and internet sites, we see the concept continues to flourish.

Ideas and Stories

The Random Acts of Kindness Foundation has a website that gives people good ideas for being kind to others. It also shares stories from readers.

In his book titled *Guerilla Kindness*, Gavin Whitsett cites Dr. Karl Menninger's "10 Rules to Cure the Blues": Do something for someone else. Repeat nine times.

Rewards for Do-Gooders

We know what kind acts do for the recipients. Research shows that kindness is just as rewarding for the doer. In his 1991 book titled *The Healing Power of Doing Good: The Health and Spiritual Benefits of Helping Others*, Alan Luks refers to a study conducted with more than 3,000 volunteers of all ages representing a wide variety of organizations. These volunteers described the feeling of euphoria that comes with helping, the reduction of stress in their lives, and their sense of calm. Most believed they were healthier than other people their age.

Practicing kindness just two hours a week, Luks said, can bring about significant health improvements including relief from sleeplessness, acid stomach, headaches, backaches, and depression.

A Father Forgets
By W. Livingston Larned

Listen, son: I am saying this as you lie asleep, one little paw crumpled under your cheek and blond curls stickily wet on your damp forehead. I have stolen into your room alone. Just a few minutes ago, as I sat reading my paper in the library, a stifling wave of remorse swept over me. Guiltily I came to your bedside.

These are the things I was thinking, son: I had been cross to you. I scolded you as you were dressing for school because you gave your face merely a dab with a towel. I took you to task for not cleaning your shoes. I called out angrily when you threw some of your things on the floor.

I'm Sorry

At breakfast I found fault, too. You spilled things. You gulped down your food. You put your elbows on the table. You spread butter too thick on your bread. And as you started off to play and I made for my train, you turned and waved a hand and called, "Good-bye, Daddy!" and I frowned, and said in reply, "Hold your shoulders back!"

Then it began all over again in the late afternoon. As I came up the road I spied you, down on your knees, playing marbles. There were holes in your socks. I humiliated you before your friends by marching you ahead of me to the house. Socks were expensive, and if you had to buy them you would be more careful! Imagine that, son, from a father!

Spontaneous Love

Do you remember, later, when I was reading in the library, how you came in, timidly, with a sort of hurt look in your eyes? When I glanced up over my paper, impatient at the interruption, you hesitated at the door. "What is it you want?" I snapped.

You said nothing, but ran across in one tempestuous plunge, and threw your arms around my neck and kissed me, and your small arms tightened with an affection that God had set blooming in your heart and which even neglect could not wither . . . and then you were gone, pattering up the stairs.

Wrong Measuring Stick

Well, son, it was shortly afterwards that my paper slipped from my hands and a terrible sickening fear came over me. What has habit been doing to me? The habit of finding fault, reprimanding—this was my reward to you for being a boy. It was not that I did not love you; it was that I expected too much of youth. It was measuring you by the yardstick of my own years.

And there was so much that was good and fine and true in your character. The little heart of you was as big as the dawn itself over the wide hills. This was shown by your spontaneous impulse to rush in and kiss me goodnight. Nothing else matters tonight, son. I have come to your bedside in the darkness, and I have knelt here, ashamed!

I Will

It is a feeble atonement; I know you would not understand these things if I told them to you during your waking hours. But tomorrow I will be a real daddy. I will chum with you, suffer when you suffer, and laugh when you laugh. I will bite my tongue when impatient words come. I will keep saying as if it were a ritual, "He is nothing but a boy, a little boy!"

I am afraid I have visualized you as a man. Yet as I see you now, son, crumpled and weary in your bed, I see that you are still a little boy. Yesterday you were in your mother's arms, your head on her shoulder. I have asked too much, too much.

Source: W. Livingston Larned, "Father Forgets," *Mikey's Humor* <http://www.youthspecialties.com/mikeyshumor/index.html>

NOT WITHOUT PRAYING FIRST

One of the most prolific hymn writers of all time was Fanny Crosby, blind from infancy, who wrote no less than 8,000 songs during her life. According to her own statement, she never attempted to write a song without first kneeling in prayer. Once, under intense pressure to meet a deadline, she tried to write words for a tune the composer W. H. Doane had sent her. No words came. Then she remembered she had forgotten to pray. She immediately fell to her knees, and when she rose, the words to one of her most famous hymns, "Jesus, Keep Me Near the Cross," came so fast her assistant could hardly keep pace in writing them down.

Adapted from Paul Lee Tan, *Encyclopedia of 7,700 Illustrations* (Dallas, TX: Bible Communications, Inc., 1979), entry 4537.

God's Miracle Potion: Water

Water is a treasure during a drought and a scourge during a flood. God used it to purge the earth during Noah's time and heal the leper Naaman in the prophet Elisha's time.

Most of us take water for granted since it is the most common substance on earth, covering roughly three-quarters of the planet's surface and comprising 60 percent of the human body's composition. Water is critical to the body's temperature regulation, digestion, and elimination of waste and secretion. It makes up 80 percent of the composition of blood.

Water's Effects on Fat

Anyone who's ever tried to lose weight knows that drinking plenty of water is recommended. But did you know that not drinking enough water can actually encourage your body to retain and ultimately *gain* weight? Water suppresses the appetite and helps the body metabolize fat. Studies have shown that a decrease in water intake will cause fat deposits to increase, while an increase in water intake can actually reduce fat deposits.

According to Dr. Donald S. Robertson of the Southwest Bariatric Nutrition Center, the kidneys can't function properly without enough water. When they don't work to capacity, some of their load is dumped onto the liver. One of the liver's primary functions is to metabolize stored fat into usable energy for the body. But, if the liver has to do some of the kidney's work, it can't operate at full throttle. As a result, it metabolizes less fat, more fat remains stored in the body, and weight loss stops.

Water Retention?

"But I'll float away!" you may be protesting. Is water retention a problem for you? Try this simple test: Place your thumb on the boniest part of your shin, press down firmly, and count to five. When you release if you can see or feel a definite indentation, you are probably retaining fluids.

Does that mean you should avoid drinking extra water? Not so! According to physicians, drinking enough water is the best treatment for fluid retention. When the body gets less water it perceives this as a threat and begins to hold onto every drop.

The body stores water in the spaces outside cell walls. This shows up as swollen feet, legs, and hands. Diuretics force out stored water along with some essential nutrients and, again, the body perceives a threat and will replace the lost water at the first opportunity. The swelling quickly returns.

According to Dr. Robertson and others, the best way to overcome the problem of water retention is to give your body what it needs—plenty of water. Remember that an overweight person needs more water than a thin one. Larger people have larger metabolic loads. Since water is the key to fat metabolism, it follows that the overweight person needs more water.

Aid to Weight Loss

During weight loss, the body has a lot more waste to get rid of; all that metabolized fat must be eliminated. Drinking enough water helps flush out waste and helps relieve constipation. If the body gets too little water, it siphons what it needs from internal sources, primarily the colon, and that usually leads to constipation.

How Much Water?

How much water is enough? Unless you have a potassium deficiency, it's difficult to drink too much. On average, an adult should drink eight 8-ounce glasses (two quarts) daily *plus* one additional glass for every 25 pounds over normal weight. More water is also important during hot dry weather and vigorous exercise. Experts suggest that the body uses cold water more quickly than warm and that water intake should be spread evenly over the day. Other drinks such as coffee, colas, lemonade, or sports drinks don't substitute for water and can even be dehydrating.

"I'm not *that* thirsty!" you say? You *will* be. An interesting thing happens when the body regularly gets the water it needs to function optimally. Body fluids are balanced, endocrine-gland function improves, fluid retention is alleviated, more fat is used as fuel (because the liver is free to burn stored fat), and natural *thirst* returns. Many people also report a corresponding loss of hunger.

Skin Benefit

But there's even more good news. Water helps us look our best. Skin, for instance, can be only temporarily moistened on the surface. Drinking water places moisture *in* the skin and helps prevent the sagging skin that often accompanies weight loss. Shrinking cells are buoyed by water, which plumps the skin and leaves it clear, healthy, and resilient. Water also helps maintain proper muscle tone, which helps us move more gracefully, stand up straighter, appear fresher, and feel better! Now *that* should put a smile on your face!

God's Property?

Some years ago a New Orleans lawyer sought a direct Veterans Administration loan for a client. He was told that the loan would be approved if he could provide proof of clear title to the property offered as collateral. The title for the property in question was complicated and he spent a considerable amount of time reviewing all pertinent documents back to 1803.

Satisfied with the depth and expanse of his examination, he submitted the information to the Veterans Administration.

Close Isn't Good Enough

He soon received this reply from the VA:

"We received your letter today enclosing application for a loan for your client, supported by abstract of title.

CHILDREN AND CHURCH

A grandson was visiting his grandmother one day and he asked, "Grandma, do you know how you and God are alike?"

Mentally polishing her halo, the grandmother asked, "No, how are we alike?"

"You're both old," he replied.

The application forms are complete, but you have not cleared the title before the year 1803. Therefore, before full review and possible approval can be accorded the application, it will be necessary that the title be cleared back before that year."

Beyond the Call of Duty

Annoyed, the lawyer wrote the VA:

"Your letter regarding titles in case #9378329 received. I note that you wish titles extended further back than I have presented. Your attention is invited to the following information to update your records for the property prior to 1803:

a) I was unaware that any educated person would not know that the United States gained clear title to Louisiana from France in 1803. This title transfer was a result of a real estate transaction known as The Louisiana Purchase.

b) France gained clear title to Louisiana by right of conquest from Spain under the Treaty of San Ildefonso (1800).

c) The land came into the possession of Spain by right of discovery in 1492 by a sailor named Christopher Columbus. He was acting on behalf of Isabella, Queen of Spain, and had her permission to claim newly discovered lands for Spain.

d) The good Queen, being a pious woman and careful about titles—almost as careful as the VA—took the precaution of securing the blessing of the Pope before authorizing the voyage.

e) The Pope is a servant of God; God created the world.

f) Therefore, I believe that it is safe to presume that God created title to that part of the world called Louisiana and thus was the original holder of the property in question."

The Offering

Here is a true story about a nine-year-old boy who lived in a rural town in Tennessee. His house was in a poor area of the community. A church there had a bus ministry that came knocking on his door one Saturday afternoon. The boy came to answer the door and greeted the bus pastor.

The bus pastor asked if his parents were home and the small boy told him that his parents take off every weekend and leave him at home to take care of his little brother. The bus pastor couldn't believe what the boy said and asked him to repeat it. The youngster gave the same answer and the bus pastor asked to come in and talk with him. They went into the living room and sat down on an old couch with the foam and springs exposed.

Church Investigation

The bus pastor asked the boy, "Where do you go to church?"

The young boy surprised the visitor by replying, "I've never been to church in my whole life."

The bus pastor thought to himself about the fact that his church was less than three miles from the child's house. "Are you sure you have never been to church?" he asked again.

"I'm sure I haven't," came his answer.

Then the bus pastor said, "Well, son, more important than going to church, have you ever heard the greatest love story ever told?" and then he proceeded to share the gospel with this little nine-year-old boy. The young lad's heart began to be tenderized and at the end of the bus pastor's story, the bus pastor asked if the boy wanted to receive this free gift from God.

Free Gift Offer

The youngster exclaimed, "Of course!" The kid and the bus pastor got on their knees and the lad invited Jesus into his little heart and received the free gift of salvation. They both stood up and the bus pastor asked if he could pick the kid up for church the next morning.

"Sure," the boy replied. The bus pastor got to the house early the next morning and found the lights off. He let himself in and snaked his way through the house and found the little boy asleep in his bed. He woke up the little boy and his brother and helped get them dressed. They got on the bus and ate a doughnut for breakfast on their way to church.

BUG BITES

The cat flea is the champion jumper of all the varieties of fleas. It has been known to jump 34 inches, which would be equivalent to a 100-pound person jumping over 1,000 feet.

Clueless at First

Keep in mind that this boy had never been to church before. The church was a real big one. The little boy just sat there, clueless of what was going on. A few minutes into the service, these tall unhappy guys walked down to the front and picked up some wooden plates. One of the men prayed and the boy, with utter fascination, watched them walk up and down the aisles.

He still didn't know what was going on. All of a sudden, like a bolt of lightning, it hit the boy what was taking place. These people must be giving money to Jesus. He then reflected on the free gift of life he had received just 24 hours earlier. He imme-diately searched his pockets, front and back, and couldn't find a thing to give Jesus.

By this time the offering plate was being passed down his aisle and, with a broken heart, he just grabbed the plate and held on to it. He finally let go and watched it pass on down the aisle. He turned around to see it passed down the aisle behind him. And then his eyes remained glued on the plate as it was passed back and forth, back and forth all the way to the rear of the sanctuary.

My Gift

Then he had an idea. This little nine-year-old boy, in front of God and everybody, got up out of his seat. He walked about eight rows back, grabbed the usher by the coat, and asked to hold the plate one more time.

Then he did the most astounding thing I have ever heard of. He took the plate, sat it on the carpeted church floor, and stepped into the center of it. As he stood there, he lifted his little head up and said, "Jesus, I don't have anything to give you today, but just me. I give you me!"

Source: Rev. Tim Gibson, *Preacher's Illustrations and Jokes Deluxe* version 3.1, Copyright 2002 by Gibson Productions, part of the Gibson Family Christian Resource <http://members.truepath.com/timshen/preach.html> (January 31, 2002).

Strange Diets

John the Baptist ate locusts and wild honey (Mark 1:6). What if you had to chow down on these things?

What Is It?

The children of Israel ate manna. Literally translated, *manna* means "what is it?" Sweet, white flakes or seeds appeared every morning on the desert floor like dew (Exodus 16:31–35; Number 11:5–6).

Jelly Roll for a Prophet?

Ezekiel was to eat a sweet roll. "Moreover he said unto me, Son of man, eat that thou findest; eat this roll, and go speak unto the house of Israel. So I opened my mouth, and he caused me to eat that roll. And he said unto me, Son of man, cause thy belly to eat, and fill thy bowels with this roll that I give thee. Then did I eat it; and it was in my mouth as honey for sweetness" (Ezekiel 3:1–3).

A Good Book

John, the author of Revelations, was told eat a book that would upset his stomach; yet he complied (Revelation 10:10).

Heavenly Waiters?

If you were dining with Elijah, you'd want to figure out how to tip a raven. (See 1 Kings 17.) Elijah, having prophesied the drought, was not welcome in town. God told him to hide in the wilderness and that the ravens would bring food to him.

And they did! The menu was not varied—bread and meat twice a day, but he got liquid refreshment straight from the brook. And dining al fresco (or picnicking) was not a problem since there was no hint of rain!

Did Eve Bite into an Apple?

"She took the fruit thereof and did eat, and gave also unto her husband with her; and he did eat" (Genesis 3:6). The actual type of fruit Eve ate is unknown. The principal behind the act, however, is clear. Adam and eve chose to disobey God.

It was not a menu choice that doomed Adam and Eve; it was disobedience.

———————————

A HUNDRED YEARS OF PRAYER

In the early days of their denomination, the Moravians at Hernbut felt the need to establish 24-hour-a-day prayer. They formed two praying bands—one band of men and the other of women, each with 24 members. These prayer bands set aside one man and one woman to pray every hour of the day, the men in one place of prayer and the women in another. This double bond of prayer, unbroken through every day, was maintained for 100 years. During this time the missionary efforts of the Moravians grew greatly, to the point where three times as many people attended their missionary churches than the home church.

Top 10 College Edits

The top 10 ways the Bible would be different if college students had written it.

10. Loaves and fishes would be replaced by pizza and chips.

9. Ten Commandments actually would be only five, but because they are double-spaced and written in a large font they look like ten.

8. Forbidden fruit would have been eaten because it wasn't dorm food.

7. Paul's letter to the Romans would be Paul's e-mail to the Romans.

6. Reason Cain killed Abel: They were roommates.

5. The place where the end of the world occurs would not be the plains of Armageddon but a blank mind during finals week.

4. Book of Armaments would be in there somewhere.

3. Reason why Moses and his followers walked in the desert for 40 years: They didn't want to stop and ask for directions and look like freshmen.

2. Tower of Babel would be blamed for today's foreign language requirement.

1. Instead of creating the world in six days and resting on the seventh, God would have put it off until the night before it was due and then pulled an all-nighter and hoped no one would notice.

Adapted from the SFSU Presidential Scholars Listserv and *eLetter for American Young Adults* 3, no. 11 (1998), <http://www.laya.com/bissues/003-11.shtml> (January 31, 2002).

Strive for Perfection

Matthew 5:48 says, "Be ye therefore perfect, even as your Father which is in heaven is perfect."

Perfection in real life outside of the grace of Jesus is not realistic. So how about *nearly* perfect? Will that do? You be the judge.

If 99.9 percent is good enough, then:

* $761,900 will be spent in the next 12 months on tapes and compact disks that won't play.
* $9,690 will be spent each day and into the future on unsafe sporting equipment.
* 1,314 phone calls will be misplaced by telecommunications services every minute.
* 103,260 income tax returns will be processed incorrectly this year.
* 107 incorrect medical procedures will be performed today.

A BIT OF CHURCH HUMOR

A woman went to the post office to buy stamps for her Christmas cards. "What denomination?" asked the clerk.

"Oh, good heavens! Have we come to this?" said the woman. "Well, give me fifty Baptist and fifty Catholic ones."

• • •

On a cold, snowy Sunday in February, only the pastor and one farmer arrived at the village church. The pastor said, "Well, I guess we won't have a service today."

The farmer replied: "Well, if even only one cow shows up at feeding time, I feed it."

* 114,500 mismatched pairs of shoes will be shipped this year.
* 12 babies will be given to the wrong parents every day.
* 14,208 defective personal computers will be shipped this year.
* 18,322 pieces of mail will be mishandled in the next hour.
* 2 million documents will be lost by the IRS this year.
* 2,488,200 books will be shipped in the next 12 months with the wrong cover.
* 20,000 incorrect drug prescriptions will be written in the next 12 months.
* 22,000 checks will be deducted from the wrong bank accounts in the next 60 minutes.
* 268,500 defective tires will be shipped this year.
* 291 pacemaker operations will be performed incorrectly this year.
* 3,056 copies of tomorrow's *Wall Street Journal* will be missing one of three sections.
* 5,517,200 cases of soft drinks will be shipped without carbonation this year.
* 55 malfunctioning automatic teller machines will be installed in the next year.
* 811,000 faulty rolls of 35mm film will be loaded this year.

Original source unknown. Forwarded by Dan Bonin via *Mikey's Humor* <http://www.youthspecialties.com/mikeyshumor/index.html>.

Doing What's Right

Charlton Heston is best known as an award-winning actor in films whose plots are taken from the Bible. In a speech titled "Winning the Cultural War" delivered to the Harvard Law School Forum on February 16, 1999, he said:

"I remember my son when he was five, explaining to his kindergarten class what his father did for a living. 'My daddy,' he said, 'pretends to be people.' There have been quite a few of them. Prophets from the Old and New Testaments, a couple of Christian saints, generals of various nationalities and different centuries, several kings, three American presidents, a French cardinal, and two geniuses, including Michelangelo.

"If you want the ceiling repainted I'll do my best."

Sense of Liberty

"As I pondered our visit tonight it struck me: if my Creator gave me the gift to connect you with the hearts and minds of those great men, then I want to use that same gift now to reconnect you with your own sense of liberty . . . your own freedom of thought . . . your own compass for what is right.

"Dedicating the memorial at Gettysburg, Abraham Lincoln said of America, 'We are now engaged in a great Civil War, testing whether this nation or any nation so conceived and so dedicated can long endure.'

"I'm not complaining, but my own decades of social activism have taken their toll on me. Let me tell you a story.

Truth Exposed

"A few years back I heard about a rapper named Ice-T who was selling a CD called *Cop Killer* celebrating ambushing and murdering police officers. It was being marketed by none other than Time/Warner, the biggest entertainment conglomerate in the world.

"Police across the country were outraged. Rightfully so—at

SEVEN WONDERS OF THE ANCIENT WORLD

1. **The Great Pyramid of Giza**
   A gigantic stone structure near the ancient city of Memphis, serving as a tomb for the Egyptian Pharaoh Khufu

2. **The Hanging Gardens of Babylon**
   A palace with legendary gardens built on the banks of the Euphrates river by King Nebuchadnezzar II

3. **The Statue of Zeus at Olympia**
   An enormous statue of the Greek father of gods, carved by the great sculptor Pheidias

4. **The Temple of Artemis at Ephesus**
   A beautiful temple in Asia Minor erected in honor of the Greek goddess of hunting and wild nature

5. **The Mausoleum at Halicarnassus**
   A fascinating tomb constructed for King Maussollos, Persian satrap of Caria

6. **The Colossus of Rhodes**
   A colossus of Helios the sun-god, erected by the Greeks near the harbor of a Mediterranean Island

7. **The Lighthouse of Alexandria**
   A lighthouse built by the Ptolemies on the island of Pharos off the coast of their capital city

---

least one had been murdered. But Time/Warner was stonewalling because the CD was a cash cow for them, and the media were tiptoeing around it because the rapper was black. I heard Time/Warner had a stockholders meeting scheduled in Beverly Hills. I owned some shares at the time, so I decided to attend.

Bold Act

"What I did there was against the advice of my family and colleagues. I asked for the floor. To a hushed room of a thousand average American stockholders, I simply read the full lyrics of *Cop Killer*—every vicious, vulgar, instructional word.

"'I got my 12 gauge sawed off I got my headlights turned off I'm about to bust some shots off I'm about to dust some cops off . . .'

"It got worse, a lot worse. I won't read the rest of it to you. But trust me, the room was a sea of shocked, frozen, blanched faces. The Time/Warner executives squirmed in their chairs and stared at their shoes. They hated me for that. Then I delivered another volley of sick lyrics brimming with racist filth. . . .

Deafening Silence

"Well, I won't do to you here what I did to them. Let's just say I left the room in echoing silence. When I read the lyrics to the waiting press corps, one of them said, 'We can't print that.'

"'I know,' I replied, 'but Time/Warner is selling it.'

"Two months later, Time/Warner terminated Ice-T's contract. I'll never be offered another film by Warners or get a good review from *Time* magazine. But . . . you must be willing to act, not just talk."

How Many Shekels?

How much is a shekel worth in U.S. dollars?

How many cubits high are the ceilings in your house? How many ephahs of grain does it take to fill a silo?

Could you buy grain from Joseph? Or bake a cake for Mary and Martha? Given the tables below, it might not be as tough as it sounds. See if you can come up with the right conclusion for each of the following situations. Use the charts that follow to calculate your answers. The correct answers appear on page 304.

Situation #1: You have two jars that hold one *hin* each. How many trips to the well will you have to make to fill your horse's new trough, which holds one *kor*?

Situation #2: Noah built the ark 300 *cubits* long, 50 *cubits* wide, and 30 *cubits* high. What were its dimensions in feet?

Situation #3: You are a merchant preparing for a long journey. You have a small bag of gems valued at 6 *talents* of silver with which to buy supplies. You buy 6 camels at 20 *minas* each; 6 saddles at 50 *shekels* each; 20 *seah* of grain at 25 *bekah* each; 4 jars each containing one *bath* of oil at 75 shekels each. How much silver do you have left at the end of your shopping?

Situation #4: From the time the harvest is completed, your family relies on your stored grain to provide bread throughout the year. On average, your family uses about nine *cabs* of grain each week. How many *homers* and *ephahs* of grain will the family need for the whole year?

Use the table that follows to calculate your answers.

Biblical Weights and Measures

Bible   *American/British*

length

cubit .... 18 inches
span .... 9 inches
handbreadth .... 3 inches

weight

talent (60 minas) .... 75 pounds
mina (50 shekels) .... 1 1/4 pounds
shekel (2 bekas) .... 2/5 ounce
pim (2/3 shekel) .... 1/3 ounce
beka (10 gerahs) .... 1/5 ounce
gerah .... 1/50 ounce

dry capacity

cor or homer (10 ephahs) .... 6 bushels
lethek (5 ephahs) .... 3 bushels
ephah (10 omers) .... 3/5 bushel
seah (1/3 ephah) .... 7 quarts
omer (1/10 ephah) .... 2 quarts
cab (1/18 ephah) .... 1 quart

liquid capacity

kor (10 baths) .... 60 gallons
bath (1 ephah) .... 6 gallons
hin (1/6 bath) .... 4 quarts
log (1/72 bath) .... 1/3 quart

Note: This table of weights and measures is based upon the best available information from ancient sources. It is not intended to be absolutely precise.

Answers:

Situation #1: You need 3 trips to fill 1 bath and you need 10 baths:
3 x 10 = 30 trips (whew!)

Situation #2:

1 cubit = 18" so	300 x 18 = 5400 ÷ 12 = 450 feet long
	50 x 18 = 5400 ÷ 12 = 75 feet wide
	30 x 18 = 5400 ÷ 12 = 45 feet high

Situation #3:

6 camels x 20 minas ea.	= 120 minas		
6 saddles x 50 shekels ea.	= 300 shekels		
		=	6 minas
20 seah of grain x 25 bekah ea.	= 500 bekahs		
		=	5 minas
4 jars oil at 75 shekels ea.	= 300 shekels		
		=	6 minas
			137 minas

6 talents	= 300 minas
purchases	= 137 minas
remaining	= 223 minas or 3 talents, 43 minas of silver

Situation #4:

9 cabs =	9/18 ephah or 1/2 ephah
	x 52 weeks = 26 ephahs
	26 ephahs = 2 homers and 6 ephahs of grain

Pen Pals with God

A significant number of people are finding that one of the best ways for them to pour out their heart to God is to become a "pen pal." Rather than only speaking to God, they write out their prayers in a prayer journal or notebook.

The Benefits of Writing

Those who have kept a prayer journal have experienced the following:

- Acknowledgment that God is sovereign and greater than they are
- Freedom from negative emotions that can build up to an explosive point
- A willingness to face needs and problems, and the feelings associated with them
- An opportunity to look objectively at their own statements about problems, needs, and desires, as well as to look objectively from time to time at their *responses* to various life situations

Practical Suggestions

Here are four suggestions for becoming a pen pal with God:

1. Make a commitment to spend a few minutes at least three times a week writing to God about what is going on in your life.
2. Start each letter with the words which have the most

meaning to you. You may write "Dear God," "Precious Heavenly Father," "My Lord," or whatever phrase depicts your greatest understanding of God.

3. Be honest in expressing your feelings, whether you are mad, sad, or glad.

4. After six months, write *yourself* a letter about what you have learned from your correspondence with God.

MORE BUG BITES

• If you have ever tried to catch a grasshopper you know what a challenge that can be. The reason? The grasshopper's eyes. A grasshopper has two kinds of eyes. Their *compound* eyes consist of thousands of little eyes that enable the grasshopper to see forward, backward, and sideways. They also have three small *single* eyes.

• In the world of the black widow spider, the female is the aggressor. She has the fangs that can penetrate skin; a male black widow's fangs are not large enough. A male black widow spider initiates courtship by touching the female. He will then begin to spin a silk wrap around her; however, the female can interrupt the proceedings and attack the male.

• Bats may eat as many as 600 mosquito-size insects in an hour, and a bat colony may devour a half million insects in an evening. Bats are the best natural controller of the insect kingdom.

Bible Animals of Mythical Proportions

The Bible is an exciting book for folks interested in the "wild kingdom." Some of the beasts described by biblical writers are of unusual, huge, or even mythical proportions. Modern writers and translators have only been able to make educated guesses about some animals' physical appearances and origins. Other animals were not real but representational in nature.

Behemoth

The word *behemoth* is frequently used in American slang to describe something of gigantic proportions. In truth, the behemoth described in the Bible was a large, amphibious animal that ate grass. The plural for behemoth is sometimes used in the Old Testament to describe either domestic or wild animals. Other Bible scholars believe the word isn't Hebrew but of Egyptian origin signifying "water ox."

References to its great size, its eating grass, the difficulty with which weapons penetrate its hide, and its frequenting of streams have led some scientists to believe that the behemoth is more like the hippopotamus than any other animal.

The remains of fossilized hippopotamuses of apparently the same species are found over most of Europe, so it may have inhabited Palestine in early historical times, although there is no scientific record of this. The remains of *Hippopotamus minutus* have been found in enormous quantities in caves in Malta and Sicily.

Leviathan

Leviathan is the transliterated Hebrew word *livyathan*, meaning "twisted" or "coiled."

The leviathan has been presumed to be a real animal—so real, in fact, that many modern-day writers have speculated that sightings of the Loch Ness Monster in Scotland may actually be a descendant of the biblical leviathan. Yet the Hebrew word has had a number of reinterpretations throughout the Old Testament. In Job 3:8 it denotes the dragon, which according to Eastern tradition is an enemy of light. In Psalm 104:26 it denotes any large animal, perhaps a whale, that moves by writhing or wriggling the body.

This word is also used figuratively for a cruel enemy, as in Psalm 74:14—"the Egyptian host, crushed by the divine power, and cast on the shores of the Red Sea." As used in Isaiah 27:1, the word may denote the Assyrian and Babylonian Empires, "leviathan the piercing or swift serpent, even leviathan that crooked or 'winding' serpent."

Cockatrice

Cockatrice translates as a "fabulous serpent." Since the animal is always referred to in a figurative sense, some assume that it is more likely a symbolic rather than real animal. Jeremiah 8:17 says, "For out of the serpent's root shall come forth a cockatrice, and his fruit shall be a fiery flying serpent."

The medieval name of cockatrice is a corruption of "crocodile" and refers to a serpent produced from a cock's egg. It is generally supposed to denote the *cerastes*, or "horned viper," a poisonous serpent about a foot long. Still, the case for the cockatrice's actual existence shouldn't be dismissed. Some believe it to be the yellow viper (*Daboia xanthina*), one of the most dangerous vipers, based upon its size and its nocturnal habits as described in Isaiah 11:8; 14:29 and Jeremiah 8:17.

Pygarg

Pygarg was probably a species of antelope. The Hebrew word *dishon* or "springing" likely refers to the antelope addax, a large animal, over three-and-a-half feet high at the shoulder and with long, gently-twisted horns. Its color is pure white, with the exception of a short black mane, and a tinge of tawny on the shoulders and back.

Unicorn

The unicorn (literally "one horn") is perhaps one of the most controversial animals in Scripture. Most Americans have been introduced to unicorns through fairy tales and children's stories and have assumed that it is a mythical beast.

Unicorn stories have been told in many parts of the world, including Syria, China, India, ancient Greece, and medieval Europe. In European stories the unicorn is depicted as a horse with cloven hooves. Although it is always shown with one horn, its body has also been depicted in many other ways, including as a sheep, a goat, or even something like a rabbit.

It is often associated with virtue and virginity. Though wild, it liked to cradle its head in a virgin's lap, while its horn ensured a skewered end for all who tried to falsely pass themselves off as so undefiled. Marco Polo searched for the unicorn, but rejected the rhinoceros in disappointment.

Keeping the Faith in the Baltics

In 1940 the independent, democratic nation of Estonia was occupied by communist Russia. Of the three Baltic countries (Estonia, Latvia, and Lithuania) the northernmost one, Estonia, shares a border with Russia. This made it a primary proving ground for communist ideology and infiltration.

Estonia Overrun

In order to quickly "Sovietize" Estonia, a mass transmigration of Russians and Estonians was begun in 1940. Specific policies aimed at restricting the role of Estonians in society, as well as restricting Estonian culture, were implemented. On March 25 and 26, 1949, at least 20,700 people were deported, and private farms and industry were turned into "collectives." About 25 percent of the population were deported to Siberia.

Churches Strangled

All of Estonia suffered great loss, but the church suffered most of all. Anti-Christian Soviet legislation systematically persecuted and closed churches. Many church leaders were martyred. Cultural and religious treasures were destroyed with the aim of severing cultural continuity and completely demolishing the church.

It was hoped that these tactics would slowly strangle the life out of the church. Yet, in the Methodist Church, for example, the number of church members more than doubled during the 50 years of communist occupation.

A Packed House

The story is told that in the early 1980s of a group of western tourists was being escorted by an official Soviet tour guide. The group stopped outside the historic St. Olav's church (home to the city's Baptist congregation). The tour guide explained that most churches were empty and that basically no Soviet citizens believed in any kind of God. By coincidence, it was Sunday at noon, and as she said these words, the doors opened and several hundred Estonians poured onto the street, still singing and praising God.

A Hidden Organ

When the Methodist churches across the rest of the Soviet Union were forcibly closed, it was only in Estonia that Methodism survived. Under the leadership of godly men and women, groups of Christians continued to meet in rented facilities after their churches were destroyed. While *parents* most often encouraged their children to go along with the Soviet indoctrination, godly *grandmothers* continued to influence the children.

The deep faith and determination of these people is demonstrated by the acts of two such grandmothers. The Soviets decided that the Methodist church in the center of the capital of Tallinn had some use to them. Instead of destroying the building, they began destroying its contents. But two grandmothers, in faith that someday God would return the structure to his service, took the organ that had been such an important part of their praise to God. For more than 40 years, they hid this instrument in the basement of a home.

Growing under Persecution

God continued to honor their faith. Even during the occupation, the "illegal" church became a point of unification for Estonian young people. A Russian congregation was formed, and both Estonian and Russian congregations actually doubled in size!

The people continued to pray for freedom that would enable them to rebuild and spread the gospel more effectively. Prayer was their only weapon.

Finally, God granted Estonia freedom and Estonia regained her independence on August 20, 1991. Not a shot was fired.

Shared Buildings

After the occupation, churches of every denomination shared facilities. The church in Tallinn, for instance, was actually owned by the Seventh Day Adventists, who used the building on Saturdays. On Sundays, the Estonia and Russian Methodist congregations each held services there for about eight years while they sought permission to buy property and build another church.

Then a strange thing happened: The Estonian government agreed to *give* the church prime property on which to build both a church and a seminary to train ministers. The only condition was that the Christians must "think *big*"—no 300–500-seat structure could be put on the property. It had to accommodate over 1,000 people for services and concerts!

Perseverance Rewarded

Today, the Baltic Mission Center stands as a testament to the faith and perseverance of the Christians there. Freedom has given the church a chance to minister in ways that were impossible under Soviet domination. Street evangelists, children's camps, and Christian radio are just some of the ways in which the saving message of Jesus Christ is being proclaimed.

People from all over the city and the region are drawn to concerts and services in the beautiful auditorium, and the seminary is training both pulpit ministers and Christian leaders for positions in government, education, and other related fields.

Thanks to the fearless faith of grandmothers who saw the children as God's property, the whole of Estonia is being won back for Christ.

PRAYER FROM SINGAPORE

God stir the soil,

Run the plowshare deep,

Cut the furrows around and around,

Overturn the hard, dry ground,

Spare no strength nor toil,

Even though I weep.

In the loose, fresh mangled earth

Sow new seed.

Free of withered vine and weed

Bring fair flowers to birth.

What Children Teach Us
Author unknown

When I look at a patch of dandelions, I see a bunch of weeds. My kids see flowers for Mom and blowing white fluff you can wish on.

When I look at an old drunk and he smiles at me, I see a smelly, dirty person who probably wants money and I look away. My kids see someone smiling at them and they smile back.

When I hear music I love, I know I can't carry a tune and don't have much rhythm so I sit self-consciously and listen. My kids feel the beat and move to it. They sing out the words. If they don't know them, they make up their own.

When I feel wind on my face, I brace myself against it. I feel it messing up my hair and pulling me back when I walk. My kids close their eyes, spread their arms and fly with it, until they fall to the ground laughing.

When I pray, I say thee and thou and grant me this, give me that. My kids say, "Hi God! Thanks for my toys and my friends. Please keep the bad dreams away tonight. Sorry, I don't want to go to heaven yet. I would miss my mommy and daddy."

When I see a mud puddle I step around it. I see muddy shoes and dirty carpets. My kids sit in it. They see dams to build, rivers to cross, and worms to play with.

No wonder God loves the little children!

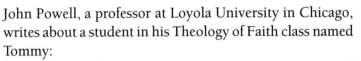

God Will Find You

John Powell, a professor at Loyola University in Chicago, writes about a student in his Theology of Faith class named Tommy:

Some 12 years ago, I stood watching my university students file into the classroom for our first session in the Theology of Faith. That was the day I first saw Tommy. My eyes and my mind both blinked. He was combing his long flaxen hair, which hung six inches below his shoulders.

It was the first time I had ever seen a boy with hair that long. I guess it was just coming into fashion then. I know in my mind that it isn't what's on your head but what's in it that counts; but on that day I was unprepared and my emotions flipped.

Strange Kid

I immediately filed Tommy under "S" for strange . . . very strange. Tommy turned out to be the "atheist in residence" in my Theology of Faith course. He constantly objected to, smirked at, or whined about the possibility of an unconditionally loving Father-God. We lived with each other in relative peace for one semester, although I admit he was for me at times a serious pain in the back pew.

When he came up at the end of the course to turn in his final exam, he asked in a slightly cynical tone: "Do you think I'll ever find God?"

I decided instantly on a little shock therapy. "No!" I said very emphatically.

"Oh," he responded, "I thought that was the product you were pushing."

I let him get five steps from the classroom door and then called out: "Tommy! I don't think you'll ever find him, but I am absolutely certain that he will find you!"

He shrugged a little and left my class and my life.

I felt slightly disappointed at the thought that he had missed my clever line: "He will find you!" At least I thought it was clever. Later I heard that Tommy had graduated and I was duly grateful.

Return Visit

Then I heard that Tommy had terminal cancer. Before I could search him out, he came to see me. When he walked into my office, his body was very badly wasted, and the long hair had all fallen out as a result of chemotherapy. But his eyes were bright and his voice was firm, for the first time, I believe.

"Tommy, I've thought about you so often. I hear you are sick!" I blurted out.

"Oh, yes, very sick. I have cancer in both lungs. It's a matter of weeks."

"What's it like to be only 24 and dying?"

It Could Be Worse

"Well, it could be worse," he said.

"Like what?"

"Well, like being 50 and having no values or ideals, like being 50 and thinking that booze, seducing women, and making money are the real 'biggies' in life."

I began to look through my mental file cabinet under "S" where I had filed Tommy as strange. (It seems as though everybody I try to reject by classification God sends back into my life to educate me.)

Banging on Heaven's Door

"But what I really came to see you about," Tom said, " is something you said to me on the last day of class." (He remembered!) He continued, "I asked you if you thought I would ever find God and you said, 'No!' which surprised me. Then you said, 'But he will find you.' I thought about that a lot, even though my search for God was hardly intense at that time. (My "clever" line. He thought about that a lot!) But when the doctors removed a lump from my groin and told me that it was malignant, then I got serious about locating God. And when the malignancy spread into my vital organs, I really began banging bloody fists against the bronze doors of heaven.

"But God did not come out. In fact, nothing happened. Did you ever try anything for a long time with great effort and with no success? You get psychologically glutted, fed up with trying. And then you quit.

Lessons of Love

"Well, one day I woke up, and instead of throwing a few more futile appeals over that high brick wall to a God who may or may not be there, I just quit. I decided that I didn't really care . . . about God, about an afterlife, or anything like that. I decided to spend what time I had left doing something more profitable. I thought about you and your class and I remembered something else you had said: 'The essential sadness is to go through life without loving. But it would be almost equally sad to go through life and leave this world without ever telling those you loved that you had loved them.' So I began with the hardest one: my dad. He was reading the newspaper when I approached him.

"Dad."

"Yes, what?" he asked without lowering the newspaper.

"Dad, I would like to talk with you."

"Well, talk."

"I mean, it's really important."

The newspaper came down three slow inches. "What is it?"

"Dad, I love you. I just wanted you to know that." Tom smiled at me and said with obvious satisfaction, as though he felt a warm and secret joy flowing inside of him: "The newspaper fluttered to the floor. Then my father did two things I could never remember him ever doing before. He cried and he hugged me.

"And we talked all night, even though he had to go to work the next morning. It felt so good to be close to my father, to see his tears, to feel his hug, to hear him say that he loved me.

"It was easier with my mother and little brother. They cried with me too, and we hugged each other, and started saying real nice things to each other. We shared the things we had been keeping secret for so many years. I was only sorry about one thing: that I had waited so long. Here I was just beginning to open up to all the people I had actually been close to.

There Was God

"Then, one day I turned around and God was there. He didn't come to me when I pleaded with him. I guess I was like an

animal trainer holding out a hoop, 'C'mon, jump through. C'mon, I'll give you three days . . . three weeks.' Apparently God does things in his own way and at his own hour. But the important thing is that he was there. He found me.

"You were right. He found me even after I stopped looking for him."

"Tommy," I practically gasped, "I think you are saying something very important and much more universal than you realize. To me, at least, you are saying that the surest way to find God is not to make him a private possession, a problem solver, or an instant consolation in time of need, but rather by opening to love. You know, the apostle John said that. He said God is love, and anyone who lives in love is living with God and God is living in him.

Teaching Time

"Tom, could I ask you a favor? You know, when I had you in class you were a real pain. But (laughingly) you can make it all up to me now. Would you come into my present Theology of Faith course and tell them what you have just told me? If I told them the same thing it wouldn't be half as effective as if you were to tell them."

"Oooh. . . . I was ready for you, but I don't know if I'm ready for your class."

"Tom, think about it. If and when you are ready, give me a call." In a few days Tommy called, said he was ready for the class, that he wanted to do that for God and for me. So we scheduled a date. However, he never made it.

Another Appointment

He had another appointment, far more important than the one with me and my class. Of course, his life was not really ended by his death, only changed.

He made the great step from faith into vision. He found a life far more beautiful than the eye of man has ever seen or the ear of man has ever heard or the mind of man has ever imagined.

Before he died, we talked one last time. "I'm not going to make it to your class," he said.

"I know, Tom."

"Will you tell them for me? Will you . . . tell the whole world for me?"

"I will, Tom. I'll tell them. I'll do my best."

So, to all of you who have been kind enough to hear this simple statement about love, thank you for listening. And to you, Tommy, somewhere in the sunlit, verdant hills of heaven: "I told them, Tommy . . . as best I could."

> ### CHILDREN AND CHURCH
>
> A Sunday school class was studying the 10 Commandments. They were ready to discuss the last one. The teacher asked if anyone could tell her what it was. Susie raised her hand, stood tall, and quoted, "Thou shall not take the covers off the neighbor's wife."

Note: This story was written by Father John Powell, now retired and advanced in years. TruthOrFiction.com talked with him. This story was fresh in his mind, and he confirmed that it is true and happened in the way that he described it.

Too Many Songs

Fanny Crosby was probably the most prolific hymnist in history. Though blinded by an incompetent doctor at six weeks of age, she wrote more than 8,000 hymns.

She entered what was then known as the New York Institution for the Blind at the age of 15 and afterward taught English and history at the school. As a pupil and as a teacher, Fanny spent 35 years at the school.

She was often asked to entertain visitors with her poems, and she frequently met with presidents, generals, and other dignitaries. She was asked to play at President Grant's funeral.

Dedicated to the Poor

Her first book of poems, published in 1844, was called *The Blind Girl and Other Poems*.

After leaving the school, Crosby dedicated her life to serving the poorest and neediest. Supporting herself by her writing, she quickly gained fame for her hymns. It is said that publishers had so much of her work that they took to using them under at least 94 different pseudonyms. Fanny sometimes used marks such as ##, ###, "*", and *** instead of a name.

Her usual fee was a mere $2, which frequently went to her work with the poor. Her mission work is legendary.

Blessed by Blindness

About her blindness, Miss Crosby said, "It seemed intended by the blessed providence of God that I should be blind all my life, and I thank him for the dispensation. If perfect earthly sight were offered me tomorrow I would not accept it. I might not have sung hymns to the praise of God if I had been distracted by the beautiful and interesting things about me."

Known and Loved

In her lifetime, Fanny Crosby was one of the best-known women in the United States. To this day, the vast majority of American hymnals contain her work. When she died, her tombstone carried the words, "Aunt Fanny" and "Blessed assurance, Jesus is mine. Oh, what a foretaste of glory divine." These last words are from one of her most beloved hymns.

> Esther 8:9 is the longest line in the Bible (89 words; 425 letters). The Bible's longest word is Maher-shalal-hash-baz (Isaiah 8:1). The shortest verse in the NIV version of the Bible is John 11:35: "Jesus wept."
>
> • • •
>
> The longest chapter in any book of the Bible is Psalm 119. The shortest chapter is found only two earlier—Psalm 117.
>
> • • •
>
> The tabernacle covering was created from ram skins and sea cow hides (Exodus 36:19).
>
> • • •
>
> Contrary to popular assumption, the Bible never says that there were three wise men. Matthew 2:1 simply says, "Magi from the east came to Jerusalem." Later they presented three gifts.

Neglected Treasure

Leonardo da Vinci's masterpiece the *Last Supper* is one of the most famous and most reproduced works of art in the modern world.

Most people have at least seen photos of it or reproductions of it on posters. It has graced the walls of cathedrals and churches around the world and been meticulously reproduced in stained glass. The painting depicts Jesus at the center of a long table with his disciples on either side of him as they dine with him for the last time before his crucifixion.

Practice Pieces?

It is possible that the artist painted several versions of this masterpiece. One was originally actually painted by da Vinci as a fresco on the wall of a monastery's dining room in Milan.

Church history records that the artist took great pains to paint each face with feelings he imagined, and he succeeded in expressing the anxiety that seized the apostles after Jesus announced that one of them would betray him. Da Vinci left the head of Christ unfinished for quite some time, not believing that he was able to give it the divine air that he thought essential to the image of Christ. Missing, too, was the face of Judas, the betrayer.

Consequences of Hurrying the Artist

The prior, monk of second-highest rank, of that monastery kept pressing Leonardo to finish the work. In response, Leonardo sometimes stood half a day at a time, lost in contemplation.

Eventually the prior lost patience and complained to the duke about Leonardo's lack of progress—whereupon the duke spoke to the artist. Leonardo still struggled with the image of his Lord, but he was suddenly inspired for the image of Judas. Historical accounts state that the duke was "moved to laughter" upon finding the image of the insistent prior as Judas's face.

Crumbling Respect

That is not the end of the story. Although the outer walls of the monastery were no doubt made of stone, apparently inner walls could be constructed from a host of other, less durable materials.

The wall began to crumble almost immediately after Da Vinci finished painting his fresco because the monks had only built the wall with loose dirt. It is reported that some early friars even cut a door through the wall, right where Christ's feet were painted.

Over time there were changes made in the monastery and the dining room became a stable, a storage room, a prison, and a barracks.

When someone finally decided to restore the painting, they almost did more harm than good. Some of the restoration was so sloppy it was scandalous. One artist in particular was so casual about the task that he gave James six fingers on one hand!

Does It Really Mean That?

Did you ever wonder about these things? Well, relax because here are the answers.

Were Giants in the Bible Really *Giant*?

Or were they just much bigger than most people of that place and time?

Most people of both Old and New Testament times were generally smaller in stature than people are today. Does it follow, then, that anyone who was simply a very tall person would have been considered a giant? If there were giants, were they oddities?

There is ample evidence that the giants of the Old Testament would be considered giants today. For instance, Deuteronomy 3:11 NIV, tells about Og, king of Bashan: "His bed was made of iron and was more than 13 feet long and 6 feet wide." Furthermore, we know that these large people were not rarities, but members of an entire race of large people who were the products of intermarriage between angels and the daughters of men (Genesis 6:4 NIV).

Goliath, who was killed by David, is known as the giant of Gath and champion of the Philistine army (1 Samuel 17:4–23; 21:9; 22:10; 2 Samuel 21:19). Goliath was almost certainly not of Philistine blood, but belonged to one of the races of giants, or aboriginal tribes. His size was most extraordinary. If a cubit was about 21 inches, he was over 11 feet in height; if a cubit was about 18 inches, he was over 9 feet in height. The enormous weight of his armor would seem to require the larger cubit. This height probably included his full length in armor, helmet and all. In either case he is the largest man described in the Bible.

Did Eve Really Have a Conversation with a *Snake*?

Or was it some other kind of creature?

Wouldn't Eve have avoided a *snake*? There is reason to assume that Eve would have been unafraid of a snake—after all, she and Adam had been given dominion over everything in the garden. Some conclude that the serpent must have had a beautiful or intriguing appearance. Genesis 3:1 only describes it as the most crafty or cunning of God's creations.

Satan chose this form, no doubt, because it was a familiar creature whose nature was most like his own. The Hebrew word used for Satan's form in the garden of Eden is *nachash* meaning "to hiss"—which also makes it the term used for a snake. But the primitive root of the word refers to "whispering a (magic) spell." When we look at the conversation between Eve and the creature, the role of the soothsayer seems to fit the creature especially well.

But *was* it really a slithering snake? In the days of the garden, we can be fairly certain that Satan, in the form of this creature, didn't slither since God condemned him to crawl on his belly as part of his punishment. He likely had legs or even wings. But the creature's progeny most certainly slithers today— so we can be fairly certain that Eve really *did* talk to Satan in the form of a snake's ancestor.

Did Methuselah Really Live to Be Over 900 Years Old?

Or were the ancient Bible years of a different length than they are today?

The author of Genesis traces Methuselah's descent through his father Enoch to Seth, a son of Adam and Eve. At the time of his son's birth, Enoch was 65 years of age. When Methuselah had reached the great age of 187, he became the father of Lamech. Following this he lived the remarkable term of 782 years, which makes his age at his death 969 years.

Some skeptics and various theologians have "solved" the mystery of Methuselah's longevity to their own satisfaction by declaring that the year meant by the sacred writer is not the equivalent of our year today. Questions about the exact time equivalents are further complicated by the existence of Samaritan texts that indicate that Methuselah was 67 at Lamech's birth, and 720 at his death.

An open-minded examination of the recorded ages now seems warranted, however, owing to recent discoveries that suggest a biological basis for such longevity. Inbreeding within a limited gene pool appears to produce longevity in some species. Certainly close inbreeding was a social and legal custom well documented in the Old Testament.

Love to Ink

When we learn to give thanks, we are learning to concentrate not on the bad things, but on the good things.
—Amy Vanderbilt

With the advent of e-mail and instant messaging, some of the finer points of friendship are less and less practiced. If you have ever received an encouraging card or letter you know how valuable they are.

What Makes a Good Note of Encouragement?

Here are several characteristics:

- It has sincere words.
- It is tangible, written in your own hand on a blank card or personal stationery, and mailed with a stamp.
- It is brief and to the point.
- It mentions the recipient's personal strengths or talents.
- It passes along a compliment that you've overheard (if it is appropriate).

Who Needs a Note of Encouragement?

Just about everybody! Here are some ideas:

- Someone who's dealing with a major upheaval in life (such as the death of a loved one, divorce, major illness, personal loss, or a job change).
- Anyone dealing with family conflict (be sure the individual is open about this fact or has confided in you).

- People with relatives who are in trouble.
- Someone whose recent victory has brought about new challenges (promotion, elected to public office).
- Anyone who is struggling with a spiritual problem or addictive behavior.

But I'm Not a Writer! What Do I Say?

One option is to thank the person for what they do, or simply point out what you admire about them.

- "Thank you for continuing to teach fourth-grade Sunday school. I can see what an influence you are on the children's lives."
- "Thank you for the great service you give whenever I come into the store."
- "Thank you for always making sure I have a dry newspaper every morning just outside my front door! Wow! What great service!"
- "I see your dedication. You are an inspiration to me."
- "We don't talk very often, but I think of you frequently and am so glad you're my friend."

Won't an E-mail Work as Well?

E-mail is fast, but a handwritten note is both a visual and tactile keepsake for the recipient. Notes on paper say, "You are important enough for this extra bit of effort—this note is not an afterthought."

Organ Transplant?

Create in me a clean heart, O God; and renew a right spirit within me. —Psalm 51:10

On July 2, 2001, Robert Tools, age 59, became the first person in the world to let doctors cut out his entire heart and replace it with a completely implanted, battery-powered, plastic and titanium AbioCor artificial heart. This was not a transplanted organ. It was brand new technology.

The heart was not hooked up to external machines or wired to some other device. It had no inherent genetic defects or unknown diseases from its previous owner. It didn't come with a few years already logged on its figurative odometer.

Man's New Creation

It was a totally new creation placed in Mr. Tool's chest and connected to his veins and arteries. It was the one and only pump his body would use to pump his blood through his lungs for oxygenation and on through his body to literally carry life to his organs. It continued to do so for 152 days.

It was man's most successful attempt thus far to create a "new heart" in himself. But it didn't really work.

Surgery?

The Hebrew word *leb* means "the heart." The same word is also used figuratively for the emotions, the will, the intellect, or for the center of anything. So what was the psalmist saying when he wrote, "Create in me a clean [or new] heart"?

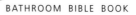

The Hebrew word for clean is *tahor,* which means "pure in the physical, chemical, ceremonial, or moral sense." The Hebrew word for create—*bara*—means "absolutely to create." This is the same word used in Genesis for God's creation of everything that is—and literally, creation from nothing. It is also the same word used throughout Isaiah to describe God's bringing forth of creation.

God's Creative Miracle

It is, then, not merely a "different" heart that the psalmist requested. It was a totally new, unused, newly-created-by-God heart that he wanted—a core or center without genetic defects and full of the disease inherited from sin.

He didn't say, "Help me, Father, to change the habits of my heart," or "Help me to change my lifestyle so that my heart will change." He didn't even pray for a "transplant" from a righteous man.

The word "Christian" appears only three times in the Bible: Acts 11:26; 26:28; 1 Peter 4:16. Early Christians called themselves followers of "the Way" (Acts 24:14).

• • •

There are 66 books in the Bible, 39 in the Old Testament and 27 in the New Testament. The 66 books of the Bible is divided into 1,189 chapters consisting of 31,173 verses. The Old Testament has 929 chapters, the New Testament 260. (King James version)

He recognized the hopeless, helpless condition of a sin-ravaged heart, and he prayed for a creative miracle from the hand of God.

Create in me a clean heart, O God!

Oops! Did I Say That?

As he helped warble the 1980s hit, "We Are the World," Willie Nelson sang, "As our God has shown us, by turning stones to bread . . ."

Well, God didn't turn stones to bread. In fact, the opposite happened. According to the Matthew 4:3–4, Satan tempted Jesus to turn stones into bread and he refused, quoting a verse from the Old Testament that "Man shall not live by bread alone."

Here are a few more quotes that are often erroneously attributed to Scripture:

- **Money is the root of all evil.** First Timothy 6:10, says the *love of* money is a root of all kinds of evil, not money itself. There is nothing inherently evil about having money. Loving money is the problem.
- **Adam and Eve shared an apple.** The Bible says they ate from the fruit of the tree of the knowledge of good and evil (Genesis 2–3). It almost certainly wasn't an apple.
- **Cleanliness is next to godliness.** This was John Wesley, in his sermon "On Dress." It is not in the Bible.
- **God works in mysterious ways.** Yes, he does, but that isn't in the Bible. William Cowper penned this one in the poem "On the Loss of the Royal George."

Oh well, you might say, "to err is human, to forgive divine." No, that's not Scripture either.

Where Islam Is Winning

At this time, Islam is the fastest-growing religion on earth. As Islam gains political strength in a nation, Christians are invariably persecuted and often killed. Here are some nations in which Islam is on the rise and Christians are suffering:

Azerbaijan—former Soviet nation. Armenian and Russian Christians still have the ability to meet and print literature, but distribution is limited; nationalists are becoming more anti-Christian.

Bangladesh—Christians are routinely denied access to public wells and are being forced from their homes by Muslim extremists.

Indonesia—More than 60,000 Christians are presently in jeopardy. Dozens of churches have been burned and thousands displaced from their homes.

Kuwait—the government has purchased large quantities of Bibles for the sole purpose of burning them.

Pakistan—breaking Law 295C (blaspheming Mohammed) is a crime punishable by death. Christians are being falsely accused of this crime.

Somalia—Christians are fleeing to neighboring countries to avoid intense Muslim persecution.

Sudan—approximately 2 million Christians have perished at the hands of Islamic fundamentalists.

Tajikistan—Christians must increasingly guard evidence of their faith or suffer persecution.

Turkmenistan—since 1997, an increasing number of

churches have been closed and Christian students threatened with expulsion from the university.

Nations in which Islam dominates: Afghanistan, Algeria, Brunei, Iran, Iraq, Kuwait, Libya, the Maldives (islands), Mauritania, Morocco, Oman, Qatar, Saudi Arabia, Syria, Tunisia, and Yemen.

Nations in which Islam is widespread and persecution of Christian population is less militant but nonetheless persistent: Egypt and Turkey.

A rabbi and a priest got into a bad car accident. Both cars were demolished, but amazingly, neither of the clergy was hurt.

They crawled out of their cars and the rabbi saw the priest's collar and said, "So you're a priest. I'm a rabbi. Just look at our cars. There's nothing left, but we are unhurt. This must be a sign from God. God must have meant that we should meet and be friends and live together in peace the rest of our days."

And the priest said, "I agree with you completely. This must be a sign from God."

And the rabbi said, "And look at this. Here's another miracle. My car is completely demolished but this bottle of Mogen David wine didn't break, surely God wants us to drink this wine and celebrate our good fortune."

And so he handed the bottle to the priest. The priest said he agreed, took a few big swigs, and handed the bottle back to the rabbi.

The rabbi took the bottle, didn't take a drink at all, put the cap on, and handed it back to the priest. The priest asked, "Aren't you going to have any?"

The rabbi replied, "No . . . I think I'll just wait for the police."

Who Needs an Advocate and Why?

The New Testament uses two words that mean advocate: *parakleôtos* means "an intercessor, consoler, advocate, or comforter;" and *rheôtoôr*, meaning "a speaker, that is, (by implication) a forensic advocate or orator." In Jesus we find the perfect embodiment of both those words.

Our Defense Attorney

An advocate is one who acts on behalf of or in defense of someone else. A defense lawyer is an advocate. Political leaders advocate for certain policies and programs.

But do we really *need* an advocate?

According to Romans 3:23, there are charges against us. But you may say, "I try to live a good life; how can you say I deserve these charges?"

The Charges

All people have broken the law of God and Satan, the "accuser" or "adversary," pointedly accuses us before the heavenly Father. We are due in court, and we need an advocate—someone who will defend us.

Satan is like the prosecuting attorney; he tries to convince God that we are guilty and worthy of punishment. The accusation is just. We *are* guilty.

The Verdict

But Christ, our advocate, in full knowledge of our guilt, chose to take the punishment on himself. He paid the penalty in our stead and in doing so earned the right to be our advocate—our defense attorney—before the Father and our eternal Judge.

Satan continues to tempt us, lure us, and snare us in sin, and then cruelly and gleefully accuse us before God.

So what is the verdict? Forgiven! Not liable to punishment! Case dismissed!

Self-Advocacy Results

What happens if we fail to *seek* an advocate? Can't we argue our own case before God? What happens if we *don't* ask Christ for his forgiveness and advocacy?

It's simple. We are *known* to be guilty. Someone must pay. It's not a case we can win without the intercession of the *one* true advocate, Jesus Christ.

Without him in the courtroom, there is but one verdict: guilty and liable for punishment. Those who have not *accepted* Christ as Savior have no advocate, no intercessor, no mediator, no defense lawyer.

Hired?

When you stand before God at the final judgment, will you be able to defend yourself? Will you be able to convince God that you don't deserve eternal punishment? No.

Jesus can only advocate for and defend his own. Once you become a Christian, you get the services of the best defense lawyer who ever lived.

Top 10 Biblical Ways to Acquire a Wife

10. Bring home an attractive prisoner of war, shave her head, trim her nails, and give her new clothes. Then she's yours!(Deuteronomy 21:11–13).

9. Find a man with seven daughters and impress him by watering his flock (Exodus 2:16–21).

8. Purchase a piece of property and get a woman as part of the deal (Ruth 4:5–10).

7. Go to a party and hide. When the women come out to dance, grab one and carry her off to be your wife (Judges 21:19–25).

6. Have God create a wife for you while you sleep. Note: this method will cost you! (Genesis 2:19–24).

5. Agree to work seven years in exchange for a wife. If you get tricked into marrying the wrong woman, work another seven years to get the one you wanted to marry in the first place. That's right—fourteen years of toil for a wife! (Genesis 29:15–30).

4. Cut 200 foreskins off your future father-in-law's enemies and get his daughter for a wife (1 Samuel 18:27).

3. Become the emperor of a huge nation and hold a beauty contest (Esther 2:3–4).

2. When you see someone you like, go home and tell your parents, "I have seen a . . . woman; now get her for me" (Judges 14:1–3).

1. Wait for your brother or close relative to die. Marry his widow. It was actually the law of ancient times! (Genesis 38:8).

Ready or Not, Here He Comes!

"The King is coming! The King is coming!"

Until that day arrives, we've got the unbelievably successful *Left Behind* series of books to remind us to watch and pray.

Left Behind

Do you know how big *Left Behind* is? Well, the official website, www.leftbehind.com, sponsors a car in NASCAR races. An article on the website of the car's driver, Randy MacDonald (www.randymacdonald.com), said that the ESPN announcer mentioned during a race that he and his wife had read the Rapture-based books.

The grandson of series creator Tim LaHaye then said, "You know you've arrived when your grandfather gets his name mentioned on ESPN during a NASCAR race." MacDonald is a Christian who is thrilled with the way the *Left Behind* logo on his car opens doors for him to witness about his faith in Jesus Christ.

Plane Happenings

Tim LaHaye, a retired pastor and prophecy teacher, has been in the ministry for more than 50 years. Prior to *Left Behind*, he had written several nonfiction books. The idea for *Left Behind* came to him on an airplane. Fittingly enough, that's exactly where the first book starts—on a plane.

The Rapture occurs and all the Christians in the world disappear, including quite a few on the plane being piloted by one of the lead characters, Rayford Steele. Flight attendant Hattie Durham, who figures prominently in several books, is as mystified as the others who were left behind. Buck Williams, the intrepid journalist, is determined to get to the bottom of what's going on.

Warm Style

The books' popularity comes in large part from the warm and personal writing style of author Jerry Jenkins. Jenkins was the sports editor of a daily newspaper when he was just 19. He became the editor of *Moody Magazine* at 25, and was later a vice president for publishing at Moody. In 1990, he decided to do freelance writing full time.

Collaborative Partnership

LaHaye and Jenkins met for the first time in 1992. You might say theirs was a collaborative partnership made in heaven. LaHaye does all the research and sends it to Jenkins in the "cave," as Jenkins calls it, where he writes—a place with no TV, phone, radio, or other distractions.

Jenkins is the one who comes up with the characters. He also does all the plotting and writing. (In a Crosswalk.com online chat, in answer to a question about characters who die in the books, Jenkins said, "I don't kill 'em; I find 'em dead.") As soon as he has a few hundred pages done, he sends them to LaHaye for review.

Jenkins admits that the books have overwhelmed even him a little bit. "I have to reread the books to keep the characters on track," he said in a Desecration Live Global chat on Leftbehind.com.

Left Behind was only supposed to be one book, so there's no master outline to follow.

Difficult but Effective

Writing these books is not as simple as following the template of the Book of Revelation. Jenkins says he experiences "heavy oppression" while writing. The enemy, to be sure, is not happy about the influence these books are having.

LaHaye and Jenkins say they've heard from more than 2,500 people who have accepted Jesus Christ as their personal Savior as a result of reading the books. They also hear from lots of Christians who are more mindful of how short life can be and who are recommitting their lives to the Lord and being more aggressive in sharing their faith.

A Publishing Phenomenon

The first book came out in 1995 and has sold more than 7 million copies. When the ninth book, *Desecration*, came out in November 2001, it had a first printing of 2.8 million copies—the largest print run in history for a Christian novel.

Only three other authors have had a first printing of 2 million or more copies: John Grisham, Tom Clancy, and J. K. Rowling. The seventh book, *The Indwelling*, debuted in the number one spot on the top four best-seller lists in 2000: *USA Today, The Wall Street Journal, Publishers Weekly,* and *New York Times*.

Spin-offs

Left Behind: The Movie, based on the first book, has had mixed reviews, many negative, but it set a new record for evangelical

Christian movies with its opening-weekend box office take of more than $2.6 million.

Left Behind is not just for adults. There's also *Left Behind: The Kids*. At the time that book #18 came out in September 2001, the series had sold more than 7.6 million copies, earning it the distinction of "best-selling contemporary Christian children's fiction series."

Criticism

With every success, of course, comes criticism. LaHaye and Jenkins have had their share. Because the books subscribe to the premillennial view—which contends that the church will be raptured, followed by seven years of tribulation, followed by Jesus Christ's return—those with a different theological viewpoint have often been strident in their criticism.

Some critics have also voiced concern that Christians will get so caught up in being "caught up," they'll forget that there's a world full of people who need food, clothing, shelter, and a hefty dose of the love and compassion of God. Only time will tell if Christians will become "so heavenly minded, they're of no earthly good" after reading all (eventually) 12 books.

Reason for the Success?

So why *are* these books (*Left Behind, Tribulation Force, Nicolae, Soul Harvest, Apollyon, Assassins, The Indwelling, The Mark*, and *Desecration*) so successful? Is it that people can't wait to see Nicolae get his comeuppance? Is it not knowing what will happen or who will die next? Is it the soap-opera quality? Or is it what Jenkins believes, that "there's a God hunger out there"?

Perhaps LaHaye is right when he says a lot of it has to do with timing, as more and more secular books concerning the end of the world find their way onto bookstore shelves.

People are certainly more focused than ever on the fragility of life, owing to the terrorist attacks of September 11, 2001. Jenkins was in midtown Manhattan that day, and found the event as unbelievable as everyone else.

Even More Plausible

"Would the attacks affect how Jenkins approached writing the remaining books in the series?" asked one participant in a CNN.com chat on October 3, 2001.

No, Jenkins said. The effect, he believes, is that when people read a *Left Behind* book in the future, the book's events will seem "all that more plausible."

In the final analysis, the message of the books is "be prepared." Otherwise, as the song says, when the end finally comes, "There's no time to change your mind/The Son has come, and you've been left behind."

A priest, a minister, and a rabbi were discussing what they would like people to say after they died and their bodies were on display in open caskets.

Priest: "I would like someone to say 'He was a righteous and honest man, and very generous.'"

Minister: "I would like someone to say 'He was very kind and fair, and he was very good to his parishioners.'"

Rabbi: "I would want someone to say 'Oh, look! He's moving!'"

Bible Questions and Answers

Q: Who was the greatest financier in the Bible?

A: Noah. He was floating his stock while everyone else was in liquidation.

Q: Who was the greatest female financier in the Bible?

A: Pharaoh's daughter. She went down to the bank of the Nile and drew out a little prophet.

Q: What kind of man was Boaz before he got married?

A: Ruth-less.

Q: Who was the greatest comedian in the Bible?

A: Samson. He brought the house down.

Q: What excuse did Adam give to his children as to why he no longer lived in Eden?

A: Your mother ate us out of house and home.

Q: Who is the greatest babysitter mentioned in the Bible?

A: David. He rocked Goliath to sleep.

Q: Why was Goliath so surprised when David hit him with a slingshot?

A: The thought had never entered his head before.

Q: Which of God's servants was the most flagrant lawbreaker in the Bible?

A: Moses. Because he broke all 10 commandments at once.

What a Name!

Here are some Bible names (found in the King James Version) that you can be glad your mother did *not* name you!

Mahershalalhashbaz (Isaiah 8:1)
Bashanhavothjair (Deuteronomy 3:14)
Chepharhaammonai (Joshua 18:24)
Chushan-rishathaim (Judges 3:8)
Kibrothhattaavah (Numbers 11:34)
Selahammahlekoth (1 Samuel 23:28)
Abelbethmaachah (1 Kings 15:20)
Almondiblathaim (Numbers 33:46)
Apharsathchites (Ezra 4:9)
Berodachbaladan (2 Kings 20:12)
Helkathhazzurim (2 Samuel 2:16)
Ramathaimzophim (1 Samuel 1:1)
Tilgathpilneser (1 Chronicles 5:6)

These, by the way, are not only difficult names to pronounce. They are the 13 longest names in the Bible.

He Hung the Planets in Place

The largest planet in the solar system is Jupiter—fifth from the sun. A giant gas planet, Jupiter's mass is greater than all other planets combined. However, few people realize Jupiter's influence on earth.

The Life Support Zone

In order to sustain life, a planet must be a certain distance from the sun. Earth is exactly where it needs to be—any closer and all living creatures would fry; any farther away and we would freeze.

Jupiter's Orbit

The planets influence each other through gravitational pull—the orbits of the various planets sustain the orbits of the other planets. Several years ago, a probe sent to Jupiter revealed two startling facts:

1. Jupiter has a nearly circular orbit. This is unusual, because most planets that far from the sun have *elliptical orbits*. If Jupiter had an elliptical orbit, life on earth wouldn't exist.
2. Jupiter's orbit has what scientists call a "tiny inclination," meaning there is only a slight difference between the angle of its orbit and the angle of the earth's orbit. This is very rare for giant gas planets like Jupiter that are so far away from the sun. If Jupiter had a slightly larger inclination, it would pull earth outside the life support zone.

More Bulletin Bloopers

Every church office assistant makes mistakes. We can all enjoy these actual bulletin bloopers.

Next Thursday there will be tryouts for the choir. They need all the help they can get.

Barbara remains in the hospital and needs blood donors for more transfusions. She is also having trouble sleeping and requests tapes of Pastor Jack's sermons.

The Rector will preach his farewell message after which the choir will sing "Break Forth into Joy."

Irving and Jessie were married on October 24 in the church. So ends a friendship that began in their school days.

At the evening service tonight, the sermon topic will be "What Is Hell?" Come early and listen to our choir practice.

Eight new choir robes are currently needed, due to the addition of several new members and to the deterioration of some older ones.

The senior choir invites any member of the congregation who enjoys sinning to join the choir.

For those of you who have children and don't know it, we have a nursery downstairs.

Please place your donation in the envelope along with the deceased person(s) you want remembered.

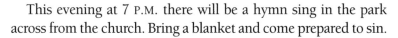

The church will host an evening of fine dining, superb entertainment, and gracious hostility.

Potluck supper Sunday at 5 P.M.—prayer and medication to follow.

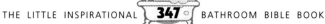

This evening at 7 P.M. there will be a hymn sing in the park across from the church. Bring a blanket and come prepared to sin.

The pastor would appreciate it if the ladies of the congregation would lend him their electric girdles for the pancake breakfast next Sunday morning.

Smile at God

A little girl walked to and from school daily. Though the weather one morning was questionable and clouds were forming, she made her daily trek to the elementary school.

As the day progressed, the winds whipped up, along with thunder and lightning. The mother of the little girl felt concerned that her daughter would be frightened as she walked home from school and she herself feared that the electrical storm might harm her child. Lightning, like a flaming sword, cut through the sky.

The mother quickly got into her car and drove along the route to her child's school. In the distance, the mother saw her little girl walking along, but at each flash of lightning, the child would stop, look up, and smile.

Flashes of lightning followed one after the other, and with each the little girl would look at the streak of light and smile.

When the mother's car drew up beside the child, she lowered the window and called to her, "What are you doing? Why do you keep stopping?"

The child answered, "I am trying to look pretty. God keeps taking my picture."

When the storms of life come your way, don't forget to *smile*!

Popular Books by Starburst Publishers®

The Little Inspirational™ Bathroom Bible™ Book
By W. B. Freeman
(trade paper) ISBN 1892016680 **$13.99**

Fifty Ways to Stand Up for™ America: Put the Spirit of July 4ᵗʰ into Everyday Life
By W. B. Freeman
Rev up your patriotic spirit with heart-warming anecdotes, how-to advice, interesting historical information, and practical tips. Learn flag flying etiquette. Discover the benefits and responsibilities of good citizenship. Be inspired to take part in your community, and find that one-for-all-and-all-for-one attitude. Make the spirit of July 4th relevant for everyday life.
(trade paper) ISBN 1892016702 **$11.99**

A Growing Heart: Stories, Lessons, and Exercises Inspired by Proverbs
Edited by Kathy Collard Miller
The profound truths of Proverbs provide wisdom for making good choices in life. Each selection includes a verse from Proverbs, an inspirational story, teachings, quotation, and idea for journaling with room to write. Lessons will guide the reader on topics such as discipline, friendship, love, parenting, wealth, and work.
(trade paper) ISBN 1892016524 **$12.99**

An Expressive Heart: Stories, Lessons, and Exercises Inspired by the Psalms
Edited by Kathy Collard Miller
(trade paper) ISBN 1892016508 **$12.99**

The **God's Word for the Biblically-Inept™** series is already a best-seller with over 300,000 books sold! Designed to make reading the Bible easy, educational, and fun! This series of verse-by-verse Bible studies, topical studies, and overviews mixes scholarly information from experts with helpful icons, illustrations, sidebars, and timelines. It's the Bible made easy!

Acts by Robert C. Girard	ISBN 189201646X	**$17.99**
The Bible by Larry Richards	ISBN 0914984551	**$16.95**
Daniel by Daymond R. Duck	ISBN 0914984489	**$16.95**
Genesis by Joyce L. Gibson	ISBN 1892016125	**$16.95**
Health & Nutrition		
by Kathleen O'Bannon Baldinger	ISBN 0914984055	**$16.95**
John by Lin Johnson	ISBN 1892016435	**$16.95**
Life of Christ, Volume 1		
by Robert C. Girard	ISBN 1892016230	**$16.95**
Life of Christ, Volume 2		
by Robert C. Girard	ISBN 1892016397	**$16.95**
Luke by Joyce L. Gibson	ISBN 1892016478	**$17.99**
Mark by Scott Pinzon	ISBN 1892016362	**$17.99**
Men of the Bible by D. Larry Miller	ISBN 1892016079	**$16.95**
Prophecies of the Bible		
by Daymond R. Duck	ISBN 1892016222	**$16.95**
Revelation by Daymond D. Duck	ISBN 0914984985	**$16.95**
Romans by Gib Martin	ISBN 1892016273	**$16.95**
Women of the Bible		
by Kathy Collard Miller	ISBN 0914984063	**$16.95**

The **What's in the Bible for . . .™** series makes the Bible applicable to everyday life. Whether you're a teenager or senior citizen, this series has the book for you! Each title features the same reader-friendly icons, illustrations, questions, and chapter summaries that are used in the *God's Word for the Biblically-Inept™* series. It's another easy way to access God's Word!

What's in the Bible for . . . ™ Couples
by Kathy Collard Miller and D. Larry Miller

ISBN 189201632X **$16.95**

What's in the Bible for . . .™ Mothers
by Judy Bodmer

ISBN 1892016265 **$16.95**

What's in the Bible for . . .™ Teens
by Mark Littleton and Jeanette Gardner Littleton

ISBN 1892016052 **$16.95**

What's in the Bible for . . .™ Women
by Georgia Curtis Ling

ISBN 1892016109 $16.95

Learn more at www.biblicallyinept.com

The Bible for Teens: Learn the Word™
By Larry Richards

In a special adaptation just for teens, the unique Biblically-Inept™ brand of simplified Bible commentary is blended with content and features aimed directly at today's youth. Popular elements from the original series such as chapter summaries, definitions, timelines, illustrations, and study questions are combined with several new features including "Your Move" and "Get Real." Finally, a complete overview of the entire Bible—from Creation to Christ to Armageddon and beyond—just for teens.

(trade paper) ISBN 1892016516 **$14.99**

Also available

Revelation for Teens: Learn the Word™
By Daymond Duck

(trade paper) ISBN 1892016559 **$14.99**

God Things Come in Small Packages: Celebrating the Little Things in Life
By Susan Duke, LeAnn Weiss, Caron Loveless, and Judith Carden

Enjoy touching reminders of God's simple yet generous gifts to brighten our days and gladden our hearts! Treasures like a sunset over a vast, sparkling ocean; a child's trust; or the crystalline dew on a spider's web come to life in this elegant compilation. Such occasions should be celebrated as if gift wrapped from God; they're his hallmarks! Personalized Scripture is artfully combined with compelling stories and reflections. (hard cover) ISBN 1892016281 **$12.95**

Purchasing Information
www.starburstpublishers.com

Books are available from your favorite bookstore, either from current stock or special order. To assist bookstores in locating your selection, be sure to give title, author, and ISBN. If unable to purchase from a bookstore, you may order direct from STARBURST PUBLISHERS. When ordering please enclose full payment plus shipping and handling as follows:

Post Office (4th class)
$4.00 with a purchase of up to $20.00
$5.00 ($20.01–$50.00)
9% of purchase price for purchases
   of $50.01 and up

Canada
$5.00 (up to $35.00)
15% ($35.01 and up)

United Parcel Service (UPS)
$5.00 (up to $20.00)
$7.00 ($20.01–$50.00)
12% ($50.01 and up)

Overseas
$5.00 (up to $25.00)
20% ($25.01 and up)

Payment in U.S. funds only. Please allow two to four weeks minimum for delivery by USPS (longer for overseas and Canada). Allow two to seven working days for delivery by UPS. Make checks payable to and mail to:

   Starburst Publishers®
   P.O. Box 4123
   Lancaster, PA 17604

Credit card orders may be placed by calling 1-800-441-1456, Mon.–Fri., 8:30 A.M. to 5:30 P.M. Eastern Standard Time. Prices are subject to change without notice. For a catalog send a 9 x 12 self-addressed envelope with four first-class stamps.